INTERVENTIONS IN ETHICS

ETHICAL THEORY
Robert B. Louden, Series Editor, University of Southern Maine

Recent years have seen a proliferation of work in applied and professional ethics. At the same time, however, serious questions have been raised concerning the very status of morality in contemporary culture and the future of moral theory efforts. Volumes within the SUNY Press Ethical Theory series address the present need for sustained investigations into basic philosophical questions about ethics.

INTERVENTIONS IN ETHICS

D. Z. PHILLIPS

State University of New York Press

First published
in U.S.A. by
State University of New York Press
Albany

For information, address State University of New York Press,
State University Plaza, Albany, NY 12246

Printed in Hong Kong

Library of Congress Cataloging-in-Publication Data
Phillips, D. Z. (Dewi Zephaniah)
    Interventions in ethics / D. Z. Phillips.
       p.   cm. — (SUNY series in ethical theory)
    Includes bibliographical references and indexes.
    ISBN 0–7914–0995–3. — ISBN 0–7914–0996–1 (pbk.)
    1. Ethics.   I. Title.   II. Series.
BJ1012.P46   1992
170—dc20
                               91–19790
                                    CIP

Contents

Acknowledgements

Most of the essays in this volume have been published previously. They appeared in the following publications and the author wishes to thank the editors and publishers concerned for permission to reprint them here:

'On Morality's Having A Point', *Philosophy*, Oct. 1965; 'Moral Practices and Anscombe's Grocer', in D. Z. Phillips and H. O. Mounce, *Moral Practices* (Routledge & Kegan Paul and Shocken Books, New York, 1970); 'The Possibilities of Moral Advice', *Analysis*, Dec. 1964; 'Allegiance and Change in Morality', Royal Institute of Philosophy Lectures, Vol. 6 1971/72, *Philosophy and the Arts* ed. G Vesey (Macmillan, 1973); 'After Virtue', new title for the Critical Notice of Alasdair MacIntyre's *After Virtue?* (Mind, 1984); 'The Presumption of Theory' in *Value and Understanding: Essays for Peter Winch*, ed. Raimond Gaita (Routledge, 1990); 'What Can We Expect From Ethics?' *Aristotelian Society Proceedings*, Supp. Vol. LXIII 1989; 'Not in Front of the Children: Children and the Heterogeneity of Morals', *The Journal of Philosophy of Education*, Vol. 14 no. 1, 1980; 'Does It Pay To Be Good?', *Proceedings of the Aristotelian Society*, Vol. LXV, 1964–5; 'In Search of the Moral "Must": Mrs Foot's Fugitive Thought', *Philosophical Quarterly*, 1977; 'Do Moral Considerations Override Others?', *Philosophical Quarterly, 1979*: 'An Argument from Extreme Cases?' *Philosophical Investigations*, Vol. 3 no. 4, 1980; 'Morality and Purpose', new title for my introduction to J. L. Stocks, *Morality and Purpose* (Routledge & Kegan Paul and Schocken Books, New York, 1969); 'How Lucky Can You Get?' in *Wittgenstein: Attention to Particulars: Essays in Honour of Rush Rhees*, ed. D. Z. Phillips and Peter Winch (Macmillan, 1990); 'Some Limits to Moral Endeavour', University College of Swansea, 1972; 'My Neighbour and My Neighbours', *Philosophical Investigations*, 1989.

The author thanks Mr H. O. Mounce for permission to reprint 'On Morality's Having a Point' which he co-authored with him.

Some modifications have been made in certain cases to avoid repetition and to provide cross-references, etc.

The papers, 'Self-Knowledge and Pessimism', 'Philosophy and the Heterogeneity of the Human' and 'Necessary Rewards, Necessary Punishments and Character' are published here for the first time.

Introduction

The essays in this collection were meant to be interventions in ethics, by which I mean moral philosophy. The interventions were thought to be necessary because of something written or said in the course of discussion. It is extremely difficult to be content with such interventions. Time and again we are tempted to do more but, for the most part, this temptation should be resisted.

Interventions in ethics are often needed because of our deep-rooted tendency to theorise in ethics. We want to give a general, theoretical account of something called Morality. We search for its essence. The intervention we need, in that event, takes the form of reminders of possibilities which the so-called essence cannot account for. The trouble is not that we have failed to locate the real essence, or misdescribed what the essence is. Our trouble lies in the assumption that there is an essence of something called Morality. We are rescued from the futile search for it by coming to pay attention to the heterogeneity of moral practices. The differences between these perspectives may be as important as any similarities they may exhibit. The differing perspectives are not incomplete; they do not await completion in some single definition of morality.

It is easy to think otherwise, if we think that moral considerations stand in need of an external justification which underwrites them. Philippa Foot thinks that morality must be shown to have a point if it is to be rational, and that its point is found in its relation to human good and harm. Such a rational criterion, she thinks, enables us to distinguish between genuine and sham perspectives, since some of them may not further human good nor avoid human harm. In 'On Morality's Having A Point', I argued that such a test for genuine morality is futile, since what we take to be human good and harm is already informed by moral considerations. Since these considerations differ for different people, unsurprisingly, there are different conceptions of human good and harm.

If the character of human good and harm is thought to be fixed, we can see how philosophers are led to conclude that there is *never* a gap between facts and values. Given the facts concerning human good and harm, moral conduct would be determined as that conduct which led to the realisation of these facts. This view was advanced by philosophers who reacted against the opposite view, namely, the thesis that there is *always* a gap between facts and values. They insisted, rightly, that we cannot attach commendatory labels to any facts we choose. They pointed out the obvious truth that, given certain facts, we draw moral conclusions from them. What they did not emphasise, however, was that drawing these moral conclusions is something people do within the context of moral practices they adhere to. In 'Moral Practices and Anscombe's Grocer' and 'The Possibilities of Moral Advice', I point out that, given different moral practices, the same facts may have a different moral significance. In such contexts people may even differ in what they take the facts to be.

If we think that there is one single phenomenon called Morality, which is underwritten by its relation to human good and harm, this will influence one's view of the nature of the moral agent. His moral actions will be thought of as rational actions, namely, actions which lead to human good and avoid human harm. Thus, a person will have reasons for his values. If he changes his values, he must have reasons for these changes too; reasons which, once again, will be related to human good and harm. In this way, if no mistake has been made, a person's new values will be more reasonable than his former values. In a social context, the account is one in which society develops rationally as it sheds its inhibitions and taboos.

In 'Allegiance and Change in Morality', by reference to examples from literature, I argue that this account of moral considerations is a caricature. People do not have reasons for their values, in the suggested sense. Rather, their reasons are their values. When reasons change, in a person or in a society, it does not follow that the change can be assessed by appeal to a common reason. What has happened is that certain moral values have been eroded by others.

Our criticisms have shown already that there is a huge gap between the heterogeneity of moral practices and perspectives and the spurious unity imposed on them by moral theories. It will not do to argue, as Alasdair MacIntyre has done, that ethical theories simply reflect the social and historical milieu in which they are constructed. In 'After Virtue?' I argue that the allure of theories in ethics has a deeper source. They all ignore the variety which moral perspectives have. In 'The Presumption of Theory' I show how Peter Winch exposes the inadequacies of moral theories in terms of this ignoring. Yet, so deep is the hold of theory on us, that many, like Onora O'Neill, think that Winch's examples of deep-going moral differences between people merely constitute preliminary data awaiting some kind of unifying theoretical resolution.

It may be thought that because of recent numerous attacks on traditional theories, the influence of theory on us is diminishing. In 'What Can We Expect From Ethics?', I show that this would be an over-hasty conclusion. For example, although Bernard Williams and Annette Baier attack ethical theories and their claims to tell us the nature of the good life, an adherence to theory is still to be found in their work. It is more difficult to detect because it appears *after* Williams and Baier have recognised the moral diversity to which I have called attention. They do not reject the question, 'What is the good life?' They simply argue that philosophers cannot answer it unaided. Philosophy must play its part in a wider, interdisciplinary, intellectual reflection. But, I argue, this reflection has hidden values. For example, it is assumed uncritically, from the outset, that the form of the good life is of a life shared in common by all those who care about living the good life. Once this is accepted, any specific moral perspective becomes a mere local practice, and cannot be accepted as the good life. But there is no reason why we should accept these uncritical assumptions. Agreement need not be the aim of our conversations with others. Our relations will be characterised sometimes by closeness and sometimes by distance. Certainly, different moral perspectives need not be seen as alternatives or optional versions of an agreed conception of the good life. To think otherwise is, in fact, an intellectualist distortion of human lives, including the lives of intellectuals.

The recognition of the heterogeneity of morals which I have insisted on, may itself lead to misunderstanding. It may be thought that moral relativism is its unavoidable consequence. This is not so. In 'Not in Front of the Children', for example, I show why recognition of the heterogeneity of morals does not give credence to absurd educational theories which advocate telling children that all moral values are equal, or are options about which they should exercise a free choice. If such theories were correct, it would be hard to account for deep allegiance to any moral perspective.

Moral theories distort what moral allegiances come to. Once again, they insist that they have to be underwritten by some kind of rationale. It has been said, for example, that there would be little point in pressing moral obligations if it could not be shown that their fulfilment is in the agent's self-interest. It is via such self-interest that moral imperatives have an effective hold on the agent's will. This general theory, in which villainy must be irrational, was never very plausible. I criticise the version of it found in Philippa Foot's early essays in 'Does It Pay To Be Good?' I see no reason to revise these criticisms. On the other hand, in making them, I sometimes speak as though I, too, were appealing to some single phenomenon called Morality. I was not content, as I should have been, to settle for telling reminders.

My reluctance to settle for interventions in ethics was also evident in my discussions of Philippa Foot's later views in ethics where moral concerns are characterised as hypothetical imperatives effectively operative for those interested in promoting the common good. I tried to counter this general thesis with a general thesis of my own. In my paper 'In Search of the Moral "Must" ' I claim that the moral 'ought', unlike the 'oughts' of prudence, aesthetics or etiquette, could not be overridden without remorse or regret by anyone who is said to care for moral considerations. This general thesis led me to treat all moral obligations, no matter what the circumstances, in the same way. In 'Do Moral Considerations Override Others?' I gave the impression that neglect of *any* moral obligation shows lack of care for moral considerations – an absurd moralism.

I still find Philippa Foot's later discussions of moral obligation unsatisfactory. She seems to find little sense in talk of moral considerations as absolute, unconditional, or inescapable, but this is because she treats such talk as expressions of a general theory to which counter-examples are easy to find. On the other hand, what I should have done, was to have concentrated on examples which give talk of moral obligations as categorical and inescapable its point, and not tried to generalise from these examples. This may have been part of what William Davie was arguing in his contribution to the dispute between Philippa Foot and myself. If so, despite my continued disagreement with his treatment of his actual examples, his argument deserved more attention than I gave it in 'An Argument From Extreme Cases?' Instead of trying to defend a general thesis against his counter-examples, I should have concentrated on those cases where the moral necessity expressed in such remarks as, 'I must help him', 'My responsibility is inescapable' is internally related to the moral perspective being expressed. If we say that, for the people involved, their obligations are categorical, this is not 'the categorical imperative' of ethical theory. When someone says. 'I just can't let him down', he need not be a Kantian!

There are further difficulties with teleological conceptions of ethics which characterise moral concerns as interest in the common good. The conception of the common good is itself a dubious one, but this apart, it is odd to speak of moral obligations as a set of interests. Moral considerations may arise in connection with our interests, but do we list these considerations among our interests? In 'Morality and Purpose' I expound J. L. Stocks' view that moral considerations do not bear on human action as a distinctive end, or as the distinctive means by which our ends are achieved. No matter what purposes we pursue, questions may be raised concerning their decency. Further, no matter how splendid the envisaged prospects may be, moral considerations say that they cannot be pursued by any and every means. For these reasons, Stocks concluded that over and above our purposes and means of achieving them, moral considerations constitute 'an additional principle of discrimination', since means and ends are subject to the demands of decency.

Some philosophers, Kant, for example, have claimed that moral allegiance and the values it extols are distinctive in that they transcend the contingencies of human life; they provide a certainty and universality which luck and chance cannot touch. Thomas Nagel and Bernard Williams are right to argue against such unrealistic claims. Nevertheless, as I show in 'How Lucky Can You Get?' the hold of philosophical theory on them leads them to distort the role of luck and contingency in human affairs. Nagel thinks that there is a contradiction between our philosophical conclusions concerning such contingencies and our moral practice of praise and blame. According to him, we simply live with such contradictions. This conclusion is unwarranted, since the contingencies to which Nagel refers, so far from contradicting our moral convictions, often play a crucial role in forming them. Williams argues that once we pay attention to the presence of luck in human affairs, we will have to revise the kind of importance we attach to moral considerations. The difficulty is in the generality of his conclusion. No doubt Williams is describing how some people may react to luck in their lives. But he is simply making a personal recommendation if he says that everyone should react in the same way. He has not established any general conclusions about the place of morality in our lives.

Instead of embracing general conclusions about contingency in human affairs, we should concentrate on particular examples of the limitations such contingency may create for our moral endeavours. In 'Some Limits to Moral Endeavour', I discuss ways in which these endeavours are often constrained by circumstances, limitations of character and sheer luck. Such constraints may lead someone to conclude that, in certain circumstances, and in certain respects, he should not even try to be better. It is often just as important to know what we cannot do, as it is to face up to what we can do. Often, we settle for less.

Some philosophers find this conclusion hard to accept. They seem to be in the grip of an *a priori* optimism about moral allegiance. This is because they define this allegiance as involving the ability to determine the course of one's life and to reconcile the conflicts which may occur within it. In 'Self-Knowledge and Pessimism', I criticise Ilham Dilman for holding such a view. Because he does not take due account of particular cases, Dilman fails to allow that while caring for moral considerations is the condition for the possibility of moral improvement, it is also the condition for the possibility of despair. For Dilman, despair about oneself in certain moral respects, can never be a form of self-knowledge.

Even when we are not in the grip of ethical theory, concentration on the general may obscure what the particular reveals. There is a generality involved in what Wittgenstein called an attitude towards a soul, our unhesitating recognition of others as human beings. In 'My Neighbour and My Neighbours', however, I question Peter Winch's claim that this generality throws light on the Good Samaritan's reaction to the plight of the man who had fallen among thieves. I do not believe that our lack of doubt about the fact that we live in a human neighbourhood, does throw much light on the Samaritan's response to a neighbour on the road from Jerusalem to Jericho. What we need is to concentrate on what is distinctive in this response.

It has been suggested that the concept of the human being is central in moral philosophy. Cora Diamond makes the claim that philosophers are not simply confused conceptually in ethics, while being clear-sighted when not philosophising. On the contrary, it is said, philosophical confusion in ethics is often a form of cultural deprivation, a blindness about what it means to be human. I do not deny the possibility of conceptual blindness, but there are other possibilities which need emphasising. Since 'being human' is not a homogeneous phenomenon, there are dangers in a general thesis which threatens to make a too-simple distinction between moral philosophers who appreciate what it means to be human and those who are blind to what is involved. There is little less ragged than the heterogeneity of the human. Here, too, philosophy teaches us differences, differences which cannot be underwritten by an appeal to 'what it means to be human'. What 'appreciation' or the lack of it involves in these contexts is itself extremely varied. Attention to particular cases is essential. This is my argument in 'Philosophy and the Heterogeneity of the Human'.

What is distinctive in particular moral responses is sometimes difficult to understand for those who do not share these responses or perspectives. Such is the case, I believe, with the claim that a good man is necessarily rewarded and that an evil man is necessarily punished. In 'Necessary Rewards, Necessary Punishments and Character', I discuss Peter Winch's treatment of this claim. My aim is not to dispute the possibilities Winch elucidates, but to explore and extend them further. I am interested in the fact that certain assumptions of outstanding goodness or of extreme evil, are assumptions necessarily made by spectators. It is an internal feature of these displays of good and evil that the agents themselves do not describe themselves in these terms. An assent to the spectator judgements of good and evil by the agents themselves would show immediately that the judgements had been misplaced.

Given my attack on theories and generalities in this collection, does this mean that there is no place for generality in ethics? What is general in ethics is struggling with conceptual puzzlement, and attempting to provide conceptual clarification and elucidation. This concern is general insofar as it is not personal. These puzzles may occur for anyone, since they arise from characteristic ways in which people speak of moral considerations. Ethical theories had grand designs which could not be realised. We should not replace them, however, with grand designs of different kinds. I am advocating a return to ethics' modest task of struggling for conceptual clarity. After all, it is not as if people have ceased to be puzzled by the various forms of language we use when speaking of moral

I

Philosophers ask, What is the point of morality? Why does it matter whether one does one thing rather than another? Surely, it is argued, if one wants to show someone why it is his duty to do something, one must be prepared to point out the importance of the proposed action, the harm involved in failing to do it, and the advantage involved in performing it. Such considerations simply cannot be put aside. On the contrary, the point of moral conduct must be elucidated in terms of the reasons for performing it. Such reasons separate moral arguments from persuasion and coercion, and moral judgements from likes and dislikes; they indicate what constitutes human good and harm.

If we take note of the role of reasons in morality, we shall see that not anything can count as a moral belief. After all, why does one regard some rules as moral principles, and yet never regard others as such? Certainly, we *can* see the point of some rules as moral principles, but in the case of other rules we cannot. How is the point seen? There is much in the suggestion that it is to be appreciated in terms of the background which attends moral beliefs and principles.[8] When rules which claim to be moral rules are devoid of this background we are puzzled. We do not know what is being said when someone claims that the given rule is a moral rule.

Normally, we do not speak of these backgrounds when we express and discuss moral opinions. It is only when we are asked to imagine their absence that we see how central they must be in any account we try to give of morality. Consider the rules, 'Never walk on the lines of a pavement', and 'Clap your hands every two hours'. If we saw people letting such rules govern their lives in certain ways, taking great care to observe them, feeling upset whenever they or other people infringe the rules, and so on, we should be hard put to understand what they were doing. We fail to see any point in it. On the other hand, if backgrounds are supplied for such rules, if further descriptions of the context in which they operate are given, sometimes, they can begin to look like moral principles. Given the background of a religious community, one can begin to see how the rule, 'Never walk on the lines of a pavement', could have moral significance. Think of, 'Take off thy shoes for thou art on holy ground', and its connections with the notions of reverence and disrespect. It is more difficult, though we

1

On Morality's Having a Point*

In 1958, moral philosophers were given rather startling advice. They were told that their subject was not worth pursuing further until they possessed an adequate philosophy of psychology.[1] What is needed, they were told, is an enquiry into what type of characteristic a virtue is, and, furthermore, it was suggested that this question could be resolved in part by exploring the connection between what a man ought to do and what he *needs*: perhaps man needs certain things in order to flourish, just as a plant needs water; and perhaps what men need are the virtues, courage, honesty, loyalty, etc. Thus, in telling a man that he ought to be honest, we should not be using any special (moral) sense of ought: a man ought to be honest just as a plant ought to be watered. The 'ought' is the same: it tells us what a man needs.

Those who agreed with the above advice must have been pleased at the way it was taken up. Its implications were worked out in some detail by Philippa Foot in a number of influential papers.[2] The attack on the naturalistic fallacy which it involves was welcomed by a contemporary defender of Utilitarianism.[3] Strong support for a deductive argument from facts to values came from a leading American philosopher,[4] while agreement with this general approach in ethics was found in the work of a Gifford lecturer, who, amid all the varieties of goodness, could not find a peculiar *moral* sense of 'good'.[5] Also, contemporary philosophers were prompted to explore the connections between morality and prudence,[6] and even to express the hope that past masters would have a salutary influence on the future relationship between philosophy and psychology.[7] It seems fair to say that the advice of 1958 produced a climate of opinion, a way of doing moral philosophy. For this reason, it is all the more important to expose the radical misunderstanding involved in it.

* This chapter was co-authored with H.O. Mounce.

considerations. Ethics, with dubious ambitions, has simply turned away from these puzzles, that is all.

It has been no part of my intention to deny that we can give reasons for our moral behaviour, elucidate where we stand morally. But we do not all stand on the same spot, and elucidations will reveal distances as well as proximities. We did not learn to speak by speaking to everyone about everything, and there is no reason to think it is otherwise where moral matters are concerned. We can come to know another in such a way that a glance is enough, but we can also be enigmas to each other.

The moral philosopher, aided or unaided, has no authority to construct a main road in ethics. He must endeavour, as far as possible, to clarify conceptual issues concerning the varieties and complexities of moral perspectives and moral endeavour. When faced by distortions and misunderstandings, he has to intervene to call attention to them. Others may intervene to show that *he* is the one who is guilty of distortion or misunderstanding. Interventions may take the form of teaching differences or elucidating philosophically neglected perspectives. But these perspectives are not underwritten by any kind of necessity or by a reflective intellectualism. Rather, to adopt Wittgenstein's phrase, 'They are there, like our life'. It may be said that if our moral perspectives and practices are different, we could not go on. To which we should reply: that is how we do go on.

It is extremely difficult to be content with philosophical interventions in ethics, but this is hardly surprising. It is in ethics, after all, part of that wider impossible task in philosophy of never saying more than we know.

do not say it is impossible, to think of a context in which the rule, 'Clap your hands every two hours', could have moral significance. Our first example shows how we can be brought to some understanding of a moral view when it is brought under a concept with which we are familiar. By linking disapproval of walking on the lines of a pavement with lack of reverence and disrespect, even those not familiar with the religious tradition in question may see that a *moral* view is being expressed. Such concepts as sincerity, honesty, courage, loyalty, respect, and, of course, a host of others, provide the kind of background necessary in order to make sense of rules as moral principles. It does not follow that all the possible features of such a background need be present in every case. The important point to stress is that unless the given rule has *some* relation to such a background, we would not know what is meant by calling it a moral principle.

The above conclusion follows from a more extensive one, namely, that commendation is internally related to its object. Mrs Foot, for example, suggests that there is an analogy between commendation on the one hand, and mental attitudes such as pride and beliefs such as 'This is dangerous' on the other. One cannot feel proud of *anything*, any more than one can say that *anything* is dangerous. Similarly in the case of commendation: how can one say that clapping one's hands every two hours is a good action? The answer is that one cannot, unless the context in which the action is performed, for example, recovery from paralysis, makes its point apparent.

Certainly, those who have insisted on the necessity of a certain conceptual background in order to make sense of moral beliefs and moral judgements have done philosophy a service. They have revealed the artificiality of locating what is characteristically moral in a mental attitude such as a pro-attitude, or in a mental activity such as commending. They have shown the impossibility of making sense of something called 'evaluative meaning' which is thought of as being externally or contingently related to its objects. One could have a pro-attitude towards clapping one's hands every two hours, and one could commend one's never walking on the lines of a pavement, but neither pro-attitude nor commendation would, in themselves, give a point to such activities.

If the point of virtues is not to be expressed in terms of pro-attitudes or commendations, how is it to be brought out? It has been suggested that this could be done by showing the connection between virtues and human good and harm. But this is where the trouble starts, for if we are not careful, we may, in our eagerness to exorcise the spirit of evaluative meaning, fall under the spell of the concept of human good and harm, which is an equally dangerous idea. Unfortunately, this has already happened, and much of the current talk about human good and harm is as artificial as the talk about 'attitudes' in moral philosophy which it set out to criticise.

The point of calling an action (morally) good, it is suggested, is that it leads to human good and avoids harm. Further, what is to count as human good and harm is said to be a *factual* matter. Thus, one must try to show that there is a logical connection between statements of fact and statements of value, and that the logical gap supposed to exist between them can be closed. Men cannot pick and choose which facts are relevant to a moral conclusion, any more than they can pick and choose which facts are relevant in determining a physical ailment. Admittedly, the notion of a fact is a complex one, but this makes it all the more important to exercise care in the use of it. Let us try to appreciate this complexity in terms of an example.

Someone might think that pushing someone roughly is rude, and that anyone who denies this is simply refusing to face the facts. But this example, as it stands, is worthless, since it tells one nothing of the context in which the pushing took place. The reference to the context is all-important in giving an account of the action, since not any kind of pushing can count as rudeness. Consider the following examples:

(a) One man pushing another person violently in order to save his life.

(b) A doctor pushing his way through a football-match crowd in response to an urgent appeal.

(c) The general pushing which takes place in a game of rugby.

(d) A violent push as a customary form of greeting between close friends.

In all these cases, pushing someone else is not rude. If someone took offence at being pushed, he might well see in the light of the situation that no offence had been caused. But what of situations where there is general agreement that an offence *has* been caused? Is the offence a fact from which a moral conclusion can be deduced? Clearly not, since what this suggestion ignores is the fact that *standards already prevail* in the context in which the offence is recognised. If one wants to call the offence a fact, one must recognise that it is a fact which already has moral import. The notion of 'offence' is parasitic on the notion of a standard or norm, although this need not be formulated. The person who wishes to say that the offence is a 'pure fact' from which a moral conclusion can be deduced is simply confused. What are the 'pure facts' relating to the pushing and the injury it is supposed to cause? A physiological account of the pushing (which might be regarded as pure enough) would not enable one to say what was going on, any more than a physiological account of the injury would tell us anything about what moral action (if any) is called for as a result. It makes all the difference morally whether the grazed ankle is caused by barging in the line-out or by barging in the bus queue. Any attempt to characterise the fact that an offence has been caused as a non-evaluative fact from which a moral conclusion can be deduced begs the question, since in asserting that a *kind of offence* has been caused, a specific background and the standards inherent in it have already been invoked.

But our opponent is still not beaten. He might give way on the confusion involved in the talk about deducing moral conclusions from 'pure facts', and agree that 'pushing' does not constitute rudeness in all contexts. Nevertheless, he might argue, where the circumstances *are* appropriate, it is possible to determine the rudeness of an action in a way which will settle any disagreement. But, again, this is clearly not the case. Whenever anyone says, 'That action is rude', there is no logical contradiction involved in denying the assertion, since although two people may share a moral concept such as rudeness, they may still differ strongly over its application. This is possible because views about rudeness do not exist *in vacuo*, but are often influenced by *other* moral beliefs. A good example of disagreement over the application of the concept of rudeness can be found in Malcolm's *Memoir of Wittgenstein*. Wittgenstein had lost his temper in a philosophical discussion with Moore, and would not allow Moore sufficient time to make his point. Moore thought that Wittgenstein's behaviour was rude, holding that good manners should always prevail, even in philosophical discussion. Wittgenstein, on the other hand, thought Moore's view of the matter absurd: philosophy is a serious business, important enough to justify a loss of temper; to think this rudeness is simply to misapply the judgement. Here, one can see

how standards of rudeness have been influenced by wider beliefs;
in other words, how the judgement, 'That is rude', is not entailed
by the facts.

The position we have arrived at does not satisfy a great many
contemporary moral philosophers. They are not prepared to recognise the possibility of permanent radical moral disagreement. They
want to press on towards ultimate agreement, moral finality, call it
what you will. They propose to do this by considering certain
non-moral concepts of goodness in the belief that they will throw
light on the notion of human good and harm. The non-moral
example, 'good knife', has been popular in this respect. The word
'knife' names an object in respect of its function. Furthermore, the
function is involved in the meaning of the word, so that if we came
across a people who possessed objects which looked exactly like
knives, but who never used these objects as we use them, we
should refuse to say that they had the concept of a knife. Now
when a thing has a function, the main criterion for its goodness
will be that it serves that function well. Clearly, then, not anything
can count as a good knife. But how does this help our understanding of moral goodness? Moral concepts are not functional. One can
see what is to count as a good knife by asking what a knife is *for*,
but can one see the point of generosity in the same way? To ask
what generosity is *for* is simply to vulgarise the concept; it is like
thinking that 'It is more blessed to give than to receive' is some
kind of policy!

Yet, although moral concepts are not functional words, they are
supposed to resemble them in important respects. The interesting
thing, apparently, about many non-functional words, is that when
they are linked with 'good' they yield criteria of goodness in much
the same way as 'good knife' and other functional words do. For
example, it seems as if 'good farmer' might yield criteria of goodness in this way. After all, farming is an activity which has a certain
point. To call someone a good farmer will be to indicate that he has
fulfilled the point of that activity. What 'the point' amounts to can
be spelled out in terms of healthy crops and herds, and a good
yield from the soil. The philosophical importance of these
examples is that they show that the range of words whose meaning provides criteria of goodness extends beyond that of functional
words. But what if the range is even wider than these examples
suggest? It is clear what the philosophers who ask this question
have in mind: what if the meaning of moral concepts could yield

criteria of goodness in the same way? If this were possible, one need not rest content with expounding 'good knife' or 'good farmer'; 'good man' awaits elucidation. The goal is to find out what constitutes human flourishing. Furthermore, once these greater aims are achieved, all moral disputes would be, in principle at least, resolvable. Anyone claiming to have a good moral argument would have to justify it by showing its point in terms of human good and harm. And, once again, not anything could count as human good and harm.

The programme is nothing if not ambitious. Unfortunately, it will not work. The reason why is no minor defect: the whole enterprise is misconceived almost from the start. As far as land farming is concerned, the confusion could have been avoided had one asked why 'farming' yields criteria when joined with 'good'. To say that this type of farming is an activity which has a point, that farming serves some end, and that to call someone a good farmer is to say that he achieves this end, is only to tell part of the story. The most important part is left out, namely, *that the end in question is not in dispute*. That is why it makes sense to talk of experts in farming, and why problems in farming can be solved by technical or scientific means. For example, farmers might disagree over which is the best method of growing good wheat, but there is no disagreement over what is to count as good wheat. On the other hand, the situation is different where animal farming is concerned. Suppose it were established that the milk yield was not affected by keeping the cattle indoors in confined quarters, and by cutting their food supply.[9] Many people would say that no good farmer would be prepared to do this, despite the economic factors involved. Others may disagree and see nothing wrong in treating animals in this way. The point to note is that here one has a *moral* dispute. We recognise it as such because of the issues of cruelty, care, and expediency involved in it. The dispute cannot be settled by reference to the point of farming in this instance, since it is agreed that whichever side one takes, the milk yield remains the same. One must recognise that there are different conceptions of what constitutes good farming. Similarly, we shall find that there is no common agreement on what constitutes human good and harm. I shall argue presently that human good is not independent of the moral beliefs people hold, but is determined by them. In short, what must be recognised is that there are different conceptions of human good and harm.

II

The above argument would not satisfy the philosophers I have in mind. For them, moral views are founded on facts, the facts concerning human good and harm. I shall argue, on the other hand, that moral viewpoints determine what is and what is not to count as a relevant fact in reaching a moral decision. This philosophical disagreement has important consequences, for if we believe that moral values can be justified by appeal to *the* facts, it is hard to see how one man can reject another man's reasons for his moral beliefs, since these reasons too, presumably, refer to the facts. If, on the other hand, we hold that the notion of factual relevance is parasitic on moral beliefs, it is clear that deadlock in ethics will be a common occurrence, simply because of what some philosophers have unwisely regarded as contingent reasons, namely, the different moral views people hold.

Many philosophers are not convinced that there need be a breakdown in moral argument. It is tempting to think that anyone who has heard *all* the arguments in favour of a moral opinion cannot still ask why he ought to endorse it, any more than anyone who has heard all there is to say about the earth's shape can still ask why he ought to believe that the earth is round. Anyone who has heard *all* the reasons for a moral opinion has, it seems, heard all the facts. Sometimes the facts are difficult to discern, but there is in principle no reason why moral disagreement should persist. Therefore, it is difficult to see how 'x is good' can be a well-founded moral argument when 'x is bad' is said to be equally well-founded. So runs the argument.

Certainly, it is difficult for philosophers who argue in this way to account for moral disagreement, since for them, moral judgements are founded on the facts of human good and harm, and the facts are incontrovertible. It is not surprising to find Bentham being praised in this context, since he too alleged that there is a common coinage into which 'rival' moral views could be cashed. The rivalry is only apparent, since the felicific calculus soon discovers the faulty reasoning. On this view, moral opinions are hypotheses whose validity is tested by reference to some common factor which is the sole reason for holding them. Bentham said the common factor was pleasure; nowadays it is called human good and harm. Whether one's moral views are 'valid' depends on whether they lead to human good and harm. But how does one arrive at these facts? One is said to do so by asking the question, 'What is the point?' often enough.

Philosophers are led to argue in this way by misconstruing the implications of the truth that a certain conceptual background is necessary in order for beliefs to have moral significance. Instead of being content to locate the point of such beliefs in their moral goodness, they insist on asking further what the point of *that* is. If one does not give up questioning too soon, one will arrive at the incontrovertible facts of human good and harm which do not invite any further requests for justification. Injury seems to be thought of as one such final halting place. To ask what is the point of calling injury a bad thing is to show that one has not grasped the concept of injury. To say that an action leads to injury is to give *a* reason for avoiding it. Injury may not be an overriding reason for avoiding the action which leads to it, as injustice is, but its being *a* reason is justified because injury is necessarily a bad thing. Even if we grant the distinction between reasons and overriding reasons, which is difficult enough if one asks who is to say which are which, is it clear that injury is always a reason for avoiding the action which leads to it?

The badness of injury, it is argued, is made explicit if one considers what an injury to hands, eyes, or ears, prevents a man from doing and getting; the badness is founded on what all men want. Mrs Foot, for example, expounds the argument as follows:

> the proper use of his limbs is something a man has reason to want if he wants anything.
>
> I do not know just what someone who denies this proposition could have in mind. Perhaps he is thinking of changing the facts of human existence, so that merely wishing, or the sound of the voice, will bring the world to heel? More likely he is proposing to rig the circumstances of some individual's existence within the framework of the ordinary world, by supposing for instance that he is a prince whose servants will sow and reap and fetch and carry for him, and so use their hands and eyes in his service that he will not need the use of his.[10]

But, Mrs Foot argues, not even this supposition will do, since the prince cannot foresee that his circumstances will not change. He still has good reason to avoid injury to his hands and eyes, since he may need them some day. But there was no need to have thought up such an extravagant example to find objections to the view that injury is necessarily bad. There are more familiar ones close at hand which are far more difficult to deal with than the case of the fortunate prince. For example, consider the following advice: 'if thine eye offend thee, pluck it out, and cast it from thee: it is better to enter into life with one eye, rather than having two eyes to be cast into hell fire' (Matt. 18:9).

Or again, consider how Saint Paul does not think 'the thorn in the flesh' from which he suffered to be a bad thing. At first, he does so regard it, and prays that it be taken away. Later, however, he thanks God for his disability, since it was a constant reminder to him that he was not sufficient unto himself. Another example is worth quoting.[11] Brentano was blind at the end of his life. When friends commiserated with him over the harm that had befallen him, he denied that his loss of sight was a bad thing. He explained that one of his weaknesses had been a tendency to cultivate and concentrate on too many diverse interests. Now, in his blindness, he was able to concentrate on his philosophy in a way which had been impossible for him before. We may not want to argue like Saint Paul or Brentano, but is it true that we have no idea what they have in mind?

A readiness to admit that injury might result in incidental gain will not do as an answer to the above argument. True, there would be a gain in being injured if an order went out to put all able-bodied men to the sword, but are we to regard the examples of Saint Paul and Brentano as being in this category? In some peculiar circumstances where this gain could be foreseen, we might even imagine a person seeking injury rather than trying to avoid it. But is this the way we should account for saints who prayed to be partakers in the sufferings of Christ? Obviously not. It is clear that Paul himself does not regard his ailment as something which happens to be useful in certain circumstances. But in any case, why speak of *incidental* gain in any of these contexts, and why speak of the contexts themselves as *peculiar*? In doing so, is not the thesis that injury is necessarily bad being defended by calling any examples which count against it incidental or peculiar? Insofar as moral philosophers argue in this way, they lay themselves open to the serious charge which Sorel has made against them:

> The philosophers always have a certain amount of difficulty in seeing clearly into these ethical problems, because they feel the

impossibility of harmonising the ideas which are current at a given time in a class, and yet imagine it to be their duty to reduce everything to a unity. To conceal from themselves the fundamental heterogeneity of all this civilised morality, they have recourse to a great number of subterfuges, sometimes relegating to the rank of exceptions, importations, or survivals, everything which embarrasses them. . . .[12]

Is it not the case that we cannot understand Brentano's attitude to his blindness unless we understand the kind of dedication to intellectual enquiry of which he was an example, and the virtues which such dedication demands in the enquirer? Again, we cannot understand Saint Paul's attitude to his ailment unless we understand something of the Hebrew-Christian conception of man's relationship to God, and the notions of insufficiency, dependence, and divine succour, involved in it. These views of personal injury or physical harm cannot be cashed in terms of what all men want. On the contrary, it is the specific contexts concerned, namely, dedication to enquiry and dedication to God, which determine what is to constitute goodness and badness. We can deny this only by elevating one concept of harm as being paradigmatic in much the same way as Bentham elevated one of the internal sentiments. We can say that injury is necessarily bad at the price of favouring one idea of badness.

Insofar as philosophers construct a paradigm in their search for 'the unity of the facts of human good and harm', they are not far removed from the so-called scientific rationalists and their talk of proper functions, primary purpose, etc. One of these, in an argument with a Roman Catholic housewife over birth control, stressed the harm which could result from having too many children. He obviously thought that the reference to physical harm clinched the matter. The housewife, on the other hand, stressed the honour a mother has in bringing children into the world. It seems more likely that the scientific rationalist was blind to what the housewife meant by honour, than that she was blind to what he meant by harm. Are we for that reason to call the honour incidental gain?

How would the scientific rationalist and the housewife reach the agreement which some philosophers seem to think inevitable if all the facts were known? It is hard to see how they could without renouncing what they believe in. Certainly, one cannot regard their respective moral opinions as hypotheses which the facts will either confirm or refute, for what would the evidence be? For the rationalist, the possibility of the mother's death or injury, the economic situation of the family, the provision of good facilities for the children, and so on, would be extremely important. The housewife too agrees about providing the good things of life for children, but believes that one ought to begin by allowing them to enter the world. For her, submission to the will of God, the honour of motherhood, the creation of a new life, and so on, are of the greatest importance. But there is no settling of the issue in terms of some supposed common evidence called human good and harm, since what they differ over is precisely the question of what constitutes human good and harm. The same is true of all fundamental moral disagreements, for example, the disagreement between a pacifist and a militarist. The argument is unlikely to proceed very far before deadlock is reached.

Deadlock in ethics, despite philosophical misgivings which have been voiced, does not entail liberty to argue as one chooses. The rationalist, the housewife, the pacifist, or the militarist, cannot say what they like. Their arguments are rooted in different moral traditions within which there are rules for what can and what cannot be said. Because philosophers believe that moral opinions rest on common evidence, they are forced to locate the cause of moral disagreement in the evidence's complexity: often, experience and imagination are necessary in assessing it. One can imagine someone versed in the views we have been attacking, and sympathetic with them, saying to an opponent in a moral argument, 'If only you could see how wrong you are. If only you had the experience and the imagination to appreciate the evidence for the goodness of the view I am advocating, evidence, which, unfortunately, is too complex for you to master, you would see that what I want is good for you too, since really, all men want it.' Such appeals to 'the common good' or to 'what all men want' are based on conscious or unconscious deception. It may be admitted that the majority of mothers nowadays want to plan the birth of their children, to fit in with the Budget if possible, and regard the rearing of their children as a pause in their careers. But this will not make the slightest difference to the housewife of our previous example. She believes that what the majority wants is a sign of moral decadence, and wants different things. But she does not believe because she wants; she wants because she believes.

The view that there are ways of demonstrating goodness by

appeal to evidence which operate *independently* of the various moral opinions people hold is radically mistaken. Sometimes, philosophers seem to suggest that despite the moral differences which separate men, they are really pursuing the same end, namely, what all men want. The notion of what all men want is as artificial as the common evidence which is supposed to support it. There are no theories of goodness.

2

Moral Practices and Anscombe's Grocer

G. E. M. Anscombe's grocer[1] teaches moral philosophers a valuable lesson, namely, that there is no need to appeal to anything beyond the facts when considering what is morally important. No appeals to a mysterious realm of evaluative meaning are necessary. If a customer orders potatoes, and the grocer delivers them to him, the grocer is justified in saying that the customer owes him for the potatoes. There is little point in the philosophers' protest that we cannot derive an 'ought' – that he owes the grocer for the potatoes – from an 'is' – that he ordered the potatoes and that the grocer delivered them – since the example illustrates the artificiality of the thesis. It will not do either to say that the facts only hold within certain social institutions, since the facts have their *meaning* within the institution of buying and selling. The grocer can say that the man owes him money on the basis of the above facts, in the context of the above institution. Certain things have happened: a man has ordered potatoes and had them delivered; other things follow: he owes the grocer for the potatoes. This is not a new theory, but a familiar story. The umpire raises his finger and the batsman walks, the jury decides and a sentence is pronounced, the priest pronounces and the man and woman are married, etc. All these facts have their meaning within certain institutions, but they do not describe these institutions; that is not what they tell us.

That the business transactions described have taken place is not absolute proof that a debt has been incurred, since the whole thing might be part of an amateur film production. What are we to say then? 'What is true is this: what ordinarily amounts to such-and-such a transaction *is* such-and-such a transaction, unless a special context gives it a different character'.[2] Normally, Anscombe's grocer does not need to look for special circumstances. Most days it is business as usual. Those philosophers who insist on there being a gap between 'ought' and 'is' *in all circumstances*, fail to recognise

14

the force of the normal implications of buying and selling, or the force of our normal ways of doing things.

But, having seen how much Anscombe's grocer has to teach moral philosophers, we must also note the way in which he obscures important moral possibilities. This can be seen in at least two ways.

First, Anscombe's grocer will not admit the possibility of serious moral or political rebellion against the institution of buying and selling. One day, an extraordinary day it is true, a man entered his shop, asked that potatoes be delivered to his house, but later denied that he owed the grocer anything. He claimed to have been protesting against the institution of buying and selling. The grocer pointed out, quite rightly, that a great deal is involved in the rebel's activity. The notion of contractual agreement runs deep in our society. We may share the grocer's doubts about how far such a rebel is going to get, but that is not the point at issue. There is something seriously wrong with a moral philosophy or a moral attitude which cannot, because of its presuppositions, recognise the seriousness of moral rebellion. Of course, not *any* rebellion will count as a moral rebellion. Lack of inclination will not count as a *moral* reason for rebellion against Anscombe's grocer. The moral or political rebel will have a story to tell. He cannot be compared with the liar, who, far from wanting to destroy the practice of truth-telling, takes advantage of it and needs it in order to achieve his ends. The liar does not rebel, he manipulates. But the rebel will have a story to tell about moral and political ideals, and alternative policies. To deny the possibility of such a story is an indication of a lack of seriousness.

Second, and perhaps more important, Anscombe's grocer's view of what people think ought to be done is a limited one. It is difficult to know to what extent he reflects Anscombe's own view, so we had better talk about his views rather than hers. Anscombe's grocer likes to know where he stands, and wants his customers to be aware of the same. One must be careful, however, in one's account of the grocer's limitations. If he were asked to justify his saying that the customer owed him money, his appeal would be to the rules of the game: 'You have ordered goods. I have delivered them. You owe me payment for them'. Normally, the grocer would go on to say, 'You must pay up'. In making this further move, the grocer does not appeal to anything beyond the facts. On the other hand, 'You must pay up' does not follow from the facts in the same way as the conclusion that the customer owes for the goods follows from the fact that the goods have been ordered and delivered. True, the fact that payment is made for goods delivered is not a merely contingent feature of the institution of buying and selling. Nevertheless, in certain situations, 'You must pay', viewed morally, may be regarded as a harsh demand rather than as a normal expectation. But would Anscombe's grocer agree with this? It is tempting to think that he would not; that for him, once the goods have been ordered and delivered, the rest is obvious. But this would be a mistake.[3] The grocer's reaction to all situations similar to the one described need not be, 'You must pay up'. It is wrong to attribute to him the view that moral truth consists in credit neither being asked for nor given. This is not the source of the grocer's limitations. His views are limited, rather, because he thinks that *whatever* his reaction is, it is the only moral possibility.

Things are different at the grocer's next door to Anscombe's flourishing businessman. He often says, 'Forget what you owe me' when his colleague says, 'You must pay up'. He does not appeal to anything beyond the facts either, but he gives them a different emphasis. It is these different emphases that Anscombe's grocer cannot account for. He knows the rules of the game, and he wants everyone to agree on what is fair or foul. He attracts all those who like to know where they stand on moral matters, and want everyone else to stand there too. Pharisees, casuists, and those moral philosophers who deny that there is a gap between 'ought' and 'is' *in all circumstances*, are among his most frequent customers.

Things are more complex next door. All the facts known, there is still room for a greater apprehension of them. There is still a question of which facts are to be emphasised or given priority. At this shop, there is always the possibility of the poor, having ordered goods and had them delivered, being told to forget their debts. Sometimes the shop is the scene of heated moral disagreement, which often ends in deadlock. Given that goods have been ordered and delivered and that the customer is temporarily unemployed, people might well disagree about what ought to be done: 'Business is business' – 'It's our duty to help ' – 'Charity encourages laziness' – 'Charity destroys self-respect' – 'It depends on how he spends his money' – 'Did he become unemployed through his own fault?' – 'I don't know about any of that, but forget what you owe me' – and so on.

Anscombe's position seems to be this: if one wants to understand a moral conclusion one can do so by seeing how certain facts are brute relative to it. Thus, once we understand that a man has ordered potatoes and had them delivered, we can see that his owing for the potatoes consists in these facts. It might also be said that the grocer's saying, 'You ought to pay' consists in these facts, given that these are the only facts. Anscombe recognises that a special context will put this business transaction in a new light, but she does not give examples. We have introduced a special consideration, namely, the fact that the debtor is unemployed. In the light of this fact there is nothing preventing Anscombe's grocer from saying, 'Forget what you owe me'. But, now, applying her conception of 'brute facts' to the *new* situation and the *new* moral conclusion, Anscombe would have to say that this moral conclusion consists in these facts which are brute relative to it. But this is precisely what the possibility of varied moral reactions shows to be mistaken. Given the new fact, the debtor's unemployment, some will conclude, 'You ought to pay up', and some will say, 'Forget what you owe me'. People may reach these conclusions for different reasons. But how can the variety of moral reactions to *the same* situation be analysed as Anscombe suggests; how can the same facts be brute relative to *different* moral conclusions; how can the varied judgements simply consist in these facts? Anscombe may say that she has no wish to apply her notion of 'brute facts' in these contexts. If so, the usefulness of the notion is extremely limited in moral philosophy, a fact which her original paper tends to obscure.

The possibility of varied moral reactions to the same facts is one of the most important features of the often confused philosophical insistence on the distinction between facts and values. The mere parading of facts will not always yield what we ought to do. Which facts do we consider important and how do we weigh them? These questions are an essential feature in the formation of moral attitudes. What cannot be denied is that facts which weigh a great deal for some people, do not weigh at all for others. It is important to recognise the diversity of moral possibilities. Otherwise, like Anscombe's grocer, we shall tend to think that no moral seriousness exists in any place other than our own. Of course, Anscombe's grocer could change with changing situations. But Anscombe's paper seems to suggest that whatever the situation, whatever changes it undergoes, there could only be one appropriate moral judgement – and that would be the judgement of her infallible grocer.

3

The Possibilities of Moral Advice

Professor Max Black tells us[1] that as a recognition of its remarkable philosophical influence, he proposes 'to assign to the principle that only factual statements can follow from exclusively factual statements the title "Hume's Guillotine"'.[2] He ends his paper by describing this principle as 'a dogma which ought by now to have been finally exploded'.[3] I assume that the 'by now' refers, not to the end of the article, but to the present state of contemporary moral philosophy, where the number of those prepared to assist in exploding the principle in question increases quarterly.

I want to consider the way in which Black thinks moral advice can be deduced from factual premisses. Certainly, in some contexts, it seems that one can argue from 'is' to 'should'. For example, as Black argues, if we know that A wants to checkmate his opponent B in a game of chess, and we see that he can only do so by moving the Queen, if A then asks us for advice, it follows that we *should* say 'Move the Queen.' But is there a transition from the chess example to an example of *moral* advice? Professor Black asks us to consider the following case:

A, playing chess with B, asks me for advice. I see that the one and only way to checkmate is to move the Queen and say 'You should move the Queen'. A bystander, C, however, who has overheard this, objects that B is in such precarious health that the shock of being suddenly mated by an inferior player might induce a stroke and kill him. C, therefore, says to A: 'You should not move the Queen – perhaps you ought to break off the game'. Is C's advice or admonition in conflict with mine? If it is, I cannot properly argue that my advice follows from the two factual premisses about A's purpose and the necessary and sufficient condition for achieving it. For the addition of further premisses –

18

for example, about *B*'s state of health and the probable consequences to him of defeat – would produce a conclusion contrary
to mine.[4]

Black underestimates the significance of his own example. As a
first reaction to it, he suggests that *C*'s comment involves a change
of subject. The introduction of moral considerations takes one
away from the question of what should be done *in this game*. I do
not want to press the point here, but the distinction between
games and morality is not as rigid as Black would make it. Consider, for example, the conflict between such attitudes as 'Win at
all costs' and 'Observe the spirit of the game.' Black says that it is
no doubt an important point that moral injunctions cannot be
limited in the same way as advice on strategy during a game, but it
is doubtful whether he has recognised the nature of the importance involved. Had he done so, he would not have tried to
establish an analogy between advice in chess, granted the absence
of so-called moral intrusions, and moral advice. In trying to do this
he is guilty of serious confusions.

Black begins by stating that *within* a given context, such as a
game, the way in which the question 'What should I do?' should
be answered may be generally agreed upon. But given that you
want to achieve *E* and that doing *M* is the one and only way of
achieving *E*, does it follow as a logical necessity that you should do
M? Black says that in the context of a game of chess, the facts
already mentioned constitute a *conclusive* reason for doing *M*. We
should not understand someone who, given the facts, advised
'You should not move the Queen.' The facts bind one to the
should-conclusion as much as the facts bind one to a factual conclusion in an argument of the form '*P*, if *P* then *Q*, therefore *Q*.' If
someone said 'Therefore not-*Q*' in this context, we should be at a
loss to know what he was up to.

Black is prepared to admit that there are differences between the
two pieces of advice. For example, in the latter, to think *P* is also to
think *Q*. Failure to think *Q* entails failure to understand *P*. Yet, it is
not so in the case of a moral *should*-conclusion. Giving moral
advice, unlike thinking *Q* given *P*, is a voluntary activity. A man
may train himself to abstain from giving moral advice, or he may
refrain from drawing a moral conclusion from the facts because of
moral deficiency. For these reasons, Black is reluctant to say that

the *should*-conclusion is entailed by the factual premisses. But once a man chooses to be involved in moral practices, the differences, for all practical purposes, are unimportant. Black says,

> If a moral conclusion is ever related to non-moral premisses in the fashion I have imagined, then, given that a moral conclusion is to be drawn, we have no choice as to what moral conclusion it shall be.[5]

Clearly, the conclusion of this argument is false, and so is its initial hypothesis. To see this one need only elaborate a little on the situation in which advice is sought during a game of chess. As well as knowing of *B*'s precarious health, and the probable effect of sudden defeat by an inferior player on him, let us suppose that various bystanders also know that *B* takes his chess very seriously indeed, and that he would be terribly upset if he thought that he had been 'given' a game; indeed, upset enough to induce a stroke. They also know, let us say, that *B* had been told by his doctor to give up playing chess because of the tension it caused in him, to which advice *B* had replied, 'In that case I'll die with my boots on.' *A* not only asks *C*, but all the bystanders, what he should do. They all know the facts we have mentioned, plus the fact that the only way to checkmate is to move the Queen. What advice should the bystanders give? Black tells us that 'The truth of the premisses restricts the performance, whether that of "advising" or something else, to a single possibility.'[6] Well, then, what is 'the single possibility' in the situation I have outlined?

If we ask, 'What advice *could* the bystanders give which would count as *moral* advice?' we can see that there are *many* possibilities. Here are some which come readily to mind.

Bystander *D* argues: 'What is more important than a man's life? After all, chess is only a game. I know that *B* has disregarded medical advice in order to play, but he is wrong in taking this attitude, and so I feel I am doing the right thing in overruling it. After all, he may never find out that he was given the game, whereas the consequences of his sudden defeat are very real. You should not move the Queen.'

Bystander *E* argues: 'How I admire *B*. He is one of the few who have seen through the shallowness of this life-at-all-costs attitude. What is life stripped of everything worthwhile? I do not share his passion for chess, but I understand it. I too should prefer to die with my boots on, rather than carry on in some kind of pretence. You should move the Queen.'

Bystander *F* argues: 'I agree with *B*. I understand him perfectly. We have played chess together for years. You should move the Queen.'

Bystander *G* argues: 'I disagree strongly with *B*'s attitude to his health, but I also think that every man has a right to his moral opinions. You should move the Queen.'

Bystander *H* argues: 'I do not propose to give positive advice. A man's life may be at stake whatever you do. I am prepared to clarify the issues involved as I see them, but you must draw your own moral conclusion.'

All these are *moral* reactions. Whether one agrees with them or not is another matter. Of course, the situation can be far more complicated; by the introduction of the fact that *B* has a family, for instance. But given that the situation is as we have described it, what is 'the single possibility' to which the facts bind us? Black says,

> Given the truth of the factual premisses concerning a man's end and the necessary and sufficient condition for attaining that end, and given one is to make some second-person 'should'-statement, one must say 'You should do *M*' – and nothing else will do. What kind of a 'must' is this? It seems to mean here precisely what 'must' means when we say that anybody affirming the premisses of a valid deductive argument must also affirm that argument's conclusion. Choice of the given 'should'-statement is enforced by the rules, understandings, or conventions governing the correct uses of 'should' and other words occurring in the argument: nobody who understands the premisses of the practical argument and knows the rules for the proper use of 'should' can honestly offer any other 'should'-conclusion. In this respect, the parallel with 'theoretical' arguments is strong. Accordingly, no special 'practical' logic is needed in such cases: the relevant principles are the familiar ones employed throughout deductive reasoning.[7]

The confusions in the above argument are due in part to a mistaken view of 'facts'. True, *within* a given moral viewpoint, the facts will bind those who share it to similar moral conclusions. But, for them, the facts already have moral import. It is not a case of

moral conclusions being deduced from non-evaluative factual premisses. Black thinks that the facts bind one to moral advice which he
regards as 'the single possibility' in the situation. But as I have tried to
show in my five examples, the moral advice one thinks one ought to
give will be determined by one's moral beliefs; it is such beliefs
which give the facts their relevance and significance. There
are no 'theoretical' rules for the 'proper' use of 'should' which
make one piece of advice the only honest possibility. To talk of 'the
proper use of "should"' is simply to beg the question: to equate
one's own moral views with 'the single possibility'. In case our five
examples of possible moral advice in the above situation are interpreted as a sign of theoretical disinterestedness, I had better put
my cards on the table and say that at the moment I do not know
what advice ought to be given in the situation I have described, or
whether positive advice should be given at all.

Another curious feature of Black's argument is his stress on a
man's end and the necessary and sufficient condition for attaining
that end. He thinks these facts bind one to a specific moral conclusion. Clearly, this is not the case. Morality does not wait on
these facts. On the contrary, people's aims and their methods of
attaining them wait on morality. A bystander would indicate his
lack of moral concern if he advised A as follows: 'B's health is
irrelevant. You want to win this game; that's all that matters. You
can only checkmate by moving the Queen, so move it.' Again, it
may be true that someone wants to extend his business, and that
the one and only way of doing so is by ruining his friend's
business. But morality says, 'Not that way.' On the other hand,
where a person's aims and methods of attaining them are moral, it
is always possible, as we have seen, for someone else to disagree
and put forward other moral proposals. There are no 'single
possibilities'.

Finally, a word about the challenge Professor Black puts to his
readers at the end of his paper. He says,

> Once Hume's Guillotine has been discredited, we may hope to
> find more important arguments containing valid transitions
> from 'is' to 'should' or from 'is' to 'ought'. If I am not mistaken,
> the following argument from factual premisses to a moral con-
> clusion is valid:
> Doing A will produce pain.

Apart from producing the pain resulting from *A*, doing *A* will have the same consequences that not doing *A* would have had. Therefore, *A* ought not to be done.[8]

On one interpretation, the conclusion of this argument can be shown to be false. If by 'consequences' Professor Black means the kind of thing Mill had in mind, it is clear that many people have thought that they ought to do *A* on moral grounds despite the absence of such consequences. For example, a man may feel that he ought to die for a cause although the cause is lost. Again, a soldier may refuse to give details of plans to the enemy under torture, although he may know that they have already discovered them. Such actions can certainly be given a *moral* point, though in Mill's sense they would be pointless.

But Black may want to include in his 'consequences' the agent's regard for his moral convictions (as opposed to the success or failure which may attend standing by them), and his remorse at failing in the time of trial. The second premiss of Black's argument could then be reworded as follows: 'Apart from producing the pain resulting from *A*, doing *A* will have the same point that not doing *A* would have had'. The challenge is then to show that pointless pain has a point. No wonder Professor Black feels confident about the argument! But confidence is bought at the price of triviality. Certainly, Hume's point is unaffected by the argument. Black tells us that pointless pain is bad, but this is to say nothing at all, since the whole moral issue concerns *what is to count* as pointless pain, and this is not something that the facts will tell us. There will be moral disagreement over what is and what is not to count as pointless. Is dying for a lost cause pointless? Black's second premiss, once it is given a *positive* content, will be a premiss which already has moral import; that is, it will say that such-and-such is pointless. Those who disagree about this pointlessness will not feel bound to the moral conclusion. There are no deductive moves to 'single possibilities' which will change this situation.

Morality is not a game, and philosophers are not people who have special insight into its 'rules'. I think Professor Black ought to take another look at Hume's Guillotine, for, unless I am mistaken, his arguments are on the block.

4

Allegiance and Change in Morality: A Study in Contrasts

INTRODUCTION

It has been said that the tendency to make use of reminders drawn from literature in discussing problems in moral philosophy is not only dangerous, but needless. Dangers there certainly are, but these have little to do with the reasons offered for the needlessness of such reminders. Reminders drawn from literature, it is said, introduce an unnecessary complexity into one's philosophising. Indeed, as Peter Winch has pointed out, according to 'a fairly well-established . . . tradition in recent Anglo-Saxon moral philosophy . . . it is not merely permissible, but desirable, to take *trivial* examples. The rationale of this view is that such examples do not generate the emotion which is liable to surround more serious cases and thus enable us to look more coolly at the logical issues involved,'[1] and it carries the implication that 'moral concerns can be examined quite apart from any consideration of what it is about these concerns which makes them important to us.'[2]

Anyone who accepts these conclusions ignores, or fails to recognise, the tension which exists between certain ways of doing moral philosophy and the novel. I am not suggesting that this tension need exist or that it is inevitable. One is faced by the contrast between complexity and simplicity: the complexity of the novel, and the comparative simplicity of contemporary moral philosophy. The student of moral philosophy may be surprised at the suggestion that his subject is simple; he may protest that it is difficult enough. But I am not equating simplicity with easiness. What I mean by the comparative simplicity of moral philosophy is the tendency to examine human conduct within narrow boundaries which the novelist does not hesitate to transgress. My suggestion

24

is that in this matter it is the philosophers who exhibit this tendency who are confused, and who have much to learn from the greater complexity of the novel.

I have argued elsewhere that the ethical theories dominating contemporary moral philosophy, though different in important respects, are characterised by optimism, order, and progress.[3] These characteristics make up what might be called an abstracted concept of reasonableness. In this essay I want to explore some features of this notion of reasonableness and to contrast these with moral reasons which are rooted in the ways people live and in their conceptions of what is important in life. I shall try to bring out the nature of the contrasts by reference to some novels by Edith Wharton. The contrast depends on showing how much separates examples suggested by prevailing moral philosophies from other moral possibilities. The difficulty is in showing the force of these other possibilities. Such a showing involves an ability not given to many. The novelist with such ability brings us to see possibilities which otherwise we might not recognise.[4]

AN ABSTRACTED CONCEPT OF REASONABLENESS

Before turning to an examination of Edith Wharton's work, more needs to be said about the notion of reasonableness I want to criticise. At first, it may seem doubtful whether different viewpoints in contemporary moral philosophy can be seen as sharing an abstracted concept of reasonableness. After all, much seems to separate those who say that there is something called human good and harm by reference to which one can assess in general what people ought to do, and those who say, not only that each person must decide his ultimate moral principles for himself, but that anything could constitute such principles for a person. Yet the differences lessen when one is told that a person must not simply be free to choose his ultimate moral principles, but must also act rationally in doing so. This latter stipulation means, it is said, that the agent's principles must be such that he is prepared to abide by them himself as well as expecting other people to abide by them. Despite the fact that it is recognised that some fanatics will legislate in such a way that their principles will make them subject, in certain circumstances, to what no reasonable man would want, the general impression one receives is that there will be a large measure of agreement in men's moral principles. Because men generally want to attain and avoid the same sorts of things, their principles, it is said, framed with such consequences in view, are unlikely to show drastic divergences. Behind this view, no less than that which makes an explicit appeal to human good and harm, is to be found the notion of what all men want, which psychologically, if not logically, tends to limit what could count as ultimate moral principles.

It is true that obstacles to the attainment of human good are recognised, but impediments, such as lack of experience and imagination, are seen as contingently related to morality. If all the facts concerning what are in people's interests were known, there would no longer be any room for disagreement about how men should conduct their lives.

Such is the philosophical neighbourhood in which an abstracted concept of reasonableness can grow. One can easily imagine a character emerging from this background. We could call him the reasonable man. Of course I am not suggesting that one could ever meet such a man. But that one could not do so is precisely the point, since the caricature is constructed on confused presuppositions which are latent in a great deal of contemporary moral philosophy. As we examine six features of the reasonable man's character, those who are acquainted with recent discussions in ethics will recognise in him, though he is nameless, a familiar friend.

The first characteristic of the reasonable man is that he has reasons for his moral allegiances. He will tell you proudly that his values are not without foundations. Since these foundations, human good and harm, serve as justifications of his allegiances, the relation between the allegiance and its grounds must be contingent. It would seem to follow that his moral principles have the status of well-tested hypotheses, well-founded generalisations, or well-grounded policies. Still, this is not something about which the reasonable man would feel apologetic. On the contrary, he will point out that if one has made a mistake in one's assessment of whether allegiance to a principle is conducive to human good, it is far better to abandon or to modify the principle than to persist in one's unreasonableness. The reasonable man is always prepared to change if called upon by reason to do so.

The second characteristic of the reasonable man follows from what I have just said. The reasonable man has reasons, not only for his allegiances, but also for his changes. If moral beliefs and actions are subject to an external measure of validity, it should not be surprising if faulty assessments are made from time to time. Change, when it comes, is justified by appeal to the same criterion that justified the prior allegiance, namely what all men want to attain and what all men want to avoid, human good and harm. Change, for the reasonable man, is always reasonable change.

The third characteristic of the reasonable man is extremely important. He believes in the unity of reason; for him, reason is one. There are many different moral beliefs, but they are all either right or wrong. This is decided by bringing them all to the bar of reason. Thus, when the reasonable man changes his beliefs, he has done so by coming to a greater appreciation of the same external measure that brought him to his initial moral beliefs.

In the light of his belief in the unity of reason we can appreciate the fourth characteristic of the reasonable man, namely, that when he changes he always changes for the better. When he changes his moral beliefs he has a deeper grasp of what is and what is not reasonable, but he is still appealing to reasons of the same kind. Therefore, since his change is a change within the same rational terms of reference, his change, being more reasonable than his former allegiance, is a change for the better.

Fifthly, since the reasonable man always changes for the better, the beliefs he has discarded or refused to believe in can be regarded as outmoded, outdated inhibitions, or as irrational taboos.

Finally, the reasonable man is likely to regard wider moral changes in society, when he agrees with them, in the same way as he regards his own moral changes. Society is progressing to a more rational morality; it is coming of age, casting off its old inhibitions and taboos. Those who resist the changes he agrees with will be regarded by the reasonable man as defenders of the status quo, as those who do not realise that we live in a real world, as being inhibited by old taboos and bound by outworn habits and customs.

No doubt additional characteristics of the reasonable man can be thought of, but I believe the six I have outlined are sufficient to illustrate one form that an abstracted concept of reasonableness can take. Adherence to such a concept obscures the essential heterogeneity of moral beliefs and the very different account of moral allegiance which is called for, once this heterogeneity is recognised. Examples play an essential role here, since in terms of the issues they present one can show, as Winch has said, that 'the seriousness of such issues is not something we can add, or not, after the explanation of what those issues are, as a sort of emotional extra: it is something that "shows itself" . . . *in* the explanation of the issues.'[5] If this is right, then what is and what is not morally important cannot be determined independently of the variety of issues that present themselves. It cannot be determined in general in terms of an abstracted notion of reasonableness. In turning to the issues which are embodied in the novels of Edith Wharton, we shall find that the notion of reasonableness we have been discussing can claim literary critics as well as philosophers among its victims.

ABSTRACTION, REASONABLENESS AND THE CRITICS

Edith Wharton is concerned with allegiance and change in morality but, for her, these notions are not abstractions. On the contrary, they are rooted in the New York of the last third of the nineteenth century and the early years of the twentieth century. She depicts the upper middle-class life of New York in the 1870s and 1880s as a life dominated by a hierarchical family system. Free and undisturbed by major crises, it laid great emphasis on tradition, decorum, and honesty in business. If its mannerly code was broken, one was expected to break it without scandal. The young men of the community practised law, but in a half-hearted way which left plenty of time for frequent dinings and European excursions. Edith Wharton is alive to the force of convention in the world she depicts. Speaking of *The Age of Innocence* she says that 'what was or was not "the thing" played a part as important . . . as the inscrutable totem terrors that had ruled the destinies of (their) forefathers thousands of years ago.' She describes people as living in 'a kind of hieroglyphic world, where the real thing was never said or done or even thought, but only represented by a set of arbitrary signs.' The easiness with which this conventionality can be appreciated has blinded critics to the moral dimension in Edith Wharton's work. Guided by very different moral beliefs, critics have abstracted selective elements from the situations and made them a picture of the whole. For example, Blake Nevius, describing old New York, says that

> The real drama is played out below the surface – the impeccable, sophisticated surface – and communicates itself, if at all, to the observer by means of signs which only the initiate can read. Hence the significance, to old New York, of certain gestures by

which the private drama is made public: that frightening portent of social annihilation, the 'cut'; the dinner invitation from the van der Luydens, the invitation to occupy a prominent box at the opera, or the presence of Mrs. Manson Mingott's carriage before the door, all signalising reinstatement; the sudden flight to Europe, which is the solution to every serious emotional crisis. These were the less arbitrary signs. By and large however the acquired manners of old New York lend themselves to what Edith Wharton termed 'an elaborate system of mystification.'[6]

Edith Wharton herself sees far more in *The Age of Innocence*. Into the society we have described comes Countess Olenska, fleeing from a broken marriage and threatening to divorce her husband. As she is an ex-member of old New York society, the influential families decide that she must be prevented from bringing scandal on herself and on them. Newland Archer is chosen to present their case to her. He is himself betrothed to May Welland in whom many critics have seen a perfect product of the society Edith Wharton was portraying. In presenting the case, however, Newland Archer's relationship with Ellen Olenska changes. What begins in criticism, ends in love. But he has put his community's case too well. He has convinced Ellen Olenska that personal happiness is not the most important thing in life. He shows her values connected with honour, time, tradition, obedience, and sacrifice. Despite their love, they part. Archer marries May Welland, but even after her death, when he has a chance to meet Ellen Olenska again, he lets the opportunity go by, convinced that nothing that could happen as a result of such a meeting would be as real as the considerations that parted them in the first place. The moral notions involved in the relationship between Newland Archer and Ellen Olenska are at the centre of the story.

Why have many critics distorted these moral notions in their discussions of *The Age of Innocence*? The answer lies in the fact that having already laid down what is to count as reasonable conduct, they cannot see anything in the novel other than a straightforward tale of a weak man trapped by a trivial society, unable to take the opportunity of freedom and a life worth living. There is no doubt in their minds that Newland Archer ends defeated.

Newland Archer's defeat, it is suggested, can be seen in the way meeting Ellen Olenska changed his attitude to May Welland. At first Blake Nevius tells us,

He is the willing accomplice of a society 'wholly absorbed in barricading itself against the unpleasant,' and his appreciation of May Welland is based on this precarious ideal: 'Nothing about his betrothed pleased him more than her resolute determination to carry to its utmost limits that ritual of ignoring the "unpleasant" in which they had both been brought up.' In the story that follows Edith Wharton tries to make clear what this innocence costs. The measure of change wrought in Archer's outlook by his experience with Ellen is suggested by a sentence occurring midway in the novel, before the echo of his earlier belief has quite died away: 'Ah, no, he did not want May to have that kind of innocence, the innocence that seals the mind against imagination and the heart against experience!' . . . When he returns to May Welland, it is to the ultimate realisation that, like John Marcher in James's 'The Beast in the Jungle,' he is the man 'to whom nothing was ever to happen.'[7]

The evaluations involved in this criticism are fairly obvious: it is reasonable to be open to change, experiment, challenge, and novelty, and unreasonable to ignore the opportunities for these things. For similar reasons, it seems to me, Edmund Wilson describes *The Age of Innocence* as follows:

> Countess Olenska – returns to the United States to intrude upon and disturb the existence of a conservative provincial society; . . . she attracts and almost captivates an intelligent man of the community who turns out, in the long run, to be unable to muster the courage to take her, and who allows her to go back to Europe.[8]

These critics ignore the moral notions involved in the relations which Edith Wharton depicts. In making the separation between Ellen Olenska and Newland Archer solely a product of weakness, Wilson is distorting the moral integrity it also exemplifies. Blake Nevius's characterisation of Newland Archer is deficient for similar reasons. In discussing them further we can see how far-reaching an influence an abstracted notion of reasonableness has had on the critics.

Wilson is wrong in thinking that Newland Archer's decision to stay in old New York is simply the result of weakness on his part. Wilson finds Newland Archer's decline after his initial protest against the old ways paralleled in Edith Wharton's later works. He claims that they 'show a dismay and a shrinking before what seemed to her the social and moral chaos of an age which was battering down the old edifice that she herself had once depicted as a prison. Perhaps, after all, the old mismated couples who had stayed married in deference to the decencies were better than the new divorced who were not aware of any duties at all.[9] If Edith Wharton's view of the new is open at times to these charges, is not Wilson in danger of precisely the same deficiencies in his attitude to the old? He tends to write them off as deference to decencies, and his language implies that there is little more to be found here than sham, arid convention, and doing the done thing. When he describes Ellen Olenska's role in the novel as a narrow failure to capture one of the more intelligent of old New York's social clan, there is an unmistakable implication that if intelligence had its way, everyone would break out of the self-imposed prison they had devised for themselves. Similarly, when Nevius contrasts the protectionism, conventionalism, and conformity of May Welland with the imagination, experience, protest, and unpredictability offered by Ellen Olenska, there is little doubt as to which side he thinks exemplifies intelligence, and which exemplifies unthinking obedience, 'the dull unthinking round of duties', to use the description which Lionel Trilling gives to 'the morality of inertia' which he claims to find in Edith Wharton's *Ethan Frome*.[10]

Of course these critics could be right, but I am suggesting that a closer examination of Edith Wharton's best work shows that they are wrong. Furthermore, they are wrong because they are in the grip of an abstracted concept of reasonableness which here takes the form of the unwarrantable assumption that intelligence must take a specific form; one that excludes the kind of intelligence and integrity one finds in Edith Wharton's old New York. The critics are in danger of abstracting a standard of intelligence and reasonableness from the variety of such standards, and using it as a means of assessing different ways of living. Insofar as they do so, they are not dissimilar to the reasonable man I characterised earlier. His first characteristic, you will recall, was his insistence that we must have reasons for our values. In relation to Edith Wharton's *The Age of Innocence* he is likely to ask for reasons for the conformity to decorum and rigid standards, and for the ignoring of opportunities for wider experience and imagination. His answer, in our time, is almost certain to be that no good reason can be found for such conformity, and that those who become its victims, like Newland Archer, are doomed to waste their lives.

'That it has all been a waste' is not an infrequent reaction on completing a reading of *The Age of Innocence*. In making such a judgement high priority is given to the importance of satisfying genuine love, talking out difficulties in frank open discussion, making up one's own mind on moral issues, and not paying too much attention to what one's parents or one's family have to say on the matter, and the conviction that since one only has one life to live, one should not allow its course to be determined by others. It is essential to understand that it is no part of my intention in this essay to criticise these moral beliefs. Still less do I want to deny that people can or should criticise different attitudes in terms of them. What I am protesting against is the equation of these beliefs with intelligence as such, such that any beliefs which conflict with them are ruled out of court as moral possibilities. In this way, conflicting beliefs can be accused of lacking intelligence and reasonableness, and the illusion created that this conclusion has been reached by appeal to a norm which is independent of the moral beliefs involved. As a result of this illusion, the moral beliefs which are said to be inferior are almost certain to be ignored or distorted. Indeed, one may find it being denied that they are moral beliefs at all.

Such is the hold of an abstracted concept of reasonableness on the thinking of certain critics. Before considering the philosophical criticisms that can be made of such an influence, it is necessary to give an account of what such abstractions ignore in Edith Wharton's work, namely, the moral ideas which enter into the relationships she depicts; one must show that these are genuinely moral ideas. This can only be achieved by waiting on the novel.

WAITING ON THE NOVEL

Can one see more than dull unthinking conformity in Newland Archer and May Welland? I believe one can, and so do other critics of the work. Louis Auchincloss says that despite Newland Archer's decision to marry May Welland and not to elope with Ellen Olenska, 'there is no feeling, however, that Archer has condemned himself and the Countess to an unrewarding life of frustration.'[11] Why is this so? It could hardly be the case if, as we have been told, the decision was merely the product of deference to duties due to lack of nerve. There must be something more positive about the decision. The key to this is to be found in what happens when, having mechanically put the case against her divorcing her husband, Archer finds himself in love with Ellen Olenska, and pleads with her to come away with him. She has perceived a moral reality in what to him was little more than decorum. When Ellen reminds him that he is betrothed and that she is married, he replies, 'Nonsense! It's too late for that sort of thing. We've no right to lie to other people or to ourselves.'[12] But Ellen Olenska is able to tell him what she has learnt from him:

'New York simply meant peace and freedom to me: it was coming home. And I was so happy at being among my own people that everyone I met seemed kind and good, and glad to see me. But from the very beginning,' she continued, 'I felt that there was no one as kind as you; no one who gave me reasons that I understood for doing what at first seemed so hard and – unnecessary. The very good people didn't convince me; I felt they'd never be tempted. But you knew; you understood; you had felt the world outside tugging at one with all its golden hands – and yet you hated the things it asks of one; you hated happiness bought by disloyalty and cruelty and indifference. That was what I'd never known before – and it's better than anything I've known.'[13]

When Newland Archer appeals to rights, their right to happiness and the fact that May Welland has no right to ask them to forgo it, Ellen Olenska simply replies, 'Ah, you've taught me what an ugly word that is.'[14]

It is true that for some time after his marriage Ellen is seldom out of Newland Archer's thoughts. He is desperately unhappy, and, without doubt, she is unhappy too. Yet, even so, when Archer does meet her again, it is to be told, 'It was you who made me understand that under the dullness there are things so fine and sensitive and delicate that even those I most cared for in my other life look cheap by comparison.'[15] The force with which Edith Wharton portrays the dullness and conventionality in society should not obscure the sterner stuff she also shows us. As Auchincloss says, 'This is the climax of the message: that under the thick glass of convention blooms the fine, fragile flower of patient suffering and denial. To drop out of society is as vulgar as to predominate; one must endure and properly smile.'[16] Sometimes, the propriety of the smile may all but hide the moral strength beneath it. This is so in the case of May Welland.

According to Nevius, 'May Welland personifies all the evasions and compromises of his (Archer's) clan, she is the "safe" alternative.' This, it is true, is how Newland Archer thought of his wife at many times, but it leaves out a great deal if it is meant as a final judgement by the reader. After his wife's death, through his son, Archer learns that there was more to his wife's character than he had realised.

> '. . . you date, you see, dear old boy. But mother said . . .'
> 'Your mother?'
> 'Yes: the day before she died. It was when she sent for me alone – you remember? She said she knew we were safe with you and always would be, because once, when she asked you to, you'd given up the thing you most wanted.'
>   Archer received this communication in silence . . . At length he said in a low voice, 'She never asked me.'
> 'No, I forgot. You never did ask each other anything, did you? And you never told each other anything. You just sat and watched each other, and guessed at what was going on underneath.'[17]

Another critic, Louis Coxe, in what I regard as the finest essay in Irving Howe's collection, asks,

> The total commitment of May to her world and to Newland Archer: is there nothing admirable in this? Nothing of the heroic? For I believe that if any character in this novel partakes of the heroic nature, it is indeed May Welland, she of the pink and white surface and the candid glance, whose capacity for passion and sacrifice her husband never knew.[18]

Finally, are we to assume that Archer's reflections on his life, culminating in this revelation about his wife, had no effect on him, that the truths he had unwittingly conveyed to Ellen Olenska had not come home to him? Hardly. At the end of the novel we see him with another chance to meet Ellen Olenska. He thinks, fleetingly, that even if at fifty-seven it is too late for summer dreams, it may not be too late for friendship and comradeship. In the end, however, he decides not to go up to her hotel room and remains in the park. He has sent his son ahead of him and imagines how he will be received.

'It's more real to me here than if I went up,' he suddenly heard himself say; and the fear lest that last shadow of reality should lose its edge kept him rooted to his seat as the minutes succeeded each other.

He sat for a long time on the bench in the thickening dusk, his eyes never turning from the balcony. At length a light shone through the windows, and a moment later a manservant came out on the balcony, drew up the awnings, and closed the shutters.

At that, as if it had been the signal he waited for, Newland Archer got up slowly and walked back alone to his hotel.[19]

If Archer is to think of Ellen Olenska at all now, it is in the context of the great decision she had once made, and which had governed most of his life. Is this a man 'to whom nothing was ever to happen'?

PHILOSOPHICAL CONSEQUENCES OF WAITING ON THE NOVEL

The philosophical consequences of waiting on Edith Wharton's novel are that the artificialities of an abstracted concept of reasonableness are revealed. The tenets of the reasonable man are shown to be equally artificial. In fact, all these tenets are reversed. Let us see how this comes about.

We have seen that Newland Archer, Ellen Olenska, and May Welland, in different ways, embody the old New York morality Edith Wharton wanted to depict. But could we say, as some philosophers insist we must say, that these characters have reasons for their values? On the contrary, their values constitute their reasons. Without taking these values into account, one cannot understand their actions or even their descriptions of situations in which action is called for. Without the values which enter into it, the choice facing Ellen Olenska is unintelligible. Before Archer convinces her otherwise, the satisfaction of true love and her own happiness would have been of paramount importance to her. She would have described her elopement with Archer as a flight to freedom. But when she becomes aware of other values, values involving suffering, denial, endurance, discipline, she can no longer see things in that way. She says that her former way of looking at things is cheap by comparison. This judgement is not arrived at, however, by cashing the two attitudes into a common coinage by which one can be demonstrated to be cheaper than the other. This is how the reasonable man would have us argue. Ellen Olenska's judgement bears no relation to such an argument. On the contrary, her judgement about her former attitude is intelligible only in terms of the new moral perspective she comes to embrace.

What has become of the claim that one must have reasons for one's values? Of course, a person can provide moral reasons for an action in specific circumstances. Ellen Olenska claimed that Newland Archer gave her such reasons without realising it. But these are not the reasons that the reasonable man has in mind. These reasons already have a moral character, whereas he is looking for a further justification for such reasons. A natural context for such talk would be those cases where a person has hidden reasons for holding moral beliefs. A so-called allegiance to moral values may turn out to be sham, hypocrisy, pretence, or self-deception. The presence of such reasons indicates that a person has a mere external relation to the values in question.

Edith Wharton depicts an external relation to values in her portrayal of Undine Spragg in *The Custom of the Country*. Undine personifies the *nouveaux riches* who were being created by the financial empires being formed in the cities of the mid-west. She comes to threaten the placid society we find in *The Age of Innocence*. Her values at any time are essentially transient, serving the constant need for new pleasures, new conquests. Undine goes from marriage to marriage unable to share any of the genuine enthusiasms or values of her husbands, or to appreciate the traditions of the families she enters into. Her attitude can be summed up by the way she reacts to a future husband's comment on her insistence on being painted by a fashionable portrait painter. The husband remarks, 'Oh, if a "smart" portrait's all you want!' to which she replies, 'I want what the others want.'[20] With such an attitude she is condemned to perpetual rootlessness. Despite the fact that she ends up by marrying someone whose love of money and status is as all-consuming as her own, our last glimpse of her sees her regretting that as a result of her divorces she can never be the wife of an ambassador!

It is precisely because Undine Spragg has reasons for her values which are externally related to those values that we see in her a fundamental rootlessness in which no form of decency can grow or flourish. The difference between Undine Spragg and the characters in *The Age of Innocence* we have discussed can be expressed once again by saying that whereas she has reasons for her values, their values were their reasons.

These conclusions have drastic consequences for the reasonable man's notion of moral change. For him, since the reasons for such change must be of the same kind as those which supported prior allegiances, change occurs within a unified rational system. The inadequacy of this view can be brought out by reference to one incident in *The Age of Innocence*.

Despite the fact that Archer's son reveals depths of character in his mother which his father had never appreciated, he can hardly appreciate them. For Dallas, the son, his parents' attitudes are dated, outmoded, eccentric. Louis Coxe says, rightly, that

> For Dallas it would have been so simple: run away with Ellen Olenska and hang what people will say. . . . Times have changed, and in this simpler and freer world of Dallas' young manhood, there are no occasions to exercise the feelings nor nourish passion. . . . Can Dallas or anyone like him begin to understand the meaning of the kind of feelings Archer has known? Have they the time? the imagination? the passion? What can the notion of a buried life mean to one who can conceive only of surface?[21]

To Dallas, the relationship between his parents is 'a deaf and dumb asylum'.

If one compares the views of Newland Archer's generation with those of his son, can one appeal to a common criterion of reason-ableness which would bring out the character of the differences between them? It is difficult to see how one could do so in general. What we see is that many of the values of one generation mean little to the other. With the social changes Edith Wharton describes so well, the old values of respect for tradition, endurance, loyalty, faithfulness, and the possibility of a buried life, that is, burying one's strongest desires, are eroded by the increasing dominance of new values characterised by frankness, openness, articulate honesty, courage, and experiment. A common criterion of reasonableness is not necessary in order to explain such changes. One need only bring out the content of the opposing values to show how they naturally militate against each other. To call one set of beliefs irrational often obscures what disagreement amounts to in this context; that the disagreement is itself an expression or a product of a moral judgement.

If these conclusions are correct, one can no longer believe, as the reasonable man does, in the unity of reason. Fundamental changes in moral perspectives need no longer be seen as the rejection and replacing of hypotheses or policies within a single framework within which moral beliefs must be determined. Old values do die, and new ones take their place. What separates Archer and his son is not a matter of different tentative beliefs within a common notion of reason but, rather, different ways of looking at the world, different conceptions of what is important in life.

If these differences in moral perspective are not recognised there is a danger not simply of distorting the reality of radical change, but also of misdescribing discarded beliefs as taboos and inhibitions. We see this latter danger exemplified to some extent in Dallas's mildly amused view of his parents' attitudes. With later generations, with which we are more familiar, amusement gives way to arrogance. It is assumed that earlier generations have wanted all along to be just as we are. It is often suggested that earlier generations are not really doing or believing what they think they are doing and believing. Their beliefs, it is said, form a prison which suppresses and confines their real desires.

The credibility of this view depends, to a large extent, on examples of ways of living already in decline, where nominal existence has outlived actual existence. If one thinks of lost generations, following old rules out of habit or from fear of social sanctions, alienated from their background, but unable to embrace an alternative, it is not hard to see how it can be said that these people are not at home in their world, that they are not doing what they think they are doing. In *The House of Mirth* Edith Wharton shows the empty respectability which results from the decline of old New York morality. Irving Howe describes the situation as follows:

> The action of *The House of Mirth* occurs in the first years of the twentieth century, several stages and a few decades beyond the

dispossession of old New York. We barely see any representatives of the faded aristocracy; what we do see in the first half of the book are several of its distant offshoots and descendants, most of them already twisted by the vulgarity of the new bourgeoisie yet, for no very good reasons, still contemptuous of it. The standards of these characters who have any claim to the old aristocracy are not so much guides to their own conduct as strategies for the exclusion of outsiders . . . they have kept some pretence to social superiority, but very little right to it. . . .[22]

In such situations as these it can be said, with justice, that things are not what they seem. What one must not do is to generalise indiscriminately from such examples. For instance, one cannot say that what Newland Archer really wants, despite what he says and does, is what his son and his generation realise. It would be distortion to say that Archer wants to follow his desires without a second thought in the way Dallas does. The notion of a buried life is important to Archer and determines the degree of importance he attaches to satisfying one's desires. To say that Archer must have been wanting all along what Dallas achieved, to say that anyone who loved the standards of old New York must have been deceiving himself, one would have to produce evidence of tension, self-deception, or alienation. When the judgement is made in the absence of such evidence, one conception of what is worthwhile in life is being made a criterion of rationality by which all other conceptions must be judged. At this stage, a moral judgement has been changed into a metaphysical thesis about what all men want and the essence of rational conduct. No such thesis can be found in Edith Wharton. Louis Coxe says that in contrasting Newland Archer, the near-rebel, with May Welland, the total conformist,

a lesser novelist would have been content to rest, in the mere showing of the processes by which an American with separatist tendencies is broken to harness and curb. [This corresponds to what Edmund Wilson saw in the novel.] That she does not leave it at this adds dimension to the book and to the novelist's vision. The emphasis rests finally upon the ways in which an individual, in more or less settled times, can come to identify his illusions with those of his world. The rightness or wrongness of such identification we may determine if we can, though for my part I would say that the triumph of Edith Wharton's realism strikes one as most sweeping in just her very refusal to draw any such line: she seems merely to say, that is the way things were for these people. Had you done differently, it would have been a different time, place, and cast.[23]

This brings us to the last characteristic of the reasonable man, namely his tendency to see the society to which he belongs as the product of a coming of age in which old inhibitions and taboos have been cast off. The confusion is in the claim that this *must* be the case, and in the a priori ruling out of the possibility of decline and loss in a society. There is no confusion in the claim that a whole society could be in the grip of self-deception. Edith Wharton, in writing *The House of Mirth*, asked herself how 'could a society of irresponsible pleasure-seekers be said to have, on the "old woes of the world", any deeper bearing than the people composing such a society could guess?' She answered: 'A frivolous society can acquire dramatic significance only through what its frivolity destroys. Its tragic implication lies in its power of debasing people and ideals.'[24] That such comments have a point is not in dispute. What is in dispute is the larger claim that the heterogeneity of morals can be reduced to some kind of rational unity.

When some beliefs and values give way to others, some may want to condemn the old ways as wrong, and even as wicked. That is their privilege. What cannot be said, in general, is that the old ways were irrational, that men had reasons for adopting them which seemed good at the time, that men discovered better reasons for rejecting them, and having thus progressed again and again, have now achieved the freedom which only reason can bring. Such wholesale judgements are invariably confused. What one can say often is that a society is better or worse than its predecessors in certain respects. Edith Wharton however shows us another possibility, namely, that of refraining from such judgements and being content to observe that whereas people once thought about certain matters in a particular way, we no longer do so.

I am not suggesting that the literary judgements about Edith Wharton, which, I have claimed, many critics ignore, can be arrived at independently of the moral beliefs or sympathies of the critics. To do so would be to advocate a concept of literary criticism as abstracted as the concept of reasonableness I have been attacking. A critic must be able to sympathise with a variety of moral beliefs in order to recognise their seriousness. A critic's moral beliefs may be such, however, as to rule out certain attitudes as trivial, and a novel which gave serious attention to these would be criticised by him for this very reason.[25] If this happened with too many moral beliefs, however, the critic's narrowness would itself count against his standing as a critic.

CONCLUSION

In the brief look we have taken at Edith Wharton's novels, we have reversed and rejected all the reasonable man's principles. If I am right in thinking that these principles underlie a great deal of contemporary moral philosophy, the reason why there should be a tension between moral philosophy and the novel is not hard to find.

I shall end as I began by calling attention to the misgivings that are felt by some philosophers about giving a detailed analysis of examples taken from literature. In his *Critique of Linguistic Philosophy*, C. W. K. Mundle is wary of what he detects as 'a method of teaching ethics (which) has become popular in parts of Wales and England. This is to read long extracts from Russian novels or Existentialist plays, describing moral dilemmas.' Mundle says that 'when well done, this is an excellent way of starting arguments about *what* you would have done in the problem situations. And, sometimes, about *why*.'[26] To this, as we have seen, Edith Wharton would reply, 'Had you done differently, it would have been a different time, place, and cast.' Mundle's concern to determine the content and justification of moral conduct goes with his conception of moral philosophy as the discovery of 'rules as to how *people in general* ought to act.' After all, he argues, since all moral problems and beliefs are called 'moral', we must be concerned with the same thing in all of them.

Our discussion of Edith Wharton's work should help us to see that the question of what we mean by allegiance and change in morality does not admit of a *general* answer. The assumption that moral philosophy can provide such an answer is but another symptom of the desire for tidiness and simplicity in ethics from which attention to literature can help to deliver us. As Eugene Kamenka has said, 'The complexity of individuals and "their" interests has long been recognised in literature, especially in the novel; it is time that it was more clearly recognised in ethics.'[27]

5
After Virtue?

Alasdair MacIntyre's book *After Virtue* (London: Duckworth, 1981) begins with what he calls, rightly, a disquieting suggestion, namely, that with respect to morality, all we possess 'are the fragments of a conceptual scheme, parts which now lack those contexts from which their significance derived' (p. 2). Unsurprisingly, the consequences are said to be far-reaching: 'We possess indeed simulacra of morality, we continue to use many of the key expressions. But we have – very largely, if not entirely – lost our comprehension, both theoretical and practical, of morality' (p. 2). The author is aware of an obvious objection to such a sweeping thesis: 'If a catastrophe sufficient to throw the language and practice of morality into grave disorder had occurred, surely we should all know about it. It would indeed be one of the central facts of our history. Yet our history lies open to view, and no record of any such catastrophe survives' (p. 3). Yet, MacIntyre argues, if the confusion is as deep as he thinks it is, 'the catastrophe will have to have been of such a kind that it was not and has not been – except perhaps by a very few – recognised as a catastrophe' (p. 3).

The problem for MacIntyre's thesis is not constituted, as he thinks, by those who do not recognise the confusion we are in, but by those who *do*. He half-suggests that theoretical and practical understanding of morality has been lost by everyone, but the existence of his own book, together with the response he thinks it makes sense to look for in his audience, would constitute embarrassments for such a thesis. Once the thesis is modified and it is admitted that there are some people (although perhaps 'a very few') who understand the situation, further difficulties arise. If *all* we have are remnants of moral discourse which, divorced from their original contexts, lack sense, from what moral source could we be informed of our confusion? Further, if, like MacIntyre, we want to rectify the situation, from where could we conjure the moral resources to do so?

According to MacIntyre, neither conceptual nor historical analyses, as commonly understood today, can help us in our predicament. Since the confusion we are in is a *moral* confusion, it cannot be understood without the application of standards. The analyses in question, on the other hand, claim to be value-free. Does it follow, as MacIntyre seems to think, that they can give no account of the confusion? Many forms of conceptual analysis and clarification in philosophy have not ignored the natural settings in which concepts have their meaning. They have emphasised such contexts in calling attention to the heterogeneity of morals as between societies or within the same society. Further, they have been able to show how confusion results when these contexts are ignored, or when new movements think they can appropriate old concepts while ignoring the conditions of their intelligibility. The condescending misunderstanding to which the practices of other cultures have been subjected would be an example of the first kind of confusion; the effects of the idiocies of the sixties and seventies on educational concepts would be an example of the second kind of confusion. The possibility of revealing the confusion of values does not depend, however, on embracing the values confused.

What of those today who think their grasp of standards is firm? Is all well with them? MacIntyre has in mind the modern radical. He says of him, 'Whatever else he denounces in our culture he is certain that it still possesses the moral resources which he requires in order to denounce it. Everything else may be, in his eyes, in disorder; but the language of morality is in order, just as it is. That he too may be being betrayed by the very language he uses is not a thought available to him' (p. 4). MacIntyre says, on the other hand, 'It is the aim of this book to make that thought available to radicals, liberals and conservatives alike' (p. 4). The comments on the radical are not without point, but they do not show what MacIntyre wants them to show. The possibility of denunciation does not depend on any belief about the language of morality being in order. Nothing is a work of denunciation if *After Virtue* is not, but MacIntyre does *not* think that the language of morality is in order. MacIntyre, furthermore, wants to go beyond denunciation; he wants to present a programme for moral recovery. But if the moral resources which make denunciation possible pose a problem, how much more of a problem is posed by the availability of moral resources which make recovery possible! Given MacIntyre's premisses, such resources could only be obtained by transcending the confusion we find ourselves in. If MacIntyre does claim to be able to offer a programme of moral recovery, however, our situation did not need to be transcended in the first place. Furthermore, since our situation is said to be historically determined, what would 'transcending' it amount to? MacIntyre never faces up to these conceptual difficulties. Instead, he comments, rather lamely, 'But if we are indeed in as bad a state as I take us to be, pessimism too will turn out to be one more cultural luxury that we shall have to dispense with in order to survive in these hard times' (p. 5). If the times *are* as hard as MacIntyre takes them to be, pessimism may well be a saving grace against a romantic optimism which, rightly located in the radical, may nevertheless be a temptation to which MacIntyre himself succumbs.

According to MacIntyre, the history of the decline by which a language of morality becomes impossible has three stages:

> 'a first at which evaluative and more especially moral theory and practice embody genuine objective and impersonal standards which provide rational justification for particular policies, actions and judgments and which themselves in turn are susceptible of rational justification; a second stage at which there are unsuccessful attempts to maintain the objectivity and impersonality of moral judgments, but during which the project of providing rational justifications both by means of and for the standards continuously breaks down; and a third stage at which theories of an emotivist kind secure wide implicit acceptance because of a general implicit recognition in practice, though not in explicit theory, that claims to objectivity and impersonality cannot be made good' (p. 18).

Needless to say, we are supposed to be at the third stage, at the extremities of decline.

The history of our decline thus outlined is understood by MacIntyre in primarily Aristotelian terms. Our confusion is due, above all, to the lack of a teleological framework for ethics. Man lacks a telos which would provide him with a conception of what is good for man. The conception of such a telos has three aspects. The first aspect concerns man's relation to practices. By a practice, MacIntyre means,

> any coherent and complex form of socially established cooperative human activity through which goods internal to that form

of activity are realised in the course of trying to achieve those standards of excellence which are appropriate to, and partially definitive of that form of activity, with the result that human powers to achieve excellence, and human conceptions of the ends and goods involved, are systematically extended (p. 175).

The standards in such practices are not determined by individual choice. Although an individual may make a practice his own, what he does is to absorb criteria and standards of excellence which, insofar as they have a reality independent of him, are impersonal. Such practices create the logical and social space in which a man can aim at something other than he is in his untutored state. If man stands in no relation to such practices, he is thrown back into a radical dependence on himself; into a situation in which it is not at all clear from where criteria for responsible choice or decision are to come. MacIntyre gives an initial definition of virtue in relation to practices as 'an acquired human quality the possession and exercise of which tend to enable us to achieve those goods which are internal to practices and the lack of which effectively prevent us from achieving any such goods' (p. 178).

This definition of virtue has to be modified as we appreciate the need to go beyond the level of practices in expounding the role of a telos in human life. We have to note that practices themselves have a history in which criticism plays an important part. 'Thus the standards are not themselves immune from criticism, but none the less we cannot be initiated into a practice without accepting the authority of the best standards realised so far' (p. 177). Further, men engage in a multiplicity of practices. They may make competing and incompatible claims on them, claims which cannot be explained away, as Aristotle thought, as being due to 'flaws in individual character' (p. 183). Again, MacIntyre says that it cannot be denied that 'some coherent human activities which answer to the description of what I have called a practice – are evil' (p. 186). For all these reasons it is obvious that it is insufficient to characterise virtues as those qualities which sustain and extend practices. There must be some way of subjecting the multiplicity of practices, with their conflicting characters and demands, to a wider context of discrimination. Without such a context, the notion of groundless choice will re-emerge, 'even if with a more limited scope for its exercise than it has usually claimed' (p. 188).

The need for moral discrimination at this more general level of human life brings us to the second aspect of the telos of man: the telos provides man with a coherent narrative content for his life; it enables him to explain the priorities in his life, the direction in which he is going. In short, the possibility of a life having a narrative content is at the same time the possibility of its having a coherent identity. In this way, MacIntyre seeks to make answering the Aristotelian question, 'What is the good life for man?' (p. 187) a condition of the intelligibility of the notions of moral integrity and constancy: 'This notion of singleness of purpose in a whole life can have no application unless that of a whole life does' (p. 189). On the other hand, MacIntyre's notion of a telos for human life is a complex one. He is not so naive as to think that we are presented first with a clear conception of the telos which we then proceed to aim for. He criticises those philosophers who have replaced Aristotle's metaphysical biology, by which the telos of human life could be determined independently of the practices men engage in, with a general account of human flourishing by reference to which our practices can be assessed. According to these philosophers, 'The virtues can then be adequately characterised as those qualities necessary to promote such flourishing and well-being, because whatever our disagreement in detail on *that* subject, we ought to be able to agree rationally on what is a virtue and what is a vice' (p. 152). The naivety of such a view, as MacIntyre points out, is found in the fact that it 'ignores the place in our cultural history of deep conflicts over what human flourishing and well-being do consist in and the way in which rival and incompatible beliefs on that topic beget rival and incompatible tables of the virtues' (p. 152). The quest for *the* good of human life which MacIntyre has in mind is very different.

> [The] quest is not at all that of a search for something already given adequately characterised, as miners search for gold or geologists for oil. It is in the course of the quest and only through encountering and coping with the various particular harms, dangers, temptations and distractions which provide any quest with its episodes and incidents that the goal of the quest is finally to be understood. A quest is always an education both as to the character of that which is sought and in self-knowledge (p. 204).

This quest is not something which a human being carries out in isolation. His moral beliefs, problems and difficulties are set for him in a wider context. Even admitting that an individual may have to work through tragic moral incompatibilities which confront him, there is still the question of the wider context in which such 'working through' is to be achieved. The need for this wider context brings us to the third aspect which completes MacIntyre's notion of a telos for man, the existence of a moral tradition in which such complexities as we have mentioned can be found. Faced with competing and conflicting demands, the individual must still go forward. 'To perform his or her task better rather than worse will be to do both what is better for him or her *qua* individual or *qua* parent or child or *qua* citizen or member of a profession or perhaps *qua* some or all of these' (pp. 208–9). It is the context of a moral tradition which makes possible the discussion and assessment of different and conflicting goods in the quest for *the* good. It is precisely such a unifying moral tradition that we lack, with the result that the virtues come to have little more than a marginal hold on our lives.

By such an analysis of the notion of a telos for human life, MacIntyre hopes to have shown the kind of conceptual framework which the concept of virtue requires. 'For there are no less than three stages in the logical development of the concept which have to be understood, and each of these stages has its own conceptual background. The first stage requires a background account of what I shall call a practice, the second an account of what I have already characterised as the narrative order of a single human life and the third an account . . . of what constitutes a moral tradition. Each later stage presupposes the earlier, but not vice versa' (p. 174). Many, in responding to MacIntyre's book, will undoubtedly concentrate on criticising the fundamental assumptions which underlie this conceptual programme. In doing so, I believe, they will miss what is the most important contribution of MacIntyre's work. On the other hand, as I shall attempt to show, that contribution cannot accord with MacIntyre's own understanding of what he is doing, and must itself be seen against the justifiable criticisms of his assumptions. This is why it is necessary to begin with the criticisms.

The criticisms which can be made of MacIntyre's assumptions are of two kinds: criticisms of his account of the history of moral philosophy and criticisms of his account of the history of moral beliefs and practices. This way of putting the matter will not please MacIntyre, because one of his main complaints is that these two histories have been treated separately; or, rather, he complains against the assumption that we are dealing with two histories. 'We all too often still treat the moral philosophers of the past as contributors to a single debate with a relatively unvarying subject-matter, treating Plato and Hume and Mill as contemporaries both of ourselves and of each other. This leads to an abstraction of these writers from the cultural and social milieus in which they lived and thought and so the history of their thought acquires a false independence from the rest of the culture' (p. 11). What we need to realise, according to MacIntyre, is that 'A moral philosophy . . . characteristically presupposes a sociology' (p. 22). This leads him to make the strong claim that 'Moral philosophy, as it is dominantly understood, reflects the debates and disagreements of the culture so faithfully that its controversies turn out to be unsettlable in just the way that the political and moral debates are' (p. 235).

There are obvious objections to MacIntyre's view of philosophy. First, if we present a strong thesis in terms of which a moral philosophy is *always* a reflection of one's moral beliefs, it will be impossible to account for the fact that people who share the same or similar moral beliefs may give differing philosophical accounts of them. On MacIntyre's view, if their philosophical accounts differ, their moral beliefs must differ, since the former are inextricably bound up with the latter. Our philosophical accounts of moral beliefs, however, may be influenced by a wide variety of considerations. For example, various relativistic views of morality have been influenced by the thought that moral laws, to deserve the name, should be akin to laws in natural science. There could surely be two people who, while they do not differ in their moral views, differ in that one is tempted by relativism for the reasons I have mentioned. I do not need to deny that this philosophical temptation may affect the content of his moral beliefs; all I need deny is that it *must*. Such a person may be rescued from his philosophical confusion by being reminded of the differences between laws in natural science and anything he might want to call moral laws. In order for this to be done, he needs to be reminded of what he knows when not philosophising. How could this be possible on MacIntyre's view, since, according to him, what a person says when philosophising is a reflection of the moral beliefs he holds when not philosophising?

A second difficulty for MacIntyre's view is that it requires a one-to-one relation between a moral philosophy and a moral viewpoint. But what of moral philosophies which try to show *differences*? MacIntyre is able to say that Kierkegaard did not question the Kantian form of morality only by concentrating on *Either/Or*. In *Purity of Heart*, on the other hand, one of Kierkegaard's main points is that although 'to will the good is to will one thing', this one thing does not take one form. On the contrary, we are given no definition of purity of heart, but examples of the *different* forms such purity may take. The differences philosophers try to show concern the multiplicity of beliefs, traditions and movements which go to make up the heterogeneity of morals. Indeed, one major criticism such philosophies will make of the theories of moral philosophy is that many of them concentrate on one or a cluster of moral characteristics, but claim to be giving a general account of something called Morality. As against this, they will endeavour to display the differences, to show the heterogeneity of morals. Displaying this variety philosophically will not be work preliminary to the formulation of a general theory, but work preliminary to rescuing us from the confused desire for such a theory. On MacIntyre's view, the possibility of reminding us of moral differences would entail the odd conclusion that the philosophers who so remind us must themselves hold differing and conflicting moral beliefs. Clearly, however, I can remind you of certain moral possibilities which I do not embrace personally. Again, I do not need to deny that a person's own moral views may place limits on what he is prepared to regard as a moral perspective. He may not be able to allow certain perspectives, which others embrace, as a moral perspective. All I need deny is that this *has* to be the case. Actually, MacIntyre's own book is an embarrassment for his thesis, for if a moral philosophy is inextricably bound up with the cultural milieu of which it is a part, how is he to refer successfully to the different moral philosophies to which he wishes to draw our attention? If his philosophical appraisal is at the same time a moral appraisal, how can we arrive at descriptions of different moral philosophies and moralities which would be acceptable to their adherents on their own terms? I doubt whether MacIntyre would be content with saying that what he is offering is a kind of moral vision of the history of moralities and moral philosophies. Clearly, he is engaged in an explanatory analysis of our condition. My point is that, right or wrong, such an analysis entails transcending the limitations MacIntyre imposes on moral philosophy.

A third difficulty for MacIntyre's claim that there is an internal relation between a moral philosophy and the cultural milieu in which it is propounded, is that this makes utterly mysterious the enterprise of reviving an Aristotelian teleology for ethics. If such a teleology is the product of the cultural milieu in which Aristotle wrote, how can it rescue us from our predicament in the twentieth century? On the other hand, if a moral philosophy is inextricably bound up with the cultural milieu in which it is written, how can there be a contemporary moral philosophy which is not itself as confused and bewildered as MacIntyre says we are?

In reply to some of these difficulties, MacIntyre may say that he was only concerned to discuss 'Moral philosophy, as it is *dominantly* understood' (p. 235, my italics). But what if what is needed is to philosophise against the stream, since the dominant moral philosophies are confused? The very possibility of such philosophical activity would, for the reasons I have noted, constitute an embarrassment for MacIntyre's views on moral philosophy. Such philosophical activity need not be postulated as an abstract possibility, since in our own century there has been a considerable amount of philosophising against the stream in contemporary ethics. In the light of emphases found there, MacIntyre's programme for the recovery of a telos for man would be cast in a somewhat different light. One of the most disappointing features of MacIntyre's survey of contemporary ethics is that one searches in vain for any mention, let alone discussion, of the work of A. I. Melden, Iris Murdoch, Stuart Hampshire or Peter Winch. This work would not fit readily into MacIntyre's overall philosophical picture, but that is all the more reason for discussing it.

Iris Murdoch, in *The Sovereignty of Good*, like MacIntyre, is concerned to show how an impoverished conception of the self has affected contemporary moral philosophy, but her strictures are informed by the philosophy of Plato, mediated through the writings of Simone Weil (another who philosophised against the stream). In a rather different way, A. I. Melden showed the artificiality of many of the ways of drawing distinctions between facts and values. By concentrating on the example of family life, he showed how facts have moral import and persons have a moral identity by virtue of their involvement in institutions, practices and traditions. In *Rights and Right Conduct*, however, Melden propounded an optimistic programme (now abandoned) by which a moral tradition was to emerge, a tradition to embrace the whole community. Rights are rights to consideration, not to satisfaction.

Family life is sustained by the fact that, despite the non-satisfaction of certain rights on specific occasions, members of the family are prepared to accept this by virtue of their acceptance of familiar procedures by which competing claims are discussed. When the demands of family life clash with other demands, such as those of work, these too will be resolved within a wider moral context. The hope was for a mode of reflection which would embrace something called a total moral community. I was reminded of these hopes in reading MacIntyre. H. O. Mounce and I criticised this optimism in *Moral Practices*. There, too, the artificiality of many distinctions between facts and values was emphasised, but we also emphasised that the transition from facts to values itself had its force within a moral practice. For MacIntyre, Hume's attempt to drive a wedge between facts and values is a symptom of the breakdown of traditions within which the transition from fact to value is unproblematic. Divorced from such traditions, the individual has no given telos. So we see the emergence of the modern conception of the individual. Yet, this reading of Hume can be challenged. Again, the point would not be to deny a changing role for the individual, but to call attention to the positive contribution Hume was making. With modest modifications, Hume can be seen as reminding us of the multiplicity of moral practices. Many of the recent efforts to show that there can be transitions from facts to values, unfortunately, miss the point. That a transition from facts to values, within moral practices or in the light of certain moral beliefs is often unproblematic has seldom, if ever, been denied. Given a clash of moral practices, however, the same facts will not, of themselves, yield agreed moral conclusions. As we have seen, MacIntyre himself rejects Aristotle's claim that a telos for man can be determined independently of the practices in which he engages. The problematic aspect of MacIntyre's view is that he thinks the internal relation between a man's telos and the practices he engages in leads to the notion of a unified moral tradition. On the other hand, 'When the distinctively modern self was invented, its invention required not only a large new social setting, but one defined by a variety of not always coherent beliefs and concepts' (p. 59). The reader gets the impression, however, that the presence of variety in this context *itself* constitutes an incoherence for MacIntyre. Why this should be so remains a mystery. There is surely a distinction between the picture of the alienated individual who cannot give himself to anything because he belongs to nothing, and the picture of individuals giving themselves to different things because they belong to different movements and traditions. Why should the latter situation be thought problematic? Is it not an accurate picture of the way things are; indeed, of the way things have always been? The alternative picture of an all-embracing social morality unifying a whole culture and its participants is nothing more than a philosophical construction. Despite the fact that MacIntyre recognises John Anderson's important insight 'that it is through conflict and sometimes only through conflict that we learn what our ends and purposes are' (p. 153), he does not emphasise Anderson's repeated point that such conflicts are not the prelude to the emergence of a single tradition. Anderson never tired of pointing out that the values of different movements could not be cashed in terms of a common coinage. In 'Morality and Pessimism' Stuart Hampshire has shown that recognising such differences does not threaten the coherence of such notions as the necessity of moral claims or the idea of absolute standards or demands. On the contrary, recognising the heterogeneity of morals helps one to see what is involved in these central features of morality. Such understanding asks MacIntyre to take more seriously his recognition, already noted, of 'the place in our cultural history of deep conflicts over what human flourishing and well-being do consist in and the way in which rival and incompatible beliefs on that topic beget rival and incompatible tables of the virtues' (p. 152). As we have seen, a man may be torn between conflicting moral demands in his life. MacIntyre, while wanting to recognise such conflicts, wants to emphasise the necessity of working through to a wider view. The virtues, in the context of a sufficiently complex moral tradition, enable one to do so. In *Ethics and Action*, Peter Winch shows, time and time again, how a 'working through' in such situations need not and, characteristically, does not, involve the postulation of a wider moral tradition. Of course, if a person has a system of values by which the obligations which confront him are in an order of priority, he would not have a dilemma in the first place. Given that he does have a dilemma, we have to recognise that the virtues create it rather than help him to work through it. When he comes to his decision, does what he has to, Winch shows how we do not need anything other than the virtues to account for the way he has worked through his predicament. What the virtue which created the obligation which remains unfulfilled means to him is shown in his attitude after he has done what he has to. For example, he will show remorse and may feel the need for penance, despite the fact that he does not repudiate his action.

I have referred to these moral philosophers first, in order to show that a concern with the character of moral endeavour need not lead to a concern with forming an all-embracing moral tradition of the kind MacIntyre envisages. The point is not to deny the possibility of such a tradition, but to deny that the coherence of moral endeavour depends on its emergence. Second, the work of the philosophers I have mentioned poses a problem for Mac-Intyre's thesis that moral philosophy is itself the product of a specific cultural milieu in the way he suggests. What I have called attention to is the variety which characterises contemporary ethics. Such a variety accords ill with MacIntyre's claim that we are in the grip of the confusions of emotivism. He argues, convincingly, that some dominant theories, such as prescriptivism, are forms of emotivism in disguise, but he would be hard put to argue that case for all the views I have referred to. What actually happens in moral philosophy resists attempts to tidy it up.

I said that criticisms could be made, not only of MacIntyre's account of the history of moral philosophy, but also of his account of the history of moral beliefs. Here, too, the desire for a tidy, unified account is in evidence. It is in this context that he seeks to give historical flesh to his abstract statement of the conditions necessary for the intelligibility of the notion of a telos for human life. These conditions were satisfied by the teleological framework for ethics inherited from the Middle Ages, a teleology which was essentially Aristotelian in character. This teleology, of course, is given a theological framework. It distinguished between man as he is and man as he ought to be. Ethics was the science by which man moved from the former to the latter state. The moral rules are the laws of God. 'To say what someone ought to do is at one and the same time to say what course of action will in these circumstances as a matter of fact lead towards a man's true end and to say what the law, ordained by God and comprehended by reason, enjoins. Moral sentences are thus used within this framework to make claims which are true or false' (p. 51). This view of reason does not survive the advent of Catholic Jansenism and Protestantism, where reason is said to be part of man's fallen state. The problem is that the distinction between man as he is and man as he ought to be is retained, but without one of the essential elements of a coherent morality, namely, the notion of how man could be if he attained his telos. Since moral injunctions had their sense from being the means of such attainment, they now hang in the air without apparent justification. The task of the Enlightenment philosophers in trying to find a justification for these moral rules, therefore, had to fail. 'They inherited incoherent fragments of a once coherent scheme of thought and action and, since they did not recognise their own peculiar historical and cultural situation, they could not recognise the impossible and quixotic character of their self-appointed task' (p. 53). Kant in the second *Critique* is recognising that a telos is needed after all to provide an ultimate rationale for man's obedience to moral injunctions. MacIntyre is able to show, convincingly, the failures of utilitarianism to provide such a rationale in the wake of the Enlightenment's failure. He also discusses illuminatingly, by reference to Weber and his successors, how the existence of conflicting traditions and a lack of common agreement, leads to the emergence of an emphasis on management and on bureaucratic values. Hopes for social cohesion were based on the hope, never to be realised, of the social sciences producing laws which would make social behaviour predictable and, hence, manageable. In this discussion, however, we see again, that a plurality of moral perspectives, for MacIntyre, is a kind of incoherence. MacIntyre is aware that 'Most liberals will argue that there is no such thing as "the" contemporary vision of the world; there are a multiplicity of visions deriving from that irreducible plurality of values of which Sir Isaiah Berlin is at once the most systematic and the most cogent defender' (p. 102). To this MacIntyre simply says, 'I will reply that belief in an irreducible plurality of values is itself an insistent and central Weberian theme' (p. 103). To which the reply is, surely – so what? The fact that Weber and others draw confused conclusions from the plurality of values is no denial of its reality. One might as well argue that because, as Anderson pointed out, theorists confusedly wanted to say that different social movements all contributed to a common good called welfare, such confusion about different movements can be used to deny their irreducible differences. The incoherence lies, not in recognising such differences, but in denying them. As we have seen, MacIntyre ignores Kierkegaard's contribution in pointing this out. For MacIntyre, on the other hand, Nietzsche is the prophetic figure who reveals the arbitrariness of these conflicting demands upon us, and challenges us to have the courage to face the situation we are in and generate our own values. For all the reasons MacIntyre has given, he concludes that the challenge, though revealing, is doomed to failure. And so we come to our present state, which is understood best by contrast with 'many pre-modern, traditional societies' where 'it is through his or her membership of a variety of social groups that the individual identifies himself or herself and is identified by others. I am brother, cousin and grandson, member of this household, that village, this tribe. These are not characteristics that belong to human beings accidentally, to be stripped away in order to discover "the real me". They are part of my substance, defining partially at least and sometimes wholly my obligations and duties' (p. 32). This conception of the self ceases to be available as we approach modernity. It ceases to be available because the self has been deprived of its telos.

It can be seen that MacIntyre's account of the history of moral beliefs is as unified as his account of the history of moral philosophy. Yet we can question the latter as we did the former. It may well be asked whether MacIntyre ignores different traditions and movements by choosing to stress *some* dominant tendencies. For example, why should we accept an 'all-or-nothing' account of our situation? Are all walks of life for all people in the same state at all times? This is not to deny the possibility of a pervasive malaise affecting diverse aspects of human life, but are all these aspects affected in the same way, to the same degree, in all places? Many would testify that some parts of their lives make more sense than others; that some movements seem in a worse state than others; that some parts of the world seem more affected by confused tendencies of thought than others. For example, the moral and social phenomena to which an essayist like Joan Didion calls our attention, existed in the same America which manifested the ways of living which Flannery O'Connor embodies in her writings. Joan Didion speaks of a time when there is no way of knowing what is 'right' and what is 'wrong', what is 'good' and what is 'evil'. Her use of inverted commas is meant to convey doubt about the very intelligibility of these concepts. But then we hear Flannery O'Connor say, 'My standard is: when in Rome do as you done in Milledgeville'. MacIntyre tells us that we have lost a theological telos, and no doubt many have, but what are we to say in the face of Desmond Doig's wonderful account of Mother Teresa? What would it mean, if a philosopher tried to tidy up this varied situation? The same question can be asked of times other than our own.

MacIntyre's own observations should have led him to see that a more complex account of moral beliefs than his is needed. MacIntyre admits that there was an internal relation between moral rules and the theological conception of man's telos. If this is so, the telos would inform what it meant to follow the moral rule. Without the telos, MacIntyre argues, the moral rules become arbitrary, devoid of any point. I do not want to deny the possibility of outmoded rules which have no more than a nominal reality. Yet, with the divorce of morality from religion what we have also is a change in the conception of moral rules, not old rules robbed of their previous foundations.

MacIntyre says, with reference to a theological telos, 'Detach morality from that framework and you will no longer have morality; or, at the very least, you will have radically transformed its character' (p. 53). But which point is MacIntyre making, for a morality of a different character is very different from no morality at all? In the same way, if love of man is divorced from love of God, the very conception of love changes. Kierkegaard shows this brilliantly in his *Works of Love*, where he is concerned to distinguish between different kinds of love. What MacIntyre does not give us is an account of kinds of morality. To do so, his would have to be a work akin in spirit to William James' *Varieties of Religious Experience*. Instead, he gives what he believes to be a unified account of a journey through the centuries from moral coherence to moral incoherence. My complaint against a philosopher who urges that moralities and moral philosophies should be understood in their historical context is that he is not historical enough.

In reacting to MacIntyre's book, it would be easy to content oneself with the kinds of criticisms I have made. If they have a point it is a far-reaching one as far as MacIntyre's whole enterprise is concerned. Yet, to content oneself with this would be to miss what seems to be the most important insights in the book. They have little to do with MacIntyre's sweeping historical theses. Rather, they have to do with central issues in philosophy concerning the very possibility of various conceptions of reality. Scepticism, at its deepest, questions the very possibility of things. So it is in relation to morality. MacIntyre succeeds in showing tendencies of thought which threaten the very possibility of morality. Most of these concern a radical individualism which, admittedly, has taken virulent forms in our recent history in the West. At least four intellectual tendencies can be seen to feed this impoverished conception of the self. The most extreme of these is emotivism, which sets the radical agent over against the world as the bestower of praise and blame on it. In such a situation, there is simply an external relation between commendation and its object, and the possibility of moral discussion and a shared morality seems a happy, but mysterious, product of coincidence. '"Moral judgments express feelings or attitudes," it is said. "What kind of feelings or attitudes?" we ask, perhaps remarking that approval is of many kinds. It is in answer to this question that every version of emotivism either remains silent or, by identifying the relevant kind of approval as moral approval – that is, the type of approval expressed by a specifically moral judgement – becomes vacuously circular' (p. 12). Prescriptivism is hardly any better off, since each major premiss in its moral syllogisms is supposed to be justified by a more fundamental principle. 'The terminus of justification is thus always, on this view, a not further to be justified choice, a choice unguided by criteria. Each individual implicitly or explicitly has to adopt his or her first principles on the basis of such a choice. The utterance of any universal principle is in the end the expression of the preferences of an individual will and for that will its principles have and can have only such authority as it chooses to confer upon them by adopting them. Thus emotivism has not been left very far behind after all' (p. 20). Despite the pretensions they expose, Nietzsche and Sartre are faced with the issue of what sense can be made of their picture of the agent, placed in radical opposition to the world, but called on to make momentous moral decisions. How are the moral possibilities which confront him to be generated if the agent is cut off from all the contexts where such possibilities could have their sense? Little wonder that in more recent times the very notion of what is permissible becomes a function of what the agent feels 'comfortable' with in himself and in his relations with others. Even being aware of the diversity of moral possibilities does not necessarily rescue us from this confusion. From a sociological perspective, these possibilities are often characterised as roles, and the self called upon to play these roles is the self of emotivism. 'The goal of the Goffmanesque role-player is effectiveness and success in Goffman's social universe is nothing but what passes for success. There is nothing else for it to be. For Goffman's world is empty of objective standards of achievement; it is so defined that there is no cultural space from which appeal to such standards could be made. Standards are established through and in interaction itself; and moral standards seem to have the function only of sustaining types of interaction that may always be menaced by over-expansive individuals' (p. 109). In these and other ways, the self of different forms of emotivism threatens the very possibility of moral discourse: 'This democratised self which has no necessary social content and no necessary social identity can then be anything, can assume any role or take any point of view, because it *is* in and for itself nothing' (p. 30).

MacIntyre is at his best in discussing the various forms which the alienation of the individual from moral discourse has taken. Once again, however, he sees this as the necessary consequence of an historical process. The possibility of certain forms of moral discourse disintegrating, however, is not confined to any specific historical era, although, when it does happen, the form it takes will be determined, of course, by the historical context in which it occurs. MacIntyre would do well to reflect on the following re-marks by Marion Montgomery in his book *Why Flannery O'Connor Stayed Home*:

> If we accelerate a view of the English poet's development from our last comfortable poet, Chaucer, down to our day when the poet must depend upon 'a felt balance inside himself,' we become aware of a shifting role for the poet in the modern world. Not that such a changed circumstance for the poet is modern only. Among the most famous lines in our language are Yeats', lamenting that 'the centre cannot hold,' that 'Mere anar-chy is loosed upon the world,' where
>
>> The best lack all conviction, while the worst
>> Are full of passionate intensity
>
> But those words, which struggle to come upon a symbol to give public status to the chaos in the interest of recovery of the centre, and conclude only expectation of some 'rough beast' slouching 'toward Bethlehem to be born,' are echoed in their desperation and pathos by a poem out of Egypt four thousand years ago, quoted by Voegelin in juxtaposition to the twentieth century:
>
>> To whom can I speak today?
>> One's fellows are evil;
>> The friends of today do not love.

To whom can I speak today?
Faces have disappeared:
Every man has a downcast face towards his fellows.

To whom can I speak today?
There is no one contented of heart;
The man with whom one went, no longer exists.

But the reality of our individual and collective experiences in the modern world do not depend upon the originality of our encounter with experience, except in so far as we are individually new to the experience (pp. 58–59).

In the end, the lack of complexity in MacIntyre's historical analysis is a major source of the romanticism to which I said he is tempted to succumb. This romanticism is found in his too-unified account of the moral systems of the past. It is also found in an equally too-unified account of our contemporary confusions. This confusion, as we have seen, is due, according to MacIntyre, to our lack of a moral tradition within which, in some sense, conflicting claims can be reconciled. He illustrates this in terms of the conflict between those who emphasise legitimate entitlement in the right people have to enjoy the financial fruits of their labours without undue interference, and those who, impressed by the arbitrariness of wealth and the inability of the poor to help themselves, emphasise the satisfaction of needs through public taxation. In Nozick and Rawls we have two intellectual articulations of these two points of view. What we lack is a tradition capable of resolving the dispute morally or philosophically. What this reveals is 'that we have all too many disparate and rival moral concepts, in this case rival and disparate concepts of justice, and that the moral resources of the culture allow us no way of settling the issue between them rationally' (p. 235). MacIntyre's romanticism is shown in his view 'that the time has come once more when it is imperative to perform this task for moral philosophy' (p. 242). This task is to be performed by him, we are told, in a further volume to which the present one turns out to be a prolegomenon. How can MacIntyre's conception of this task be made consistent with his own insistence on the impossibility of an individual's generating a moral tradition in a vacuum? Alternatively, if MacIntyre's next book is seen as the expression of a tradition already with us in some sense, he cannot also contend that our culture lacks the moral resources which such traditions need.

I do not want to deny the examples of disintegration in moral discourse to which MacIntyre calls our attention. They do not constitute the whole story, as I have said, and we actually proceed, individually and collectively, in ways far more ragged than Mac-Intyre would have us believe. Yet, where such disintegration is present, MacIntyre's romanticism takes the form of an optimistic conviction that something *can* be done, *must* be done. Like Beckett's Estragon, MacIntyre says, 'I can't go on like this', to which I think we ought to reply with Vladimir, 'That's what you think'.

6

The Presumption of Theory

Peter Winch's *The Idea of a Social Science*[1] and his paper 'Understanding a Primitive Society'[2] received widespread critical attention, but this has not been the case with his papers in moral philosophy reprinted in *Ethics and Action*. Why not? In all three contexts, Winch attacks the presumption of theory; theory which claims that *it* possesses the criteria of what is rational or worthwhile in human life. That presumption is so deeply engrained in contemporary moral philosophy that its practitioners have virtually ignored Winch's challenge to it. It is not surprising, therefore, on the rare occasions the challenge is recognised, to find it, as we shall see in the second part of the paper, misunderstood.

In the philosophy of the social sciences and anthropology, the presumption of theory can lead to the following posture: '*We* know that Zande beliefs in the influence of witchcraft, the efficacy of magic medicines, the role of oracles in revealing what is going on and what is going to happen are mistaken, illusory. Scientific methods of investigation have shown conclusively that there are no relations of cause and effect such as are implied by these beliefs and practices. All we can do is to show them how such a system of mistaken beliefs and inefficacious practices can maintain itself in the face of objections that seem to us so obvious.'[3] By a consideration of examples, which is able to throw light on the possibilities of meaning which are shown in Zande magical beliefs, possibilities in terms of which people make sense of their lives, Winch believes that his treatment of these examples does help to bring out the significance which Zande practices *actually* have. Yet, it is important to note that the main thrust of his argument would not be affected even if he were factually mistaken in this instance. The citing of such *possibilities* would still be of logical importance in weaning us away from the idea that what *we* find important, the ways in which *we* make sense of our lives, are underpinned by a necessity, such that this is all that *could* be important or make sense to anyone. In this respect, there would be a parallel with Wittgenstein's references to 'other possibilities' in *On Certainty*.

Winch's essays on ethics involve equally radical consequences for the presumption of theory. He insists that 'philosophy can no more show a man what he should attach importance to than geometry can show a man where he should stand'.[4] Unlike Winch's disputes with philosophers of social science and social scientists, however, his disputes with moral philosophers are not over-common examples, such as Zande witchcraft. On the contrary, he has had an uphill battle to bring examples to their attention, examples which constitute telling counter-cases to the general claims of moral theories. Winch said, in 1964,

> In moral as in other branches of philosophy good examples are indispensable: examples, that is, which bring out the real force of the ways in which we speak and in which language is not 'on holiday' (to adapt a remark of Wittgenstein's). It is needful to say this in opposition to a fairly well-established, but no less debilitating, tradition in recent Anglo-Saxon moral philosophy, according to which it is not merely permissible, but desirable, to take *trivial* examples. The rationale of this view is that such examples do not generate the emotion which is liable to surround more serious cases and thus enable us to look more coolly at the logical issues involved. On such a view what is characteristic of the ways in which we express our moral concerns can be examined quite apart from any consideration of what it is about these concerns which makes them important to us. But 'a moral use that does not matter' is a mere chimera. The seriousness of such issues is not something that we can add, or not, after the explanations of what these issues are, as a sort of emotional extra: it is something that 'shows itself' (again I deliberately echo Wittgenstein) *in* the explanation of the issues. And an issue the seriousness of which does *not* show itself will not be one that presents for our scrutiny those features of morality that we find philosophically puzzling.[5]

In presenting his examples to us, Winch has the Wittgensteinian characterisation he gives to Kierkegaard's work in *Purity of Heart*: Winch does not attempt to *say* what moral action is; he *shows* what it is by portraying various cases. Characteristically, philosophers try to tidy up this all-too-evident heterogeneity. Failure to do so, they seem to think, would commit one to saying that *anything* could be the object of moral approval or disapproval. Winch is committed to no such view. He criticises

> moral philosophers who have made attitudes of approval and disapproval, or something similar, fundamental in ethics, and who have held that the *objects* of such attitudes were completely irrelevant to the conception of morality. On that view, there might be a society where the sorts of attitude taken up in *our* society to questions about relations between the sexes were reserved, say, for questions about the length people wear their hair, and vice versa. This seems to me incoherent. In the first place, there would be a confusion in *calling* a concern of that sort a 'moral' concern, however passionately felt. The story of Samson in the Old Testament confirms rather than refutes this point, for the interdict on the cutting of Samson's hair is, of course, connected there with much else:[6] and pre-eminently, it should be noted, with questions about sexual relations. But secondly, if that is thought to be mere verbal quibbling, I will say that it does not seem to me a mere conventional matter that T. S. Eliot's trinity of 'birth, copulation and death' happen to be such deep objects of human concern. I do not mean just that they are made such by fundamental psychological and sociological forces, though that is no doubt true. But I want to say further that the very notion of human life is limited by these conceptions.[7]

How these limiting conceptions are expressed, or how they are linked with other conceptions, including moral conceptions, varies enormously in different cultures, different societies, within the same society and even between individuals. Yet, these conceptions give us a foothold in our efforts to understand the possibilities presented to us.

These possibilities, however, are not determined by moral theories. For example, Winch says,

> Hare's formalistic account of moral language seems to leave him with a problem about the source of the specific content of people's moral evaluations. He tries to overcome this (in *Freedom and Reason*) by taking an agent's own interests, desires and

inclinations as a datum and then transmuting them into genuine moral judgements by means of the mechanism of universalization.[8]

Leaving aside difficulties in this notion of transmutation and granting its possibility in the individual case, insuperable problems remain for any notion of a recognised *shared* moral authority. These problems are presented by Alasdair MacIntyre in *A Short History of Ethics*:

> MacIntyre asks why one agent's moral evaluation, the content of which springs from a consideration of his own interests and inclinations, should carry any authority at all for another agent who perhaps has quite different inclinations and interests. Will it not be simply a lucky chance if two agents manage to arrive at even roughly the same evaluations in this way? Moreover, even if they do manage to agree, will not each man's evaluation have authority for him only in so far as they are backed by his own interests and inclinations?[9]

Hare relies on his large assumption about the psychological unity of mankind, fanatics apart, to get out of these difficulties. The efficacy of Hare's assumption depends on ignoring the variety of examples Winch and others have brought to his attention. That Hare is ill-disposed to such examples, especially to examples from literature, is therefore not surprising.

Winch is far more sympathetic to MacIntyre's own suggestion that, in order to understand the authority moral considerations have for us, we must pay attention to the social parameters within which possibilities of good and evil are given; possibilities in terms of which people endeavour to make sense of their lives. The diversity which proved problematic for Hare's analysis at the level of individuals, thus takes a more promising form at the level of social practices. When MacIntyre speaks of different practices, Winch says, 'he means not merely different views about the specific needs human beings have, but also different views about the sense in which human beings can be said to have needs at all, and about the *kind* of importance in human life those needs have.'[10] Moral philosophy cannot provide a neutral standard by which an individual can choose between these diverse moral practices, since, as MacIntyre shows, the conception of such a standard is confused, a typical presumption of theory. 'MacIntyre maintains[11] that it is "arbitrary and illegitimate" in examining the logical structure of different moralities to specify as *the* logical form of moral argument that form which is characteristic of any one of them.'[12]

Winch's claim against MacIntyre is that he, too, falls prey to the presumption of theory, by claiming, inconsistently and surprisingly, that the Aristotelian conception of human nature is superior to conceptions of human nature in Christianity, the Sophists and Hobbes, and that this can be demonstrated philosophically.[13] In opposing theories of human nature, Winch concludes that 'what we can ascribe to human nature does not determine what we can and what we cannot make sense of; rather, what we can and what we cannot make sense of determines what we can ascribe to human nature.'[14] This conclusion does not contradict what Winch said about limiting conceptions in human life. It would do so only if those conceptions were thought of as given prior to the diverse ways in which we make sense of our lives, whereas their position as 'limits' is shown by the role they play *in* that diversity.

Moral theories distort the ways in which moral considerations are *constitutive* of certain ways of thinking. Moral theories can claim to be guides to conduct only because they conceive of morality itself as such a guide. The theories create a dualism between the agent and his world. The agent is depicted as acting *on* the world, effecting changes by so doing. Why should the agent bring about some changes rather than others? Morality, it is said, will guide us as to which changes should be made. Winch examines the various forms this assumption has taken in moral theories: an assumption which obscures the ways in which moral considerations may be constitutive of a person's thinking.

When a person proposes to act in certain ways, he may be faced with familiar obstacles: lack of money, lack of friends, lack of opportunity, etc. It can hardly be thought that morality is a guide around *these* difficulties. In fact, so far from ridding us of obstacles, morality seems to create obstacles to what we want to do. A man may contemplate acting in a certain way, but morality says, 'Not that way'. Winch comments: 'Morality, we are told, is a guide which helps him round his difficulty. But were it not for morality there would be no difficulty! This is a strange sort of guide, which first puts obstacles in our path and then shows us the way round them. Would it not be far simpler and more rational to be shot of the thing altogether? Then we could get on with the business in hand, whatever it is.'[15] As Winch says, this is the essence of Glaucon's case in Book II of the *Republic*. Each individual, he argues, would, if he could, pursue his own ends without regard for anyone else. Given that this is true of everyone, however, considerations of prudence restrict unrestrained self-interest. Rules become necessary to regulate the proceedings. By abiding by these rules, the odds are that an individual will obtain more than he would in a general free-for-all. But if a given individual could transcend these common conditions, for example, by possessing a ring that would make him invisible, he would no longer have any reason for abiding by the rules. Of course, the rest of society will condemn him, but, privately, every individual would take the possessor of the ring to be a fool if he did not take advantage of his situation. Glaucon's challenge has haunted moral philosophers and they have tried to answer it in their various theories.

Mill, by appealing to the notion of general interest, tried to show why an individual should abide by moral rules, even when it is not in his self-interest to do so. The notion of 'general interest' runs into the difficulties we have already mentioned which dog any attempt to found a *shared* moral authority on the basis of an individual's desires and inclinations. More consistently, but no less problematically, Philippa Foot tried to show, in her early papers, that moral considerations give *every* man a reason for satisfying them. This reason, she argued, had to do with the cost and penalties a person would have to pay if he ignored these considerations, cost and penalties which are unlikely to be avoided. But, as Winch says,

> Glaucon would have agreed . . . that most men are not in fact strong enough to free themselves from the shackles of convention and the question is: But suppose that somebody could, what then? And anyway situations in which men actually can and do act in ways which they know to be wrong and get away with it are not, after all, far to seek. What can be said to show them that they would not be fools not to do so?[16] *Moral* reasons can clearly not be used here as that would beg the question at issue.[17]

These tensions show why Glaucon's question cannot be answered on its own terms. The moral theories we are considering presumed that it can. But, Winch says,

the question is: What advantage would morality bring? And the
form of the question suggests that we must look *outside* morality
for something on which morality can be based. But the moment
we do this, then 'what is commended is not morality itself', for
surely if the commendation is in terms of some further advantage, the connection between that advantage and morality can
only be a contingent one. And it does not matter how strong a
contingent connection it is; it will still not be 'morality itself'
which is being commended.[18]

How, then, are moral theories going to commend the good to us
without falling foul of these criticisms? G. E. Moore and others
who appealed to intuition, said that when we say something is
good we are simply stating a fact about it. But, as Winch says,
'surely some further argument is needed in order to show why a
man should aim at producing something of that kind.'[19] Moore
simply says, 'it is self-evident that men ought to do what will
produce good things'. But, again, as Winch says, following John
Anderson, Moore

> smuggles into what is supposed to be simply a property of
> something the idea of an essential relation which that thing is
> supposed to have to something else: namely, being desired by,
> or required of, human beings. So he gives the impression of
> having offered a reason why men should behave morally with-
> out in fact having done so.[20]

If we want to appreciate the ways in which moral considerations
can be constitutive of a person's perspective, it is important not to
think of morality as the agent's guide in choosing between alternative courses of action. 'It may be at least as important to notice *what
he considers the alternatives to be*, and, what is closely connected, the
reasons he considers it relevant to deploy in deciding between
them.'[21] The agent has a perspective on the situation. Indeed, it
may be helpful to say that he *is* that perspective, one that may be
informed by moral considerations. The moral possibilities expressed in his perspective are not self-generated, as Sartre
thought, but are given in the language available to him in his
culture. On the other hand, to understand what a person makes of
these possibilities, how they enter his life, how they do or do not
hang together there, we must understand, not the culture, but *him*.

Notice that Winch does not identify the agent's perspective with his will. He is anxious to avoid Kant's conception of the good will as the only thing which is good without qualification. The difficulty is, by now, a familiar one: once Kant gives his formal definition a positive content, namely, acting from a sense of duty, it is clearly not something which we can regard as good without qualification. To so regard it would be to force ourselves to call pure, actions we want to call corrupt, and to call corrupt, actions of moral purity or simplicity. Kant, quite rightly, wants to preserve the difference between acting from moral considerations (a sense of duty) and acting from inclinations external to morality. But, as Winch points out, there is just as much difference between doing something from a sense of duty, and, for example, simply paying a debt, making a gift, or being absorbed in play with one's children, as there is in the distinction Kant wants to preserve. Indeed, a person may criticise himself for simply being able to do from a sense of duty, what others can be absorbed in.

In criticising moral theories, Winch is not wanting to replace them with one of his own. The presumption is in wanting there to be a theory here at all. In contrast, he asks us to wait on the possibilities he puts before us. He is not advocating them, or asking us to agree, morally, with them. How could he be, since he shows us differences? In seeing how the differences are just as important as similarities between moral points of view, we begin to appreciate what is involved in speaking of views, differences, disputes, problems and disagreements in these contexts. We are rescued from the presumption of theory.

Yet, having said this, it brings us to the important question of how different moral possibilities *are* to be recognised. As one might expect, Winch gives no *general* answer to that question. He says:

It is very common in philosophical discussion to find that a way of speaking and thinking which seems perfectly intelligible and acceptable to oneself is met with incomprehension by other people; and of course vice versa. In such circumstances one is bound to ask whether what one wants to say really does make sense or not. . . . Discussion will take the form of raising difficulties and trying to see one's way round them. Sometimes one will think one has dealt with the difficulties satisfactorily; sometimes that the view under criticism meets with difficulties so insurmountable as to be really incomprehensible. But if one recognized the possibility of being mistaken in one's initial belief that one had understood what was being said, or that one had shown it to be unintelligible, one can equally, after discussion recognize that one may have over- or underestimated the difficulties which have emerged in its course. But that does *not* mean that one's views are subject to the test of some ultimate criterion, the criterion of what does and does not belong to human nature.[22]

The presumption of ethical theorists consists in laying claim to an ultimate criterion to determine the content of morality. They are like those philosophers of the social sciences and anthropologists we mentioned at the outset who *know* what constitutes the essence of rational behaviour. The importance of Winch's work is in showing that a readiness to wait on examples in discussion carries with it no presumption about such an ultimate criterion.

It means only that new difficulties and perhaps new ways of meeting the difficulties, are always lurking below the horizon and that discussion continues. Sometimes, if one is lucky, the discussion clarifies or extends one's conception of what is possible for human beings. But it is no use saying that this is contingent on what *is* or *is not* possible for human beings; for our only way of arriving at a view about that is by continuing to try to deal with the difficulties that arise in the course of the discussion.[23]

I have quoted this passage at length because it describes so well Winch's own style of discussion in moral philosophy; a style of discussion with which I have been acquainted, not only in Winch's writings, but ever since I was one of his first honours students thirty-five years ago in Swansea. By presenting us with telling examples, he weans us away from the presumption that theories are necessary in ethics. He gets us to see that in their more ambitious claims, language is idling or on holiday in such theories. The state of contemporary moral philosophy would be very different if this lesson were taken to heart.

II

Given the lack of critical reaction to Winch's essays on ethics, it was something of a surprise to find Onora O'Neill calling attention, not only to them, but to what she identifies as a distinctive Wittgensteinian tradition in ethics.[24] She says, 'The wintry ethics of logical positivism and the cold spring of meta-ethical inquiry have supposedly been supplanted by a new flourishing of substantive ethical writing' (p. 5). This has taken two very different forms. On the one hand, there are the Wittgensteinian writings she has mentioned. On the other hand, especially in the United States, there are discussions of substantive legal, social and political problems. I shall simply note that, with respect to the latter, O'Neill concludes that while actual problems are discussed, insufficient reflectiveness is involved in the over-simplistic solutions we are offered. In contrast, she praises those influenced by Wittgenstein for the greater reflectiveness in their writings, a reflectiveness particularly evident in the use they make of examples. Yet, having said this, O'Neill has a major complaint against these writings: she accuses them of being 'more remote from moral life and in particular from the practical resolution of moral problems' (p. 6).

It is important to grasp at the outset that O'Neill has a conception of moral philosophy as a guide to human conduct. She never comes to grips with the fact that Winch is *challenging* that conception. For her, he is simply seen as someone whose examples lack the power to give us the moral guidance we need. O'Neill fails to appreciate that Winch is not offering examples which *await* our moral judgements. He is presenting *examples of people making moral judgements*. Winch wants us to note the complexity involved in these judgements. People not only show different priorities in judging between alternatives, but often differ in what they take the alternatives to be. What is an alternative to one person may not even be considered to be an alternative by another person. Winch is emphasising that philosophy's task here, as elsewhere, is *descriptive*, one of noting that this is how it is, where moral considerations are concerned. The presumption of theory is to think that this variety awaits an ordering to be determined by criteria it possesses. Opposing such a view, Winch says, 'All we can do, I am arguing, is to look at particular examples and see what we *do* want to say about them: there are no general rules which can determine in advance what we *must* say about them.'[25]

O'Neill observes, rightly, that Winch's examples are not

theory-led, but she still calls them 'the pivot of moral thought' (p. 11). The examples, she is assuming, are meant to be a pivot for *our* reflections about what we ought to do: 'The Wittgensteinian approach to ethics by examples, depends on the possibility of arriving at "what we *do* want to say" in the course of reflecting on the example' (p. 12). Having made this assumption, her complaint is that the examples Winch offers us take far too much for granted to give us the moral guidance we need. 'The method must presuppose sufficient community of moral views – an ethical tradition, perhaps, or a shared ideology – for there to be something which "we" (whoever "we" may be: and this is a large question) do want to say about a given example' (p. 12). But, O'Neill argues, in our fragmented world, it is just such a shared community of moral views that cannot be taken for granted. As a result, the examples Winch offers lack power, the power they need to guide us in solving our most pressing problems.

Given that O'Neill has misunderstood what Winch is trying to show, it might be said that there is little point in pursuing her criticisms any further. This reaction is a premature one, since O'Neill's failure to grasp the point of Winch's examples is illustrative of the very tendencies in moral philosophy which Winch is combating. It is profitable, therefore, to examine O'Neill's complaints against Winch's examples in greater detail. We can find, in her paper, at least six complaints she brings to bear against a Wittgensteinian use of examples in moral philosophy, especially examples taken from literature.

The first complaint I shall note is the most interesting, namely, that *there are important differences between appreciating literary depictions of problems and facing problems oneself.* This is something Winch does not discuss, but it is something he would not deny. But O'Neill does not develop the differences either in any interesting way. The nearest she gets to doing so is when she says:

> Literary examples impose a spectator perspective; and in context the imposition is without costs . . . we do not have to do anything beyond 'deciding what we do want to say' about the example and making sense of it. We do not have to decide whether to turn Raskolnikov in or whether to find Billy Budd guilty. The concern shown by Wittgensteinian writers on ethics for detailed examples understood in their context conveys an atmosphere of moral seriousness and closeness to moral life. But this is in some ways illusory (p. 17).

What are *some* of the important differences between appreciating problems depicted in literature and facing problems in one's own life? We may reject the depiction of a character's development in literature as inconsistent or unrealistic. We may criticise a work saying, 'After a promising start, it falls apart.' But when loved ones, friends or acquaintances develop in ways we did not expect, we cannot put these developments aside as 'inconsistent'. They have happened, whether we like it or not. Things do fall apart after promising starts, but the 'falling apart' *is* our situation. People and events cannot be put aside like books. That is why learning to live with them is so very different. On the other hand, what our situations are, the possibilities open to us, would be very different but for the influence of literature, indirect though that influence may be. There are important, but difficult issues to be raised here, but they are not the ones O'Neill pursues. Her remaining five complaints are very different in kind.

Her second complaint against literary examples is that *the problems depicted in them are not our problems*. She says,

> Typically, the focus is on examples of completed action in a context which invites moral consideration or assessment, rather than on less complete examples of a situation which raises moral problems or dilemmas, as though the primary exercise of moral judgement were to *reflect* or *pass judgement* on what has been done rather than to decide among possible actions (p. 11).

The first thing to be said in reply is that a problem does not have to be ours before we can learn from it. The whole point of Winch's depiction of *different* possibilities, is to show us *how* different moral reactions and judgements can be. Consider, for example, Sophocles' depiction of Oedipus' absorption with what he has done. Winch says,

> Oedipus did not intend to kill his father and marry his mother; he would have acted differently if he had known the true nature of what he was doing but was in a position in which, in an important sense, it was not within his power to know this. On Kantian principles what we *must* say here is that Oedipus is in no way responsible for his actions (at least under these descriptions) and that no question of blame can possibly arise.[26]

Notice that Winch has no philosophical objection to anyone who holds this *moral* view:

Now I realise that many people would in fact say this and I have nothing to say here against someone who, as a matter of fact, takes such a view. I do, however, have something to say against a philosopher who argues, on Kantian lines, that this is the only possible coherent view to take.[27]

Once again, the object of Winch's attack is the presumption of theory. The Kantian may hold on to his own moral view that Oedipus should not blame himself, but come to see as a moral possibility, the coherence of his doing so. He may come to see, as Winch says, that 'The pity we feel for Oedipus is inextricably connected with our realisation of what he has *done* and with our understanding that these are actions for which he could not help blaming himself.'[28] The Kantian, while holding on to his moral view, is freed from the confusion of thinking that all moral possibilities *must* conform to it. So even where moral views do not change, appreciation of other possibilities is not the voyeurism O'Neill is tempted to make it. Even less can be said for her remark that Winch's conception of ethics flourishes 'mainly in the academies of a formerly imperial power', where, unsurprisingly, it focuses 'predominantly on judging what has been done' (p. 16). Embarrassingly for this piece of pseudo-sociology, the Wittgensteinian tradition in ethics has never been the dominant one in the context which, allegedly, should have made it so. On the contrary, it has combated the dominant tradition in which, sometimes, a kind of 'conceptual imperialism' seemed to flourish. After all, one of the main thrusts of 'Understanding a Primitive Society' was against the assumption that we possess, in our culture, all we need to understand cultures other than our own; an assumption which, on Winch's view, led to a condescending misunderstanding of Zande witchcraft. So far from being someone satisfied with current moral concepts, whatever they might be, as O'Neill suggests, Winch says: 'Our blindness to the point of primitive modes of life is a corollary of the pointlessness of much of our own life.'[29]

O'Neill's third complaint against literary examples is related to her second: *the invoking of literary examples takes an agreement in moral construals for granted, whereas, in our lives, the character of our construals is what we are uncertain about.* She points out that

it is the authority of the text which imposes a largely shared interpretation of examples. . . . Nobody can reasonably specu-

late whether the interpretation of such examples hinges entirely
on factors of which the author has neither told nor hinted. (It is
hardly open to a Wittgensteinian to adopt principles of interpretation – whether radically subjectivist or deconstructive – which
call in question the possibility of a shared, open reading of the
text.) Consider how impertinent it would be to construe *Macbeth*
as a murder mystery by adducing extratextual hunches, or to
wonder whether Raskolnikov wasn't perhaps mistaken in
thinking he had murdered Alyona Ivanovna, who survived his
assault and was finished off by someone else, so that his entire
experience of agitation, guilt and remorse is just misplaced.
Even in a poor whodunnit extratextual importations are suspect;
they are totally destructive of the literary examples on which
Wittgensteinian ethical reflection builds (p. 14).

O'Neill argues that the presentation of the literary examples
determines the way they are construed by us. If her argument is to
have any force, by 'construal' she must mean 'moral construal'.
But does the authority of the text determine that *latter* construal?
Sophocles' text certainly presents Oedipus as blaming himself for
what he has done. His reaction is depicted as a moral reaction.
That much the text asks us to recognise. The reader may be unable
to accord it this descriptive status. But if he can see what Sophocles
wants to show us, he need not agree morally with what he sees.
O'Neill is therefore, wrong, when she says that the Wittgensteinian use of examples suggests 'that we can deliberate only in so far
as we share the practices of those with or about whom we deliberate' (p. 14). If O'Neill were correct, Winch would have to contend 'that one is under an obligation to admire every single
manifestation of integrity'. As Winch says, this would be a 'quite
absurd moral doctrine'. He then gives an example of a terrible
morality:

> The concentration camp commandant towards the end of Irwin
> Shaw's *The Young Lions* exhibited integrity of a peculiarly revolt-
> ing sort from the point of view of Western liberal morality. He
> was morally revolting because of the unspeakable role he was
> playing; to say he was playing it with integrity is, for most of us,
> an additional count against him, not a point in his favour.[30]

The fourth complaint O'Neill brings against the use of literary examples is that, *unlike the open-ended situations of life, these examples are complete and determinate.* She says:

> Unlike those who discuss pre-packaged examples drawn either from literary texts or from the outlook of some group of specialists, agents must first come to an appreciation or appraisal of actual situations and possibilities for action. To suppose that they can instantly recognize their situation as having a certain specification simplifies, indeed falsifies, the predicament agents face. An agent may initially not even realize that this is a situation which requires or permits action. Even one who sees this much may be at a loss as to how the situation should be described or construed (p. 24).

It can be seen from this passage that O'Neill's objection seems to be to *any* determinate example, not simply to literary examples. It is extremely simplistic to suggest that all situations depicted in literature are 'complete', determinate, while all situations in life are open-ended. The determinate or the open-ended may be found in *either* context. Since O'Neill calls literary examples pre-packaged, I shall simply provide one counter-example from the countless cases which we can appeal to.

In Alice Munro's short story, *Something I've Been Meaning to Tell You,*[31] we meet two sisters, one of them, Et, envies the other's good looks. It is no surprise to her when her sister takes up with the local Romeo. Unexpectedly, however, he goes off with an older woman. Et helps her sister to get over a botched suicide attempt. Her sister marries her dull history teacher, a man much older than herself. Before long, the local Romeo is back in town and the original affair has resumed. Et is sad to see the husband deceived, but her attitude to what is going on is a complex mixture of admiration, condemnation, envy and longing. The husband's health is not good, and Et keeps checking the level of the rat poison kept in the house. The lover goes to the city for a short stay. Et has no reason to think that he will not return. Yet, when the husband, in the sisters' presence, says how much he misses him, Et finds herself blurting out that she had heard that he had taken up with another woman, reminding her sister that it had happened once before. The next morning, her sister is found dead in bed and the bottle of rat poison is missing. The local doctor puts death down to a heart-attack. Et's words were not premeditated.

She wanted to bring things to a head somehow, but didn't quite know how. After the event, as the days and even years roll by, she wonders how to weigh her words. Sometimes she sees them one way, sometimes another. Whether she blames herself depends on the aspects under which she sees them, but they are never presented in a settled, determinate form. In old age, playing cards regularly with her sister's husband, there are times when she feels he should know what has happened. Often, it is on the tip of her tongue to say, 'There's something I've been meaning to tell you', but the years roll by and she never does. We, as readers, are invited to share the terrible ambiguities and ambivalences of the story. After all, what would be the 'something' which Et would tell? Further, what would the 'telling' amount to?[32]

It is not hard to find situations in our lives which share these ambiguities. Do we always know what we mean by our words? Did we mean to be honest or to hurt? When events occur subsequent to our words, do we always know the part to assign to our words in these events? The situation may remain permanently ambiguous, its shifting aspects not permitting any determinate description. In calling attention to such situations, O'Neill is not recognising their possible permanence. On the contrary, for her, such situations are simply *preliminary data* awaiting further moral reflection. This is shown more clearly in her fifth and sixth complaints concerning what she takes to be Wittgensteinian attitudes towards moral dilemmas and moral disagreements.

O'Neill's fifth complaint is that '*Many Wittgensteinian writers insist that deep moral conflicts cannot be resolved, so that there are ineliminable and tragic clashes of moral outlook*' (p. 16, n. 18, my italics). Let us apply this complaint to moral dilemmas. She is perfectly ready to admit that there are moral dilemmas. She cites Sartre's example of the young man who is torn between caring for his mother and joining the Free French.[33] She describes the dilemma as theory-led, but it is extremely odd to regard devotion to his mother or to the Free French as theory-determined. She says rightly, however, in the light of such examples, 'that moral principles and codes cannot make our decisions for us' (p. 10).

On the other hand, for O'Neill, these dilemmas are *preliminary* data, awaiting the kind of moral thinking which will make it difficult for them to be irresolvable. She accuses the first three essays of my *Through a Darkening Glass* of arguing that deep moral conflicts *cannot* be resolved. No such argument appears there. She responds, 'But one does not have to hold all moral disagreement is tragic and irresolvable because some is' (p. 16, n. 18). I would not dispute that. The *a priorism* concerning moral dilemmas has not been on the part of Wittgensteinian ethics, but on the part of those who insist that the irresolvability of a moral dilemma *must* be due to its being underdescribed. The dogmatism is theirs, not ours. For example, R. W. Beardsmore is quite ready to admit that many could not be faced with the dilemma of the wife who had to choose between her husband's life and becoming the mistress of a Nazi officer. For them, 'adultery' is ruled out on moral grounds. Beardsmore has no philosophical argument with this moral standpoint. He does object, however, to a philosophical claim that dilemmas of this form *cannot* arise for anyone. He considers such an argument by G. E. M. Anscombe.[34] 'No one, she tells us, can know in advance that there will be, in any given case, only two alternatives to choose from. There may always be a third way out of the difficulty.' Beardsmore replies:

> Her argument is objectionable for two reasons (a) because we may take our examples from novels or from our own experience, in which case we *already* know what the possibilities are, and (b) because if it is true that no one can know 'a priori' that there will be only two possibilities, then it is also true that Miss Anscombe cannot know 'a priori' that there will not be. And it is just this knowledge that she seems to be claiming.[35]

O'Neill, surprisingly, pays no attention to Winch's discussion of the moral dilemma in which he shows why it is made artificial if it is thought of as the product of a clash of Kantian-like principles. For her, the force of the dilemmas 'derives from certain moral positions and principles which, tragically, lack the resources to resolve the problems they generate' (p. 10). The example Winch considers is from the film *Violent Saturday*: 'a gang of bank raiders hide from the police on the farm of a strict, Dukhabor-like religious community, one of whose most fundamental guiding principles is non-violence. At the climax of the film one of the gangsters is about to shoot a young girl member of the community in the presence of the community's elder. With horror and doubt on his face, the elder seizes a pitchfork and hurls it into the gangster's back.'[36]

Winch says, 'According to a neo-Kantian position like Professor

Hare's, the elder has had to make a "decision of principle", which consists in either qualifying, or perhaps even abandoning, the principle of non-violence according to which he has hitherto tried to live.'[37] But, as Winch points out, there are features of the situation which show such an analysis to be misplaced. It is clear that the elder thinks he has committed a *wrong* in killing the gangster. It is equally clear, however, that in acting, the elder did what he had to do.

Winch concludes:

> I said that, having killed the gangster, the elder knew he had done something wrong; but I also said that, if he had not killed the gangster, he would not have been able to forgive himself; i. e. that would have been wrong too, though perhaps in a different way. That the modalities involved on the side of killing the gangster are moral modalities is also clear from the fact that, in order to explicate them, notions like that of the innocence of the girl whose life was threatened and that of protecting the defenceless would have to be introduced. But it would be wrong to introduce them in the form of principles for the sake of which the elder was acting. They were involved in what I have called the 'perspective' of the action, but that perspective is not to be understood in the form of Kantian 'maxims' or Harean 'principles'. It will be objected that my account leaves no room for any discovery of, or decision concerning *'the* right' thing to do in such a situation and thus makes morality useless as a guide to conduct. But my whole point is that there *is* no room for the notion of 'the right thing to do' in such a situation and that this shows yet again that morality is *wrongly* conceived as a guide to conduct.[38]

O'Neill's sixth complaint against Wittgensteinian ethics is that by concentrating on examples of unbridgeable moral disagreements, *the examples will have 'little appeal for those whose lives confront them continually with heterogeneous practices'* (p. 16, my italics). O'Neill emphasises, with Kant, 'that there can be no complete rules for judging particular cases' (p. 8). Kant writes:

> Judgement will be the faculty of subsuming under rules; that is of distinguishing whether something does or does not stand under a given rule. . . . General logic contains, and can contain

no rules for judgement. . . . If it sought to give general instructions how we are to subsume under these rules, that is to distinguish whether something does or does not come under them, that could only be by means of another rule. This in turn, for the very reason that it is a rule, demands guidance from judgement . . . judgement is a peculiar talent which can be practised only and cannot be taught.[39]

O'Neill says that Kant goes on to liken judgement to 'mother wit' and to insist that 'its lack no school can make good'. She comments: 'However, he presumably means only that there can be no *algorithms* for judging and no formal instruction, for he allows that "sharpening of the judgement is indeed one of the benefits of examples"' (p. 8).[40]

It is in this complaint that O'Neill's misunderstanding of the role of examples in Winch is seen most explicitly. For her, the examples await our moral judgement. She does not appreciate that they are examples of *differences involved in what it means* to make moral judgements. For her, as for Kant, different moral construals of situations are construals of *prima facie* moral significance (see p. 24) which are to be subsumed under a higher synthesis. It may involve 'coming to appreciate the actual case in a specific way, as falling under one rather than another set of descriptions and hence judgeable in the light of some rather than other practices or principles' (p. 24). O'Neill does not see that moral ideas may be *constitutive* of the descriptions people give of situations. Incredibly, she thinks that, in literature, 'the problem of rival appraisals of situations is greatly reduced' (p. 24), whereas, in fact, it is hard to imagine any literature of significance which does not give prominence to it. In any event, she misconstrues the *nature* of the problem.

One of O'Neill's concerns, one she shares with Kant, is for consistency in moral judgement. The principles of universalisability in ethics attempts to capture that concern. Winch acknowledges the importance of the principle with respect to the judgements an individual makes. Unless these judgements were consistent, it would be hard to attribute any moral seriousness to him. In particular, it would be a strong indictment against him if he did not judge himself as he judged others, and sought to make an exception in his own case. What Winch does *not* accept, however, is the further claim of the universalisability thesis, namely, that in order

for an individual's judgement to count as a *moral* judgement, it
entails his holding that anyone else, morally judging the same
situation, *must* reach the same conclusion.

Winch argues against this further claim of the universalisability
thesis by considering his reaction to Vere's decision in Herman
Melville's *Billy Budd, Foretopman*, to condemn Billy Budd to death.
Let us grant that Winch *has* shown that Vere is faced by a moral
dilemma, that he is confronted by the 'ought' of private conscience
and the 'ought' of military duty. Winch says that he could not have
come to the same conclusion as Vere reached. He says: 'In reaching
this decision I do not think that I should appeal to any considerations over and above those to which Vere himself appeals. It is just
that I think that I should find the considerations connected with
Billy Budd's peculiar innocence too powerful to be overridden by
the appeal to military duty.'[41] According to supporters of the
universalisability thesis, Winch *must*, if his moral view is to be
called a *moral* view at all, come to the conclusion that Vere came to
the wrong decision and acted wrongly. But he does not want to say
this: 'The story seems to me to show that Vere did what was, for
him, the right thing to do.'[42] Now, someone seeing what the story
seeks to show, may disagree, morally with Vere's decision. Winch
has no philosophical objection to such a moral reaction. With
respect to his own different moral reaction, 'The issue . . . is not,
of course, whether [others] would happen to agree with this
particular judgement of [his], but whether [he is] saying anything
intelligible and coherent at all, whether [he is] in fact making any
genuine moral judgement in speaking thus.'[43]

Only through the presumption of theory would we be led to
deny the *possibility* of the moral differences between Winch and
Vere. Such differences exist not only as between individuals, but
also as between practices. O'Neill says,

> Precisely because of the variety and transience of ethical prac-
> tices, to which Wittgensteinian writers draw our attention, we
> cannot easily lead our lives without raising questions which are
> not just internal to but about local practices. In doing so, how-
> ever, we can still leave open the question of whether there is a
> rational or neutral standpoint from which all problems can be
> resolved (p. 16).

She accuses the Wittgensteinian failure to raise these questions of conservatism. True, the writers she refers to can make little of the notion of 'a rational or neutral standpoint' in this context, but they have not failed to raise the questions O'Neill refers to. What *is* true is that they deny that there is any *general* answer to them. People's reactions to the existence of moral perspectives different from their own will vary. Those reactions will themselves be informed, partly, by moral ideas. Moral ideas enter into the criticisms made in such contexts. One perspective may be hostile to another, even if the other seeks to cooperate. Compromise depends on how much value is placed on what it facilitates. Some will place high value on peace and commodious living, while others may be prepared, if necessary, to go down fighting. One practice may erode another or be swallowed up by a stronger or more prestigious one. When a person meets another who has values different from his own, either may change. All these possibilities have been emphasised by Wittgensteinian writers. Both at the level of individuals and practices, O'Neill complains, 'There is no neutral standpoint from which to discern who is the missionary and who is seducing missionaries into "going native"' (p. 15). But this complaint, like her others, only has force if one harbours a conception of moral philosophy as a guide to human conduct. If one sees that relations between perspectives are themselves *moral* relations for the most part, one ceases to be beguiled into a search for a 'neutrality' in which language is idling and even corrupting.

Winch does not deny that 'it is an important task for philosophy to make clear the distinction between corrupt and non-corrupt forms of the thought that something is worthy of admiration'. On the other hand,

neither it, nor any other form of enquiry, can show what *is* worthy of admiration. The idea that it can is itself a form of corruption and always involves an obscuring of possibilities. . . . Philosophy may indeed try to remove intellectual obstacles in the way of recognizing certain possibilities (though there is always the danger that it will throw up new obstacles). But what a man makes of the possibilities he can comprehend is a matter of what man he is. This is revealed in the way he lives; it is revealed *to him* in his understanding of what he can and what he cannot attach importance to.[44]

III

Given that O'Neill has all these complaints against Wittgensteinian ethics, what alternative does she offer? She says, 'Kant presumably would have held that the shared capacities to reason and under-stand preclude radical incommensurability' (p. 23). For this reason, in his later writings, he 'turns to this issue, and discusses strategies by which we might arbitrate between competing construals of a situation, so emerging in reflective judging' (p. 23). When we see what these strategies amount to, we find that O'Neill's promises of a procedure which *contrasts* with Wittgensteinian ethics turn out to be rather empty.

The strategy we are offered is one whereby

> we may move towards overcoming discrepancies between dis-parate appraisals of one situation. They are strategies, one might suggest, not for finding that one shares a view with others but for seeking to share one. They can be thought of as strategies by which we seek to escape our 'private horizons' by following the maxim 'always to try to expand rather than to narrow one's horizon'.[45] When we adopt such strategies our 'reflective act takes account of the mode of representation of everyone else, in order, *as it were*, to weigh its judgement with the collective reason of mankind' (p. 26).[46]

But what is this supposed to amount to and what is it supposed to achieve?

First, we are told that these strategies

> are indispensable when there is disagreement, and so the need to apprehend and appreciate others' appraisals and connect them to our own . . . Even if we aim at manipulative or hostile rather than morally acceptable interaction with others we will be thwarted if we do not regulate our activity by such maxims. The worldly-wise need good judgement (p. 26).

So this is what we are offered: know there are moral points of view other than your own! But this is precisely part of what the Wittgensteinian discernment of differences emphasises. This is the situation which, earlier, O'Neill found problematic.

But, second, the strategies are supposed to take us beyond this recognition. O'Neill says that we may need not only to see what other views of a situation are, and how they differ from our own, but may need to arbitrate discrepancies. One maxim which may guide us here is the so-called 'maxim of enlarged thought' which enjoins us 'always to think from the standpoint of everyone else'.[47] Once we seek to share others' standpoints, and so become aware of incompatabilities between standpoints, further reflection may lead us towards reappraisals in which coherence is restored (p. 126).

If sharing others' viewpoints simply means recognising their existence, this leaves untouched the differences between them and the diversity of the relations between them. But, then, O'Neill speaks of *reappraising* standpoints and of *restoring* coherence without the slightest indication of what such 'reappraisal' amounts to, and as if the mere existence of moral differences constitutes a 'lack of coherence'. Compared with this, there is far more substance in the way Wittgensteinian writers have tried to show the variety of ways in which different moral perspectives may affect each other, and take account of each other.[48] It has far more substance than O'Neill's empty claim that 'our search for appraisals of actual situations is guided by considerations of coherence and interpretability to all parties' (p. 27).

Despite the emptiness of these promises, O'Neill presents alternatives in a disparaging light: 'To have reached the same "decision" by the toss of a coin or by mere whim would be something entirely different' (pp. 28–9). This would be her reaction, I suspect, to Winch's wanting to say of Vere, 'He did what was right for him.' Winch is aware of such reactions:

> To them it will seem that to speak as I have just spoken is to concede that anything goes in matters of morality, that morality is not a rational universe of discourse at all. . . . It will be said that if I do not admit that the right thing for him to do would be the right thing for anyone to do in the same circumstances, I am ruling out any possible distinction between what a man thinks he ought to do and what he in fact ought to do. And if that is so, how can it matter to a man *what* he thinks is right; since whatever he thinks is right will be right.[49]

Part of Winch's response is to say, 'It was clearly important to Vere that he did the right thing and he did not think that whatever he thought would be the right thing would in fact be so.'[50] Winch would say that this was *shown* in what Vere did. But if 'shown' is to mean anything, there must be *some* check such that some forms of behaviour would be reason for saying that a man did *not* do what was right for him, even though he may say he did. Without this check, to say that a man did what was right for him, would be no more, as far as O'Neill is concerned, than 'the toss of a coin'. It is all the more surprising, therefore, that O'Neill ignores the three examples Winch gives of such a check.

First, the circumstances surrounding the way in which Vere reached his decision may have been such as to show that moral considerations did not enter for him at all. For example, he may have applied the rules mechanically. We must always be alert to the possibility that we are missing features of a moral reaction different from our own, but there will be circumstances which cannot be called a genuinely moral context at all – 'our common understanding of moral ideas enabling us to judge what is and what is not a genuinely moral context'.[51] Winch's appeal to 'common understanding' has far more substance to it than O'Neill's appeal to the 'maxim of enlarged thought'.

The second set of limiting circumstances Winch presents are those 'cases where a man acts with every sign of moral concern, but where his ideas of right and wrong differ so profoundly from our own, that we are unwilling to accept his claim that he acted rightly.'[52] As Winch points out, the first set of circumstances constitute *logical* limits to what can be regarded as a genuinely moral context, whereas the second set of circumstances are an expression of our *moral* disagreements. The realism of these limits, which will be different for different people, contrasts favourably with O'Neill's appeal to 'the collective reasoning of mankind' and her claim that 'our search for appraisals is guided by considerations of coherence and interpretability to all parties' (p. 25).

The third set of circumstances Winch brings to our attention are those in which a person says he is concerned with moral considerations, but is, in fact, insincere or deceiving himself in saying so. He cites the behaviour of Raskolnikov after his murder of the moneylender as an obvious example.

We can see that O'Neill's fears that without a more 'systematic' approach in ethics, moral perspectives become hopelessly relativistic are unfounded. O'Neill hopes that 'the attempt to make sense of the nuances and complexities of situations, which is one of the most attractive features of Wittgensteinian ethical writing, might be incorporated in a more systemic form within an account of practical reasoning' (p. 27). What we have seen, however, is that the presumption of theory distorts and obscures the nuances and complexities involved in moral considerations. Had O'Neill seen this, she would not have wanted to go beyond Winch's examples. Instead, she would have been content to wait on them.

7

What Can We Expect From Ethics?

From time to time, in the history of ethics, it has been claimed that we can establish reasons for moral conduct in such a way that anyone who is not persuaded by these reasons is thereby convicted of a failure in understanding. This was thought to be the task of ethical theory. Recently, the very conception of an ethical theory has come under attack once again. But while critics reject the answers ethical theories have offered, they have not rejected the task they set themselves. They simply argue that philosophy cannot achieve this task unaided. For example, Bernard Williams suggests that we ask, 'Must any reflection on the good life require that a reflective intellectualism be part of the answer?'[1] *What we need to reject, however, is not the answers intellectuals have provided, but their conception of the task they are engaged in.* This suggestion will disappoint those philosophers and intellectuals who see themselves as a new priesthood, or as prophets of history, but that makes the rejection of their misconceived task no less urgent. I shall argue for its rejection by reference to the work of J. L. Stocks, Annette Baier and Bernard Williams.

Before we can appreciate how reluctant we are to give up the task I have referred to, we must remind ourselves of the rejection of two well-known theoretical answers which were offered in the pursuit of it. Williams defines a positive ethical theory as 'a theoretical account of what ethical thought and practice are, which . . . implies a general test for the correctness of basic ethical beliefs or principles' (p. 72).

The first positive ethical theory which was rejected sought to demonstrate the correctness of moral considerations by attempting to show that *every* person has a reason to heed them. To this end, efforts were made to show that acting justly is in every person's interests,[2] or to show that moral principles are ascertainable by human reason and binding on all rational creatures.[3] Sometimes it has been suggested that what is rational *is* what is in every person's interest.

Attempts to effect a marriage between morality and rationality, however, have proved singularly unsuccessful. We cannot give every person, no matter what his disposition, a reason, on his own terms, why he should heed moral considerations.[4] A rogue need not be irrational in the pursuit of his aims. On the contrary, he may see what he wants clearsightedly, and appreciate how to get it with the greatest economy of effort. Even if people were persuaded to heed moral considerations on their own terms, we would have to recognise that those terms include fear of punishment, desire for respectability, concern about what the neighbours would say; in short, everything Plato rightly condemned as popular virtue.[5]

Why should moral considerations have to be assessed and justified in terms of people's interests? If rational actions are thought of as means to predetermined ends, moral considerations, so far, have not entered the picture. Moreover, when they enter, they do so, as J. L. Stocks points out, 'as an additional principle of discrimination'.[6] It may be undeniable that something is wanted, but the question remains whether what is wanted is decent. Given that what is wanted is decent, it remains the case that it cannot be pursued by every and any means. Means and ends come under a common moral scrutiny. Nevertheless, if someone wants what is not decent, or pursues what he wants with no respect for decency, there is little point in denying that he wants what he says he wants, or that, given his aims, they are pursued rationally. The moral critic, in appealing to moral considerations, does not pretend that they conform to such a person's interests. Why should he, since these are the very interests he wants to change? If the possibility of ethical theory depends on giving every person a reason to be good, without such change, it is a possibility which cannot be realised. On this conclusion, Stocks, Baier and Williams are agreed.

The second positive ethical theory which was rejected, sought to establish tests, internal to morality, for the correctness of moral beliefs and actions. The tests took the form of determining the essence of a good action, an essence which, it was argued, can then be used as the standard of moral rectitude. As we know, Utilitarians told us that a good action is one which contributes to the greatest happiness of the greatest number and Kant said that a moral action is one done from a sense of duty. But the internal search for the essence of morality is as futile as the search for external justifications of morality. Again, on this matter, Stocks, Baier and Williams are agreed. Stocks says that, when he looks at the varieties of moral endeavour,

> There is obviously an enormous gap between this chaotic material and the tidy ethical systems which philosophers offer us as the result of their reflection upon it. The philosopher does not trouble much to show the steps by which from that starting-point he arrived at this result. It often seems as though he had been content to generalize from his own limited experience assuming that it was typical or authoritative.[7]

Williams says:

> If there is such a thing as the truth about the subject-matter of ethics – the truth, we might say, about the ethical – why is there any expectation that it should be simple? In particular, why should it be so conceptually simple using only one or two ethical concepts, such as *duty* or *good state of affairs*, rather than many? Perhaps we need as many concepts to describe it as we find we need, and no fewer (p. 17).

Baier says:

> In a pluralistic society like this one there is no escaping the fact that there is a plurality of moral traditions, that what people learn at their parents' knees varies from one ethnic or religious group to another. This substantive moral disagreement is a fact that no reforms in the teaching of introductory ethics will conjure away. Catholic hospitals will make different decisions from non-Catholic hospitals on many cases, whatever we do in our classes. What I am deploring is not the variety of moral traditions and the disagreement that brings when these traditions co-exist in one nation. I am deploring the additional and unnecessary variety and conflict produced by insisting on turning every moral judgement into an instance of a law or principle that has its niche in a moral theory. The array of moral theories that philosophers have produced do not match the array of working moral traditions in this society, or in the world at large.[8]

As each theory produces its favoured essence, confusion is compounded. Conforming to such essentialism leads, as Peter Winch has pointed out, to our having to call corrupt what we would normally regard as pure, and having to call pure what we would normally regard as corrupt. Consider, for example, acting from a sense of duty as the proposed essence of moral action. In response to Simone Weil's example of a father absorbed in play with his children, Winch says that he can easily imagine another father regarding such absorption as a form of purity, and its lack, in himself, as a form of corruption. Perhaps he finds that he plays with his children only from a sense of duty. But a theory which makes acting from a sense of duty the essence of moral action, decrees that he should call the father he admires corrupt, and that he should regard his own lack as a form of purity.[9] To cling on to theory in such contexts is absurd.

But if we reject these two positive ethical theories, what task is left for ethics to perform? Stocks, Baier and Williams reject the theories, but they do not reject, entirely, the questions such theories thought they were answering. Stocks says that every student must have been struck by the relative impurity of works in ethics:

> by reason of this impurity the moral philosopher does in fact assert ethical values, recommend lines of action, advocate reform of existing institutions – all things which as a practical man he has a perfect right to do, but none of themselves activities pertaining to a philosopher. The philosopher, I should say, in virtue of his philosophy, cannot prove anything to be good or bad.[10]

Stocks says that the impurity in these works of moral philosophy 'certainly makes them more attractive to the non-philosophic reader, but is apt to cause confusion in the reader's mind as to the task of philosophy and the contribution to be expected from it' (CPD pp. 117–18). Yet, as we shall see, confusion also ensues when theoretical answers, but not theoretical tasks, are rejected. The explicit rejection of ethical theories by Stocks, Baier and Williams makes it easy to miss the remaining confusions in their conceptions of ethics' tasks. These confusions can be seen in the roles they assign to critical reflection.

Stocks argues that, although ethics cannot give a foundation or external justification for moral conduct, it can help, indirectly, in telling all human beings how they ought to live. Ethics does this by 'attempting to make explicit and evident assumptions as to the nature of good which are for the practitioner largely concealed within the concrete detail of his judgements and decisions' (*CPD*, p. 128). Stocks thinks this is an important task, since 'When men do not know the faith by which they live, they will be apt inadvertently to betray it' (*NSP*, p. 115). For example, he thinks that confusions in Marxism can be demonstrated 'by showing them on the evidence of the actual achievements of humanity what man's fundamental beliefs really are' (*NSP*, p. 116). Through critical reflection, Stocks claims, the philosopher 'will be telling the practical man what he is really aiming at all the time' (*CPD*, p. 123). Stocks assumes, then, that beneath the luxuriant variety of moral judgements lies 'the nature of the good' which critical reflection on human achievement will reveal. This assumption determines the ethical theorist's tasks:

> the would-be theorist of conduct has to face the mass of chaotic material above described and attempt to reduce it to some degree of order. He has to show that this multiplicity is at bottom a unity, that this unorganized sequence of decisions and judgements has none the less its own inner organisation and can be plausibly regarded as the expression of a single principle or a few fundamental ideas which are in intelligible relation to one another (*CPD*, p. 125).

When we wait on the multiplicity of moral perspectives and practices, we see that they are not a multiplicity waiting to be reduced, or shown to be, a unity. Neither do they constitute chaotic and unorganised material waiting for ethics to reveal its inner order. Rather, individuals and groups are related to each other in varying degrees of agreement and disagreement. Removal of any confusion which may be present is not going to change that fact. In *that* respect, ethics has no tidying-up task to perform. But it was by means of this task, according to Stocks, that ethics was to help us, indirectly, in making explicit the principles underlying the good life. Thus, the help turns out to be as illusory as the task. Williams says,

> the aim of theory is not simply, or even primarily, to understand conflict. . . . The aim of theory is to resolve it, in the more radical

sense that it should give some compelling reason to accept one intuition rather than another. The question we have to consider is: How can any ethical theory have the authority to do that? (p. 99).

Baier and Williams, however, have their unexamined assumptions too. They continue to regard 'What is the nature of the good life?' as the most basic question for critical reflection. They uncritically ascribe a character to the good life from the outset. *Whether attainable or not, the good life must be uncoerced and shared in common by those who care about living a good life.* Such a life must not be forced on people by circumstances beyond their control. If it were, as Williams says, 'The most schematic code against interference and mutual destruction may be enough for parties who may have a shared requirement to live, not a requirement to share a life' (p. 103). On the other hand, Williams says, 'If the agreement were to be uncoerced, it would have to grow from inside human life' (p. 103). But if critical reflection has no authority to take us beyond the multiplicity of moral practices, neither does it have the task of postulating, as the good life, one that must be shared in common. Of course, Williams and Baier may desire the emergence of such a life, but that desire is not underpinned by a critical reflection which rules out alternatives.

Why do Baier and Williams seek, philosophically, to go beyond the multiplicity of moral practices? They do so from a conviction that we need to distinguish between practice and prejudice as we search for the nature of the good life. Reflective self-consciousness about our practices, they claim, is an unavoidable part of our modernity. We have inherited the insights of two great unmaskers of practices, Freud and Marx, while the social sciences have put our practices in a new light. What does this critical light show?

First, practices may harbour bad faith. If they do, they cannot constitute the good life. We must remember, however, that bad faith is occasioned. It needs a specific context and distinctions of contrast to give accusations of bad faith some purchase. Had she noted this requirement, Baier would not have found such an accusation 'a charge so hard to rebut that it is easy to turn it on anyone and everyone'.[11] I admit that a practice may be so riddled with bad faith that it cannot survive exposure, but Baier speaks, sometimes, almost as if this state of affairs were the rule:

I therefore take it for granted that I, like the next person, am *not* fully aware of whose cause I may be furthering by the saying of it. False consciousness can now be taken as the successor concept to 'original sin' – of course one is liable to it. That which distinguishes any sheep from the large herd of the goats will not be their escaping it, but their awareness of it and their attempt to find some method of 'redemption' from its evils (pp. 231–2).

Such a general application of the accusation of bad faith, robs it of the cutting edge Baier needs if there is to be a distinction between practices which are the product of bad faith and those which are not. In familiar examples, a specific virtue is distorted by bad faith. The primary relation to the virtue will not be one of bad faith, otherwise we could not speak of distortion. But the primary relation has not been tested for bad faith and survived. Rather, the issue of bad faith simply does not arise. Those for whom it *always* arises have turned an accusation into a slogan. Baier writes as though our *primary* response to moral practices should be a questioning one:

> To care about what we care about is to make risky investigations not only into the question of whether we really care, but into why and with what 'reason' we care about the persons and things we do.[12]

Little sense can be made of moral practices without taking account of the diverse, unreflective moral reactions at their core. Certainty in moral matters, as with empirical matters, need not depend on risky investigations. Often, it does not depend on anything at all. What is true is that *the same* unreflective moral reactions cannot be taken for granted in all practices. The mere *possibility* of bad faith in a practice will not show that its adherents doubt its virtues. Further, the exposure of bad faith will not change the fact that a multiplicity of practices exists.

Second, Baier and Williams note that critical reflection brings to light practices based on metaphysical confusions. They are extremely confident that religious practices fall into this category. Recently, Reformed epistemologists have argued the opposite: that it is unbelief which is the ideological product of bad faith.[13] Both sides make totalitarian epistemological claims, thus obscuring real conflicts between religious and secular practices. They fail to appreciate that metaphysical legitimations may be intellectually inadequate accounts of what can be believed independently of them. For example, the praise in the psalms does not depend on the argument from design, and a programme of social welfare need not depend on the notion of the common good.

The history of metaphysical accusations made in the name of progressive thought is decidedly mixed. If anything could be disposed of by such accusations, it seemed that primitive practices could. Yet Wittgenstein had occasion to say that some of the intellectuals who reflected on these practices were more primitive than the primitives – a remark which still outrages many 'progressive' thinkers. If this rebuke is taken to heart, it should shake the confidence of those who think critical reflection will eliminate a sufficient number of practices to prepare the way for the shared, good life. We have every reason to suppose that a multiplicity of moral practices would survive critical reflection. This being so, we can ask of critical reflection the same question that Williams asked of ethical theory: what authority does critical reflection have to adjudicate between them? A curious feature of Baier's and Williams' reflections is their relatively uncritical acceptance of the power of theories in the social sciences in this context. Baier certainly responds enthusiastically to them:

Engineers need theories of physics and chemistry; cooks need knowledge about what is edible, what is digestible, what tastes will result from certain combinations of ingredients and processes such as grinding, fermenting, baking, freezing. Moral agents also need theories, or rather the reliable facts good theories produce – facts about the way people react, about the costs and consequences of particular ways of life, on those who adopt them and on their fellow persons. We need psychological theories and social theories, and, if we are intent on political change, theories about political power and its working, and about economics (p. 233).

Williams is more ambivalent. For him it is an obvious truth that reflection characteristically disturbs, unseats' traditional ethical concepts (p. 148). He thinks that 'an *explanation* of these local judgements and of the conceptual differences between societies will presumably have to come from the social sciences' (p. 150). On the other hand, he acknowledges, 'Perhaps no existing explanation goes very deep, and we are not too clear how deep an explanation might go' (p. 150). But by the end of the book, conceptual reservations have not prevailed:

> we need to have some reflective social knowledge, including history, that can command unprejudiced assent if the better hopes of our self-understanding are to be realized. We shall need it if we are to carry out the kind of critique that gives ethical insight into institutions through explanations of how they work and, in particular, of how they generate belief in themselves. . . . ethical theory should not suppose that it can do without such social understanding, or that by a pure moralistic stand it can detach itself from these issues. It needs this understanding in order to answer questions about itself that it cannot ultimately avoid, about its relations to social life, its social or psychological connections with practice, and the ways in which it might hope to turn its supposed rational authority into power (p. 199).

The future for ethics, it seems, is to play its part in this multi-faceted reflection:

> How truthfulness to an existing self or society is to be combined with reflection, self-understanding and criticism is a question that philosophy, itself, cannot answer. It is the kind of question that has to be answered through reflective living. The answer has to be discovered or established, as the result of a process, personal and social, which essentially cannot formulate the answer in advance, except in an unspecific way. Philosophy can play a part in the process, as it plays a part in identifying the question, but it cannot be a substitute for it (p. 200).

Baier and Williams make much of the fact that we have witnessed the demise of ethical theory. But they make little of the fact that we have also witnessed the demise of equally ambitious theories in anthropology, sociology, psychology, politics and economics. What is more, as with ethical theory, their demise was due to their conceptual pretensions. We have to remember also that if our culture gave us Freud and Marx, the breeders of suspicion, it also gave us Wittgenstein who made us suspicious of suspicion.[14] Wittgenstein reminded us that suspicion has to be occasioned.

Doubt is not the norm. Indeed, philosophical doubt and suspicion, in the very generality of their intended application, became idle. Baier and Williams are suspicious of moral practices, but we have reasons to be philosophically suspicious of their suspicions.

For Baier and Williams, the world of traditional ethical theory is a world well lost. The mode of critical reflection with which they want to replace it, is similar, in many ways, to the hermeneutic cultural conversation with which Richard Rorty thinks we should replace epistemology. Both conceptions have hidden values. Agreement on a shared way of life is the aim of Rorty's hermeneutics. The conception of such a way of life is not given prior to the conversation, but is supposed to emerge in the course of it. The agreement reached is a flexible one, ready to accommodate novelties as they appear on the cultural horizon. But why should everyone assume that it is good to agree with everyone else? Conversations need not have agreement as their goal. After many conversations, the participants may seem stranger to each other than they did at the outset. Rorty fails to take the good philosophical advice: 'Anything your reader can do for himself leave to him.'[15]

The Enlightenment conviction that philosophy could give a rational foundation and justification of moral practices is, as we have seen, confused. Baier's hope for critical reflection is that it will pursue another Enlightenment project which has hardly been tried. It will tell us which practices are necessary for co-existence and, by so doing, lead us to practices which are more civilised than our present ones. Williams' hopes are more complex. He insists that critical reflection must take account of ethical diversity:

> If we become conscious of ethical variation and of the kind of explanation it may receive, it is incredible that this consciousness should just leave everything where it was and not affect our ethical thought itself (p. 159).

But how is ethical thought to be affected? To be aware of diverse moral practices is to be aware that we are faced with alternatives. Were it not for these alternatives, one's own local practice might have been held on to as the good life. One would have been brought to a knowledge of the virtues it proclaims. But since the good life must be one shared in common, the local practice cannot be the good life. Thus, Williams argues, we have to reach 'the notably un-Socratic conclusion that, in ethics, *reflection can destroy knowledge'* (p. 148). Consideration of other possibilities emerges as *itself* a good. Williams says:

> A society given over to 'experiments in living', in Mill's phrase, is not one that simply increases the chances of living in the best way. It is one sort of a society rather than another, and there are various forms of living that it rules out; indeed those ruled out could include those most worth living. However, this means only that diversity and freedom of inquiry are, like confidence, some goods to be encouraged among others, not that they fail to be goods (p. 172).

The ideal goal of critical reflection is practical confidence which shows itself in a way of life in which there is an uncoerced sharing of values. Williams asks,

> how people, or enough people, can come to possess a practical confidence that, particularly granted our world, will come from strength and not from the weakness of self-deception and dogmatism (p. 171).

Since the emergence of such self-confidence is, for the present, *only a hope*, Williams says 'We should not try to seal determinate values into future society' (p. 173). On the other hand, Williams is convinced of *the form* the hope for the good life must take. To sustain it, Williams argues,

> We cannot consistently leave out the reflective consciousness and practices of free inquiry needed to sustain it and to make use of it . . . To try to transmit free inquiry and the reflective consciousness is to transmit something rather than nothing, and something that demands some forms of life rather than others (p. 173).

I do not deny that some people react to moral diversity as Williams does. It is a reaction characteristic of a certain perspective. But Williams would not be content with this conclusion. He does not want his reaction to be one among many, part of the ethical diversity. Rather, he wants his conception of *the form of the good life* to be the product of critical reflection on that diversity. This is the possibility I deny. There may be critical reflection within diverse perspectives. *Philosophical* reflection notes this diversity. It is not itself a form of critical reflection which underpins any one of these reflective perspectives. Philosophical reflection alone, or aided by other intellectual disciplines, does not in itself underpin the notion of the good life as the uncoerced sharing of values in common. I think Williams would be reluctant to accept this conclusion. This can be shown by reference to the traditionalist who, given Williams' arguments, can be treated as something of a limiting case. Williams says:

> One reason why conservatives and traditionalists attack reflection is that they fear the uncertainty that seems to follow from it, the situation in which the best lack all conviction. The result they fear is something to be feared, and they are right to detest a certain liberal posture that makes a virtue out of uncertainty itself, and, in place of conviction, enjoys the satisfactions – the equally intellectualist satisfactions – of a refined indecision. But these traditionalists and these liberals share the error of thinking that what conviction in ethical life has to be is knowledge, that it must be a mode of certainty (pp. 168–9).

But why need a conservative or traditionalist fall into this category? A traditionalist who comes to realise that a way of life is no longer possible, need not be uncertain about it. He calls it the best life to live, and calls what he has to do now making the best of a bad job. Williams will want to remind him of what he has come to know: 'that in the process of losing ethical knowledge, we may gain knowledge of other kinds, about human nature, history, what the world is actually like' (p. 168). Possession of this new knowledge is supposed to affect practitioners of practices in such a way that 'if they think about their earlier beliefs, they will now see them as the observer sees them, as knowledge they do not share' (p. 167). But the traditionalist may have had this knowledge already. He appreciated the way things were going, and saw, clearsightedly, that old ways cannot be maintained, directly, by policy. But this knowledge, even if newly acquired, need not lead him to deny that the old ways are the best ways, or prevent him from describing his present life as settling for less. In 1942, Wittgenstein wrote:

> Put a man in the wrong atmosphere and nothing will function as it should. He will seem unhealthy in every part. Put him back

into his proper element and everything will blossom and look healthy. But if he is not in his right element, what then? Well, then he just has to make the best of appearing before the world as a cripple.[16]

Any suggestion that he is committed to regarding this knowledge as *compensation* for what he has lost, is simply a recommendation. That recommendation comes from a certain perspective, but that perspective is not itself underpinned by philosophical reasoning, or some wider form of critical reflection.

Why wouldn't Williams be content with this conclusion? Part of the answer is found in his assumption that *reflection itself* involves regarding diverse moral practices as *alternatives* in the culture. Williams distinguishes between dead options and live options. Dead options are ways of living in other cultures or in remote times, which it would make no sense to try to live now. Real options are perspectives already held by people, or ones we could go over to in our present historical situation without self-deception. But *does* reflection show that a person *must* regard current perspectives which he does not hold as real options for him? Peter Winch has pointed out[17] that one characteristic of moral differences which separate people, is not simply the different choices they make when faced by the same alternatives, but the differences in what they are prepared to count as alternatives. What will count as options for some, will not be regarded as options at all by others. To insist that all current perspectives *must* be viewed as alternatives or options is to distort these various reactions and relations. Williams seems guilty of such distortion when he says:

> we must not simply draw a line between ourselves and others. We must not draw a line at all, but recognise that others are at varying distances from us. We must also see that our reactions and relations to other groups are themselves part of our ethical life, and we should understand these actions more realistically in terms of the practices and sentiments that help to shape our life (p. 160).

What is the force of these 'musts'? What I am insisting on is that these remarks have no more status than recommendations from within a certain perspective. Some, like Williams, will not draw lines between themselves and others. Others will draw lines. Not all people will draw lines in the same place or in the same way. Relations between people, in this respect, will vary enormously. Philosophical or critical reflection does not determine the character of such relations; it does not determine that the diverse reactions must be seen as data to be used as we endeavour to move in the direction of a shared, good life.

Because Baier and Williams think otherwise, they seem to have little difficulty with Mill's phrase, 'experiments in living'. Baier regards different ways of life as long-term social experiments in determining how we ought to live. She argues: 'Unless we know the fate of communities that tried to implant and live by the moral principles we consider, how can we have an empirically tested opinion about their soundness?' (p. 242). This may make us wonder what we are supposed to do in the meantime. Williams recognises the difficulty when he says that as well as having to live after reflection, 'we have to live during it as well' (p. 117), but he does not reject Mill's notion.

Moral judgements are not experiments in moral judging. We cannot make a community's 'fate' the empirical test of its morality, in the way Baier suggests, since, often, what we take to be a community's fate will be informed by the moral judgements we make. Williams even says, 'The only serious enterprise is living' (p. 117). I may engage in various enterprises in the course of my life, but it would never occur to me to call my own life or 'living' an enterprise! We may speak of 'experiments in living' in special contexts. For example, after the Bolshevik revolution, certain groups lived together in an effort to find some alternative to the institution of the family. It is important that *the participants themselves* thought of what they were doing as an experiment.[18] But family life in Swansea, Pittsburg and Berkeley is not an experiment in living, and it is hard to see any sense in so describing it. Of course, there are many occasions when people want to see how various plans and relationships work out, but it does not follow that their ideas of what it is for them to work out are experimental. Things can become uncertain in all sorts of ways, but waking to another shaky day is not to wake to an experimental one.

At best, the hope for the emergence of the shared, uncoerced good life is an ideal within a certain perspective. This ideal may be used in criticising other perspectives. There is no philosophical objection to that. How could there be? What is objectionable is the suggestion that philosophical or intellectual reflection *itself* endorses this ideal, and the abstracting of the ideal from the viewpoint to which it belongs to be used as an *intellectual* critical norm by which other practices are to be assessed. An attempt is made to link the philosopher with a specific perspective. What the philosopher needs to note is that there are other practices which do not share Williams' ideal. Some of these advocate violent conflict. Others may insist that the importance of 'manners', in Henry James' sense, is not to bring people together, but to keep them, *civilly*, apart. When told that other practices *must* be seen as alternatives for *them*, some will respond robustly as Flannery O'Connor did when she said: 'My standard is: when in Rome do as you done in Milledgeville.'[19] Once we recognise these possibilities and conclusions, we can see the confusion involved in thinking that the nature of the good life can be determined by a successor to ethics called critical reflection. *There is no such successor, and, in this context, nothing to determine.*

Where does this leave ethics? Clearly, back with the multiplicity of moral practices. This will seem singularly unpromising to Baier and Williams, since this is where they want to begin, not where they want to end. The desire to go beyond the multiplicity of practices simply illustrates that it is as difficult in ethics, as it is elsewhere in philosophy, to know where to stop.

It will seem to Baier that the stopping-places I have argued for do nothing to allay Alasdair MacIntyre's suspicion that 'behind the masks of morality (lie) what are in fact the preferences of arbitrary will'.[20] But why should this worry be caused by anything I have said? Expressing a moral conviction is not like expressing a personal preference or a sudden feeling. A person who expresses a conviction may have reflected on moral matters and be able to elucidate what it means to him if challenged. Of course, he may come to see that he was wrong, that is, become convinced by elucidations of other values. It is in such contexts that talk of 'right' and 'wrong' has its natural home where moral questions are concerned.

To Williams, it may seem as if these conclusions are tantamount to saying 'that we cannot really think much at all in ethics' (p. 74). He says: 'It is this negative option that philosophers normally had in mind when in the past they said that philosophy could not determine how we should think in ethics' (p. 74). This misses the main point at issue. As the following quotation from Rush Rhees illustrates, it is not denied that adherents to moral views can give reasons in defence of their convictions. What is denied is that no one can fail to accept these reasons without thereby being accused of a failure in understanding. It is also denied that there are further intellectual reasons which show why these must be accepted as good reasons. Reasons which weigh with one person, may not weigh at all with another. Rush Rhees says,

> If a man is determined to fight for liberty (for the furtherance of liberty in this society) – then fine. But if he says he is determined to fight for liberty, *for the reason that* . . . then I lose interest. . . .
> It is not as though 'there is something *about* a liberal society from which anyone can see that liberty is important'. No doubt there would be differences between a liberal society and an authoritarian one; different institutions (free and frequent elections, limitations on police powers: 'inviolability of the domicile', etc.) and different methods of enforcing them. And I might describe these. I might emphasize that in the authoritarian society 'people are never allowed to' do this and that, and I might call this tyranny – although this is no longer pure description. The man devoted to order and strong government might answer that he does not find tyranny so very objectionable; things like insecurity, uncertainty, time-wasting disputes, the want of any clear regularity in the life of a community, not knowing what we can expect – these are greater evils for the mass of the people than any tyranny would be. And so on. It is not that he and I understand something different by 'liberty'. We may agree on that. In other words, if I do care about liberty, then I shall want to defend the freedom of the press, the inviolability of the domicile, etc. We might even say that caring about liberty *means*, *inter alia*, wanting to defend these institutions and practices. But then we should add that I do not have any reason for wanting to defend them.[21]

Williams might well respond to this example of moral and political disagreement by saying:

> We can go on, no doubt, simply saying that we are right and everyone else is wrong (that is to say, on the non-objectivist view, affirming our values and rejecting theirs), but if we have arrived at this stage of reflection, it seems a remarkably inadequate response (pp. 159–60).

But if, as I have argued, we have reason to suspect 'this stage of reflection', perhaps we ought to look again at the response Williams finds inadequate. Rhees elaborates on it as follows:

Someone says: 'But if you cannot prove it, then you may be wrong yourself; and you may be wrong when you say that *he* is.' Well, what does this show? Sometimes I see afterwards that I *have* been wrong. But how do I see this? Not by any conclusive proof of the universal practical reason. I see it by being convinced that I ought *not* to have done this: i.e. once again by being sure. 'We could never find out that we have made mistakes, unless we sometimes made no mistakes.' When you tell me that I am wrong, then you are not uttering a logical absurdity; what you are saying makes sense, and I can understand it. In fact I should not have had the trouble in *coming* to any decision otherwise. So I admit that my decision 'may be wrong' if this is all that is meant. But this does not mean that I must say 'And yet I know I may be wrong' – as though I am hesitant or wavering. Often enough I am hesitant; but not on *these* grounds. Fr. R. emphasized the importance of *responsibility* in connexion with moral decisions. Well, exactly.[22]

The reference to responsibility in moral matters should bring us back to an issue which Williams discusses at the outset of his book, but which, unfortunately, he does not develop: the question of whether ethics can be a subject. Socrates asked how we ought to live. Williams comments:

It would be a serious thing if philosophy could answer the question. How could it be that a *subject*, something studied in universities (but not only there), something for which there is a huge and technical literature, could deliver what one might recognize as an answer to the basic questions of life? (pp. 1–2).

Socrates thought, wrongly, that an answer to such questions must be one that any person could recognize as an answer he might arrive at himself. But, despite this view, Socrates did not think that ethics could be a subject, he just 'talked with his friends in a plain way' (p. 2). But, Williams argues, there is no way back to Socrates, no way in which we can shed the weight of the texts in ethics. The reason he gives is a curious one: 'Moral philosophy has the problems it has because of its history and its present practices' (p. 2).

But the issue concerns how we should stand to this history and these practices. One does not have to deny that Descartes was a great philosopher in order to hold that one of our primary philosophical tasks is to bring words back from their Cartesian to their ordinary use. In ethics, too, one of our primary tasks is to bring moral considerations back from the theories philosophers have wanted to make of them. On that issue, as we have seen, Stocks, Baier and Williams are agreed. The alternative, however, is not to seek an heir to ethics to grapple with the question of the nature of the good life. In *this* context, the need *is to give up the question*.

Our discussion has shown where generality in ethics does not reside. There is no general justification of moral considerations by means of which they can be commended to everyone. There is no general definition of a good action. We cannot say that whatever is the nature of the good life, it must be an uncoerced one lived in common, with a reflective intellectualism as a necessary part of it. On the other hand, if all we can do is to note the variety of moral perspectives and traditions, we may wonder why we need a subject called ethics for an observation which can be made by any imaginative chronicler of our times.

Is there nothing general in the subject called ethics? Certainly there is. What is general in ethics is conceptual elucidation and clarification. A philosopher may bring out the character of a specific moral perspective. Whether he adheres to that perspective or not, he may want to elucidate its character, perhaps because he sees it ignored or distorted by those who write about ethics. On the other hand, a philosopher may simply discuss a specific virtue, say, truthfulness or courage. If his writing possesses sufficient character, he may even deepen our conception of what a particular virtue can be. Think of the discussions of patience by Socrates, Kierkegaard and Simone Weil. Contributions of this kind may be among the finest fruits of philosophical reflection in ethics. They do not depend on any claim that these conceptual elucidations and extensions are underpinned by a reflective intellectualism of a philosophical or some other kind.[23] I am not ignoring the complexities involved in this context. I realise that what people are prepared to regard as moral perspectives is itself partly determined by their own moral and psychological dispositions.[24] It is therefore difficult, at times, to say whether a problem is a moral or a philosophical one. In any event, there is no substitute for continuing with discussion.

More generally, moral considerations have always occasioned

philosophical perplexity. The point of calling such perplexity general is that it is not peculiar to any individual. It may arise for anyone. We say we have obligations we *must* keep. What kind of necessity is that? People have described obligations as inescapable. What are they getting at in saying this? How can a person worry about the right thing to do if any answer he arrives at must be personal? Can we always speak of '*the* right thing to do'? Are all moral dilemmas resolvable? Certain ways of talking may puzzle us. What does it mean to speak of 'the common good'? What does it mean to say that a good man is necessarily rewarded and that an evil man is necessarily punished?

These are simply *some* examples of conceptual elucidations or extensions and puzzles moral considerations may occasion. Thus, while I do not deny that Williams is reflecting the present philosophical climate when he says, 'The distinction between the ethical and the meta-ethical is no longer found so convincing or important' (p. 73), in some ways I find it a matter for regret. I hasten to say, however, that I am not advocating a return to the linguistic labelling of moral terms as 'emotive', 'performative', 'imperative', 'prescriptive', 'attitudinal', 'cognitivist', 'non-cognitivist', 'realist', 'non-realist', etc. What I am advocating is a return to ethics' modest task of engaging with conceptual elucidations and clarifications. After all, it is not as if people have ceased to be interested or puzzled by such matters, or laid them to rest. Ethics, with unrealisable intellectual ambitions, has simply turned away from them, that is all.

But what of the larger claim? What of the expectation that ethics, some other intellectual discipline, or some interdisciplinary enterprise, can play an essential role in determining the nature of the good life? A first comment in one of Stocks' papers shall be the last comment in this one:

> In Boswell's *Life of Johnson* the following entry may be found under the year 1775: 'In July this year he had formed some scheme of mental improvement, the particular purpose of which does not appear. But we find in his "Prayers and Meditations", page 25, a prayer entitled "On the Study of philosophy, as an instrument of living" and after it follows a note, "This study was not pursued"' (*NSP*, p. 99).

8

Not in Front of the Children: Children and the Heterogeneity of Morals

There is an argument about moral education in educational circles which goes like this: in order to avoid indoctrination children should not be taught any definite moral values. In exposing the child to definite moral judgements and beliefs, the impression is given that something is settled which in fact is a matter of opinion. There is a great variety of moral opinions on most questions. One moral opinion is just as valid as any other. Therefore respect for the child demands that we inform him of the variety, allowing him to decide between the moral views when he is old enough to do so.

This is a bad argument. How does it come about? The phrase which needs further examination is the one which states that one moral opinion is just as valid as any other. This phrase is in fact a misleading way of expressing a correct philosophical conclusion regarding the heterogeneity of morals. For various reasons philosophers may want to deny the heterogeneity of moral beliefs. They may try to give them a spurious unity. This cannot be done. I do not want to argue for this conclusion here (see the previous chapters), since my purpose is to question what is thought to follow from this conclusion even if we grant it. When philosophers have stressed the irreducible heterogeneity of morals they have wanted to emphasise that moral beliefs are not hypotheses awaiting some kind of verification. Neither are they conclusions based on a system of antecedent reasons. This being so, moral values do not stand in need of further proof. They are not founded on experiential data as is a prudential policy. Neither are they based on a set of deductions such that their contradictories have no application, being unintelligible. Moral beliefs express what people find morally important. These beliefs express parameters of right and wrong. The beliefs cannot be contrasted with knowledge. The term 'belief' in this context is synonymous with 'conviction'. It is not a conjecture or the expression of doubt. A man who believed that such and such was the case empirically would have something less than the ideal. He has a belief, but he might have had knowledge. A man who expresses his moral beliefs expresses his convictions. Not anything can be a moral belief. In order for a belief to be a moral belief it must be related to a range of characteristic notions: truth, loyalty, kindness, generosity, courage, patience, etc. Not all such notions need be present in a single or related cluster of moral beliefs, but unless some of them were present we would not know what would be meant by calling these beliefs moral. Nevertheless, despite these conceptual limits, there is also an irreducible variety of moral opinions. Not only may some of these moral notions play no or little part in a person's moral beliefs, but even when many of them are present they may still be given a radically different order of priority by different people. This being so, a philosopher is confused if he argues as if there were only one specific set of moral beliefs. He may try to show that although it is alleged that there is a variety of moral beliefs, there is only one set of such beliefs, the rest being logically counterfeit in some way or other. This is what cannot be done. It is in this context that it may be denied that one moral belief or set of moral beliefs is valid and the rest invalid. Because of this denial it may be thought that the only proper conclusion to draw is that *all* the moral beliefs are equally valid. It is this conclusion which needs to be questioned. When philosophers of the persuasion I have in mind hold that it cannot be said that some moral beliefs are valid and others invalid, they are not *using* the concepts of validity and invalidity in this context, but denying that they should have a use here. They are denying that moral beliefs are beliefs which stand in need of a further justification in terms of criteria of validity and invalidity which are supposed to be independent of them. Moral beliefs are not incomplete expressions standing in need of some more ultimate rational justification. To think, therefore, that such philosophers would say that all moral beliefs are equally valid is absurd, since this would commit them to the general application of a term which they do not want to use even in the particular case. What the philosophers are saying is that there is a variety of moral beliefs. As far as philosophy is concerned, among this variety, one moral belief is as much a moral belief as any other. This remark is *not a moral judgement*, although it must be admitted that sometimes a man's moral views will lead him to refuse to call some conflicting views moral while others will be prepared to call them moral. Nevertheless, in the main, the philosophical remark is a descriptive one; it recognises that a belief or cluster of beliefs belongs to the family of cases we call 'moral'. The term is not being used here in the way it is used when we wonder what is the moral thing to do. In this latter context 'moral' is used in the sense of 'morally right'. But if we say that there are many moral points of view, we are not saying that there are many morally right views. We are characterising the views, but not judging them. The characterisation is of considerable practical importance. There is a great deal of difference between arguing with someone who shares our own moral views but who has wandered from them, and arguing with someone whose moral views are different from one's own. In the first case, one can appeal to the deviant to come back on the rails. In the second case, there is no agreement about the rails. It is condescension to take for granted that all disagreements are in fact deviations from our rails, that all 'moral views' different from our own are in fact disguised deviations from our own. Moralities different from our own are not rationalisations of immorality. On the other hand, there is no contradiction in saying that a point of view is a moral point of view and holding at the same time that the view is morally wrong. Because this possibility is forgotten, recognising the variety of moral opinion may be thought to lead to the confused educational argument with which I began the chapter. In fact, recognising the variety should help one to appreciate the confusions in the argument.

To say that there are differing conceptions of right and wrong is to say that people hold different things to be morally important. That being so, how could these people hold that all moral beliefs are equal? If someone has moral beliefs, it must matter to him that some things are believed or done and not others. A man who says all views are equal has no views. If he does not discriminate between judgements he has no judgements of his own. The characterisation of a variety of views as moral views by the philosopher cannot possibly imply that the people who hold these views think that all moral views are morally equal. As we have seen, a person who thought all moral views to be morally equal would have no moral views. It would be odd to make something a condition of holding a moral view which would in fact be the negation of the very possibility of having such a view.

We are now in a position to appreciate the confusions involved in the educational argument. A philosophical conclusion is first misunderstood and then turned into a piece of meaningless neutrality. All the philosopher said was that a certain variety of views was a variety of moral views. But none of these moral views could be what they are if those who adhered to them said that all moral views are morally equal. Out of whose mouth could such a judgement come? Yet, this is what some educationalists propose that children should be told: 'All moral views are equally valid'. What we have seen is that such a remark could not be an intelligible comment from a philosophical or a moral point of view. The philosophical comment to the effect that there is no overriding experiential test or independent criteria of rationality to which all moral views are answerable, or by which one could arbitrate between them, is turned by the educationalist into the remark that all moral views are equally valid.

Let us now look back to the educational suggestion that children should be told that all moral views are equally valid. These are to be among the earliest things children are to hear about morality. The irony is that they will hear it characterised in a way in which no one who held moral views would talk. Telling children that all moral views are equally valid is not the move in the interests of neutrality it claims to be, but simply a product of the philosophical confusion I have outlined.

It is said that once one has told children that all moral views are equally valid, the child will be able to choose between them when he is old enough. We have already seen, however, that the initial ascription of equality to moral views falsifies the ways in which moral views are held. What actually happens is that early on in life children will be introduced to values of various kinds. They may or may not make these values their own. If they do, it is not because they have *further* values with which to assess *these* values. On the contrary, it will be because they come to see the values as important in themselves. Later in life, whatever their beginnings, they may come into contact with other values, different ways of looking at things. The initial perspective may withstand the new challenge, or it may not, but again the moral preference will be in the terms of the values concerned. There is no common coinage into which all the views can be cashed and which will establish their priority. This being so, a person who has no values at all will never have any reason to make a moral choice. If a person has no moral values he has no grounds for making a distinction between what he ought or ought not to do. Yet this is the position children would be in were the educational advice followed. The idea is that a child will wait until he is old enough to choose before acquiring any moral views. The idea seems to be to put the child in the best possible position to choose. What the policy would actually achieve is to rob the child of anything moral about which he could make a choice, or in which he could find reasons for choice when the occasion for it comes. A choice must be *about* something and must be informed *by* something. The educational suggestion we have considered does not provide ideal conditions for choice. On the contrary, it destroys the very possibility of choice. It is the educationalist's suggestion, not moral values, which should not be expressed in front of the children.

9

Does It Pay To Be Good?

In her paper to the Aristotelian Society in 1958, entitled 'Moral Beliefs',[1] Mrs Foot says that she agrees with the assumption found in the *Republic*, 'that if justice is not a good to the just man, moralists who recommend it as a virtue are perpetrating a fraud' (p. 100). The example of justice is incidental to the main contention, namely, that virtues can only be recommended if they constitute a good to the virtuous man. If virtues do not constitute such a good, they are frauds. It becomes essential, therefore, given the above assumption, to decide in general whether virtues do constitute a good to the virtuous man; in other words, to decide whether it pays to be good.

Mrs Foot argues that those who accept Thrasymachus's premiss – that injustice is more profitable than justice – and yet want to deny his conclusion – that a man who has the strength to get away with injustice has a reason to follow this as the best way of life – are in a dubious position. I shall argue that, on the contrary, it is Mrs Foot's position which is the dubious one, and that if adopted, reduces morality to expediency, and principle to policy.

First, I must make clear the choice of grounds on which I wish to challenge Mrs Foot's argument, since it is challengeable from at least two positions. These positions can be illustrated by a consideration of what Mrs Foot has to say about the fact that in seeking a justification for one's advocacy of just conduct, the chain of reasons offered must come to an end somewhere. She advocates caution, since it is all too easy to bring one's justification to a halt too soon. The request for justification in this context can be interpreted either as an attempt to justify in general the fact that justice is a moral virtue, or as an attempt to justify one's concern about justice in a particular situation. Mrs Foot pursues the latter course, and this is the one I wish to follow, but a brief word first about the alternative interpretation.

According to the view of the justification of morality I have in mind, it is not denied that my reasons for acting in a certain way

110

can be given in terms of moral considerations or moral principles, but the enquiry is pushed back a step further by asking why we have the moral rules we do. The answer is given sometimes in terms of social cohesion, the needs of society, the greatest happiness of the greatest number, and so on. What all these answers come to is that we observe the moral principles we have because it pays to do so. I think this view is radically mistaken, and were it my intention to argue against it in this paper, I should do so by examining the relation of certain fundamental moral distinctions such as truth and falsity, justice and injustice, to the concept of community. I think it can be shown that we do not adhere to moral precepts in order that we might have a harmonious society, but that, on the contrary, the very notion of social existence has moral implications. The relation between moral rules and society is not a contingent one. Nowell-Smith suggests that because these rules are so useful it has become difficult for us to imagine society without them (*Ethics*, pp. 226 ff.). He says that robbers must have rules if robbery is to pay, whereas what ought to be said is that robbers must have rules if there is to be robbery. My remarks here are sketchy and need working out, but apart from stating that the mistake of seeking a justification of moral rules as such in terms of the needs of society rests largely in a failure to take account of the moral implications in the very notion of society, I do not wish to pursue the point further. One reason for this is that I think it has been argued conclusively elsewhere,[2] and another is that Mrs Foot herself devotes her attention to the question of the justification of just action in the particular case: 'Can we give anyone, strong or weak, a reason why he should be just?' (p. 100).

Her answer to this question, an answer to end all further questions apparently, is that a man *needs* justice in his dealings with his fellow men whether he is strong or weak. Surprisingly, she thinks the need is so great that a man cannot get along without satisfying it. Judging from Mrs Foot's presentation of the matter, the question appears to be straightforwardly empirical. In case I do her an injustice, I shall quote the relevant passage at length.

> Those who think that he can get on perfectly well without being just should be asked to say exactly how such a man is supposed to live. We know that he is to practise injustice whenever the unjust act would bring him advantage; but what is he to say? Does he admit that he does not recognise the rights of other

people, or does he pretend? In the first case even those who combine with him will know that on a change of fortune, or a shift of affection, he may turn to plunder them, and he must be wary of their treachery as they are of his. Presumably the happy unjust man is supposed, as in Book II of the *Republic*, to be a very cunning liar and actor, combining complete injustice with the appearance of justice: he is prepared to treat others ruthlessly, but pretends that nothing is further from his mind. Philosophers often speak as if a man could thus hide himself even from those around him, but the supposition is doubtful, and in any case the price in vigilance would be colossal. If he lets even a few people see his true attitude he must guard himself against them; if he lets no one into the secret he must always be careful in case the least spontaneity betray him. Such facts are important because the need a man has for justice in dealings with other men depends on the fact that they are men and not inanimate objects or animals. If a man only needed other men as he needs house-hold objects, and if men could be manipulated like household objects, or beaten into reliable submission like donkeys, the case would be different. As things are, the supposition that injustice is more profitable than justice is very dubious, although like cowardice and intemperance it might turn out incidentally to be profitable (pp. 103–4).

In no way does Mrs Foot deny the logical possibility of the rogue she depicts succeeding and finding his villainy profitable. All she says is that things being as they are, it is as a matter of fact unlikely that injustice pays. Some of us may doubt Mrs Foot's assessment of human conduct. Is it for nothing that people have wondered for so long why the wicked prosper? Her account is rendered plausible by the fact that she implies, though she says otherwise, that the happy unjust man will act unjustly whenever an opportunity arises. But why need we think that the unjust man always acts unjustly? He is more likely to conform to the practice of justice in most cases, and act unjustly only when it really pays to do so. Deceit depends to a large extent on a pre-established stock of goodwill. But there is little point in lingering over the factual question of whether a life of injustice is likely to profit a man. It is more important to note that despite the empirical character of Mrs Foot's argument, it has, underlying it, presuppositions concerning the nature of the importance we attach to moral actions.

In reply to the question why I should deal justly with my fellow men, Mrs Foot would reply, presumably, 'Because it is likely to pay or profit you to do so'. She is prepared to conceive of situations where things might be different; situations where human beings can be manipulated like inanimate objects or beaten into reliable submission like donkeys, but thinks that things are not like that. I should have thought that many a despotic sheikdom or the Nazi treatment of the Jews approximated to such a state of affairs. Mrs Foot takes no account of the fact that probabilities vary with the situation. In some cases, probability will be on the side of injustice proving profitable. For example, it is easy enough to imagine a ruler having such power over his subjects that any relaxing of his ruthless rule would lead to a loss of profit. It does not profit him to show a regard for the vast majority of his subjects. He simply keeps a strong contented army. What is Mrs Foot to say about such a situation? If she wishes to be consistent she must say that since such a ruler is strong enough to get away with injustice, injustice and its profits are a sufficient reason for holding that the life the ruler leads is the best life he could lead. On the other hand, many people would want to say that the ruler was not living the best life he could lead, and that despite the fact that he found injustice profitable, he ought to deal justly with his subjects. One might put the matter provocatively by asking whether it profits a man to gain the whole world if he loses his own soul? Or, in case anyone should think that the previous question depends on one's holding religious beliefs, one could ask whether it profits a man to gain the whole world by committing despicable deeds? There seems to be a clash between two rival conceptions of what constitutes profit in a man's life. There is no dispute over the obvious profits which the ruler's injustice has brought him: wealth, gratification of his desires, ease, comfort, and so on. But a judgement is being passed on these profits which calls them unprofitable. This judgement is a moral judgement. Its possibility shows conclusively that the relevance of morality does not depend on whether it pays or not.

Mrs Foot has tried to find a non-moral justification for moral beliefs, and such an attempt always fails; it distorts the kind of importance which moral considerations have for us. It is due to her attempt to find a justification for adherence to justice in this way that Mrs Foot is led into such curious contradictions in the last paragraph of her paper. She says,

The reason why it seems to some people so impossibly difficult to show that justice is more profitable than injustice is that they consider in isolation particular just acts (p. 104).

Mrs Foot is not, as one might think at first reading of the long passage I referred to, making the point that on the whole it is more profitable in each individual's life to act justly rather than unjustly. In order to appreciate her argument, I think, one must imagine a scene often talked about from pulpits, namely, that of a man setting out on the journey of life. If he asks at the outset of the journey what he will need, what will benefit him on the journey, one answer is Justice. It is more likely that justice will benefit him on the journey than injustice. All will not run smoothly. Presumably, he must put up with an occasional unprofitable just act, since probability where justice is concerned, is always on the side of profit. But this probability is not the probability of the course of any particular life, but the probability of the courses of people's lives in general. The individual who pursues justice may find that as a matter of fact justice has not paid in his life. Mrs Foot gives a striking example of this, namely, of a person being prepared to die rather than let an innocent man be convicted of a crime of which he is accused. She says of this person:

For him it turns out that his justice brings disaster on him, and yet like anyone else he had good reason to be a just and not an unjust man (p. 104).

The good reason Mrs Foot refers to is the probabilities which faced such a man when he chose to practise justice. As it happens, his choice has led to disaster, but, as Mrs Foot says, 'like anyone else he had good reason to be a just and not an unjust man'. Notice the use of the past tense here – he had good reason – which again conjures up the picture of a man equipping himself with the essentials for the journey of life. But what of the man facing death because of his adherence to justice? Mrs Foot replies:

He could not have it both ways and while possessing the virtue of justice hold himself ready to be unjust should any great advantage accrue (p. 104).

We are told 'that if a man is just it follows that he will be prepared, in the event of very evil circumstances, even to face death rather than to act unjustly' (p. 104). It seems to me that on Mrs Foot's argument, such preparedness is unintelligible. A mysterious gap exists between one's initial choice of the way of justice, and one's acceptance of death as its result. If I ask, Why should I die? and the answer given is, 'Because your practice of justice involved the risk of death', it can only be accepted on the assumption that my practice of virtue is carried on independently of the initial reason for its adoption, namely, the likelihood of profit. It is as if Mrs Foot were saying, 'Once you choose justice you must accept what justice brings.' If I ask why, the answer is simply, 'Because you are just.' The reason why I am just, namely, because I expect justice to pay, now seems to disappear in the background. The role of such a reason begins to appear more and more like murky mythology: we are given a reason for accepting the consequences of just actions without reason. If, on the other hand, the likelihood of profit remains our reason for acting justly, I see no reason why, if there are people other than those whom Mrs Foot describes as 'too timid or too stupid to ask questions about the code of behaviour which they have been taught', there could not also be people who, at some time or other in their lives, question whether the initial justification for acting justly, namely, that it generally pays to do so, applies in their case. After all, the only relevance of the general survey of the results of virtue was to give the individual some idea of what was likely to be in store for him if he practised justice. But there may come a time when a man is better placed to assess whether justice pays in his own life than those who rely on general probabilities. Such a time is when a man faces death as the result of his policy to act justly. He no longer needs the general survey of probabilities. Death makes it always unprofitable to play the game which justice demands. Compared with all the profitable results which the pursuit of justice has led to in the past, death tips the balance. One cannot look to future events for redress, since death is not an event in the game, but the end of the game. Unless one is prepared to say that one must accept the path of justice even when one's reasons for choosing to walk it have now been proved to be false, one cannot give an intelligible account in terms of Mrs Foot's argument of why anyone should die for the sake of justice.

Mrs Foot assumes that if a man's just actions bring about his death, they have ended in disaster. She fails to see that for anyone concerned about justice, death for the sake of justice is not a disaster. The disaster for him would be to be found wanting in face of death, and to seek the path of injustice and compromise. Mrs Foot cannot give an account of anyone who sees death as a good; who dies for the sake of justice. She can only give an account of someone who dies as a result of justice, although, as I have tried to show, the justification for doing so is obscure, to say the least. Death cannot appear in Mrs Foot's list of profits, since profit is always understood in terms of results in relation to the individual. Death cannot be profitable, since that in terms of which profitableness is to be assessed, namely, myself, no longer exists. Mill, on the other hand, in his remarks on martyrdom, is able to show how one's own death can be regarded as a good, since for him, what makes it good is the fact that it contributes to the greatest happiness of the greatest number. Mill says: 'A sacrifice which does not increase, or tend to increase the sum total of happiness' Utilitarianism 'considers as wasted' (*Utilitarianism*, Everyman Ed., p. 16).

Whatever one thinks of Mill's answer, Mrs Foot is precluded from making any use of it, since she says explicitly:

> Even if the general practice of justice could be brought under the motive of universal benevolence – the desire for the greatest happiness of the greatest number – many people certainly do not have any such desire. So that if justice is only to be recommended on these grounds a thousand tough characters will be able to say that they have been given no reason for practising justice, and many more would say the same if they were not too timid or too stupid to ask questions about the code of behaviour which they have been taught (p. 102).

In striking contrast to both Mill and Mrs Foot, Kierkegaard, in *Purity of Heart*, a book which anyone seriously interested in moral philosophy ought to take account of, says of the death of Jesus:

> And yet eternally understood, the crucified one had in the same moment accomplished all (trans. Steere, Fontana ed., p. 121).

Kierkegaard locates the value of the death of the martyr, not in the contribution which the death makes to something called the general happiness, nor in the fact that the martyr must put up with it as an unprofitable consequence of a policy which is on the whole profitable, but in the death itself. It is because the death of Jesus was what it was that Kierkegaard says that in dying Jesus had accomplished all. This brings us back again to the fundamental disagreement about the nature of profit in moral action, about the sense in which it pays to be good. In this disagreement, the differences between Mill and Mrs Foot are relatively unimportant, for each locates the value of just action in considerations which refer beyond the action itself to its results. Kierkegaard condemns this attempt at justifying morality in non-moral terms, and it matters little whether the justification concerned refers to the benefits of one or to the benefits of all, since what is being criticised is the view of moral action which these positions imply. I want to devote the remainder of this paper to a consideration of the force of Kierkegaard's criticisms.

Kierkegaard believes that something can be said in general about all actions performed because of our moral beliefs. He says that such actions must be performed from a love of the good. He contends that to will the good is to will one thing. Before considering the relation of his position to Mrs Foot's argument, it is advisable to show that Kierkegaard's position is a philosophical one. This is partly because the talk about 'willing one thing' might tempt one to think that Kierkegaard's answer is an empirical one. When we are told that to will the good is to will one thing, we might ask what the one thing is: is it this, that, or the other thing? Kierkegaard describes the task awaiting anyone who interprets his answer in this way:

> If one should consider this matter properly must he not first consider, one by one, each goal in life that a man could conceivably set up for himself, mentioning separately all of the many things that a man might will? And not only this; since each of these considerations readily becomes too abstract in character, is he not obliged as the next step to attempt to will, one after the other, each of these goals in order to find out what is the single thing he is to will, if it is a matter of willing only one thing? (pp. 47–8).

Philosophically, such enumeration will never bring one to see the importance of moral action, but not because the task is endless, but because the enquirer 'at the outset . . . took the wrong way and then continued to go on further and further along this false way' (p. 48).

Kierkegaard is not interested in the specific objects of people's wills, but with what it means to will the good. His 'one thing' is not some thing or other. Furthermore, if we separate the moral objects of people's wills from the multitude of things which people will, it cannot be said that Kierkegaard is interested in any of these in particular either; that is, he is not concerned with this or that moral principle or belief. When he says that to will the good is to will one thing, he is concerned with the form of morality and not with its content. He is well aware of the distinction between what things are good and the concept of moral goodness. Kierkegaard recognises that moral philosophy is concerned solely with the latter; that it is not the business of philosophy to advocate moral beliefs, but to ask what it means to have moral beliefs. Hence the point of his remark that his 'talk is not inquisitive' (p. 161).

Kierkegaard's point, then, that to will the good is to will one thing, is a philosophical and not an empirical observation. Yet, why does Kierkegaard choose to express it in this way, by saying that to will the good is to will *one* thing? Why not two things, three things, or many things? He does so in order to stress that a moral action has a certain unity, that its importance is internally related to the action itself. Insofar as the importance of the action is externally related to the action, Kierkegaard says it is an instance of what he calls 'double-mindedness'. It is at this point that Kierkegaard's argument becomes relevant as a criticism of Mrs Foot's position, since she says that the reason we commend justice as a virtue is because on the whole it pays one to pursue it. Kierkegaard shows that if the reason for moral actions is said to be beyond the actions themselves, it follows that actions are morally indifferent for anyone who acts according to this rule. I want to elaborate on Kierkegaard's arguments.

Actions are morally indifferent for a person when it no longer matters to him whether he does one thing rather than another. If one claims to have moral beliefs or to act according to moral principles, it does make a difference to one whether one does one thing rather than another. I shall try to show how, if one thinks that non-moral reasons can be given for moral actions, the attempt at so explaining moral beliefs leads one to deny them.

Let us assume that the point of virtue is its profitableness. I wish to say that if I give alms to a beggar in order to impress my employer and obtain an increase in salary, it does not make a difference to me whether I do one thing or another. At first this seems absurd. Of course my action made a difference to me: it made a difference to my employer's opinion of me, and it made a difference to my salary. My action was a purposive action; it functions as means to my end. The end is all-important, the means relatively unimportant. *As it happened*, the means turned out to be giving alms to a beggar, but helping a blind man across the street, bribery, breaking up an uneven dog-fight, flattery, or a thousand other things might have done just as well in securing the desired end. Whether one does this or that is contingently related to the end one is aiming at.[3] The same conclusions follow if one considers the person who performs 'just' actions, not for the sake of profit, but to avoid punishment for failing to do so. As Kierkegaard says of him, '*He does continually what he would rather not do*' (p. 76).

To hold a moral principle, it is essential that the principle be distinguishable from what a man wants. Mrs Foot, on the other hand, thinks that 'the nature of justice can be shown to be such that it is necessarily connected with what a man wants' (p. 101). I am not denying the possibility of the convergence of duty and desire in given instances, but it must always be possible to specify what would constitute a clash between one's moral beliefs and one's desires. If one provides a non-moral reason for moral action, whether it be pleasure, happiness, or profit, as long as the pleasure, happiness or profit envisaged is one's own, such a clash is inconceivable. This is true of any attempt to explain moral conduct as means to some personal end. One must distinguish between moral beliefs and the expedient use of moral beliefs. Kierkegaard speaks of the man for whom expediency and profit are the rule in *Either/Or*. He is called, 'the lover of the momentary', 'the man whose interest is in the particular', 'the sensualist', and so on. The portrait is a deliberate caricature, but is meant to illustrate the lack of consistency involved in a life of expediency.

> One is struck by seeing a clown whose joints are so limber that all necessity for maintaining the human gait and posture is done away. Such are you in an intellectual sense, you can just as well stand on your head as on your feet, everything is possible for you. . . . A man who has a conviction cannot at his pleasure turn topsy-turvy upon himself and all things.[4]

There is a deceptive consistency about Mrs Foot's picture of the just man. She is able to say that 'The man who has the virtue of justice is not ready to do certain things' (p. 104). Yet, we must remember her fundamental reason for thinking this so, namely, that it is unlikely to pay a man to do these things. I do not see how Mrs Foot can distinguish between the man who loves justice, and the man who performs 'just' actions because it pays to do so. Even if we accept the argument that in fact justice pays, we can imagine people performing just actions for other reasons, namely, for the sake of the actions themselves. Would Mrs Foot find such conduct morally praiseworthy? If so, what would be her reasons for calling such conduct moral?

Kierkegaard wants to say that all things are not possible for a man who has moral beliefs. Mrs Foot would like to say the same, but she employs a concept of possibility which does not allow her to say so. True, if I am performing an action because it will bring me profit, it is not open to me to do anything which will lose me that profit. So far this is simply the model of all purposive action: if you want *A*, you must do *B*, *C* and *D*. But this has nothing to do with morality. It may be that in order to profit in life I have to keep my promises, tell the truth, act justly, show kindness, and so on. But it may be the case that what profits me is breaking my promises, lying, injustice, and callousness. If all I am concerned about is what profits me, I shall choose the course which is most likely to bring me these profits. Mrs Foot says that justice is profitable, but that has nothing to do with morality. If injustice were profitable, she would have to advocate pursuing it.

Let us consider a concrete example. My father has committed murder, I know that he has, and the police have come for him. I refuse to hand over my father to them. Someone asks me why I refuse to do so, to which I reply, 'I can't.' What kind of impossibility is involved in the answer? According to Mrs Foot, the fundamental reason for my action, assuming we think it moral, is the place which this action has in the general profitableness of moral actions. So I do not hand over my father to the police because, generally speaking, this kind of action pays. The impossibility of my action is a contingent matter. There is nothing in the action itself which makes it impossible for me to do it, since if it did not pay not to do it, I would do it. This is a travesty of the reasons I should give for not handing over my father to the police. What I should say, in fact, would be, 'Because he is my father'. Mrs Foot would not be content with this answer. She says that 'the affection which mothers feel for children, and lovers for each other, and friends for friends, will not take us far when we are asked for reasons why a man should be just' (p. 102). Mrs Foot's answer, namely, profit, takes us away from moral considerations altogether. The impossibility of my being able to give up my father to the police does not depend on profitableness or unprofitableness, but on what it means to give up my father to the police. It is *that* that I could never do, whereas the man who does not do it because of profit *could* do it; it is simply a contingent matter that he does not. Furthermore, if I try to show one of Mrs Foot's thousand tough characters why he should not leave his father destitute in his old age, I shall never do so by convincing him that it will profit him to do so, or that such actions generally profit people. Perhaps, as a result of the latter arguments, he decides to look after his father. No matter, for what I have taught him to have is a regard for profit, not a regard for his father. Perhaps Mrs Foot will say that this is but another instance of concentrating on particular just acts. I should reply by saying that it is only by taking account of actual situations in which men make stands for their moral beliefs that the nature and importance of such beliefs come to be appreciated.

Finally, a word about a neglected concept in contemporary moral philosophy, namely, remorse. No analysis of moral action in terms of the means–ends distinction can account for remorse, unless one believes with Nowell-Smith that it does not differ importantly from embarrassment! (See *Ethics*, p. 26). On Mrs Foot's account, I should not leave my father destitute in his old age because it is highly probable that it will not pay me to do so. Suppose that I go on regardless, and then find out that she is right. I may feel frustrated because I have not achieved the profit I had hoped to gain, in much the same way as I might feel frustrated at not getting a job. But this is far from remorse. One cannot explain remorse unless one realises that the just man cares about just actions. Mrs Foot's picture of the man who possesses the virtue of justice is a caricature: it is a picture of a person who performs actions which are just in their externalities. A man can perform 'just' actions without being just. If one thinks of moral goodness as a function of man in much the same way as cutting well is the function of a knife, one cannot account for praise and blame in moral discourse.[5] We do not blame the knife for being a bad knife, but we do blame a person for a bad action, unless his reasons for the action show that our assessment of what the action amounted to was mistaken. The reasons we have for acting place our actions in intelligible contexts where they can be judged by other people. If my actions were mere means to my ends, it would be impossible to feel remorse because of them, but since they are ends in themselves as far as morality is concerned, what I do and why I do it can occasion remorse; remorse because I have committed such despicable deeds. Actions are ruled out for the just man, not because they would not profit him, but because they are what they are. If unjust actions are performed by the just man he feels remorse because he discovers that he is the kind of man for whom such actions were not ruled out after all. The means–ends distinction, then, which plays such an important part in Mrs Foot's argument is foreign to morality. Kierkegaard asks the man striving to be decent:

> What means do you use in order to carry out your occupation? Are the means as important to you as the end, wholly as important? Otherwise it is impossible for you to will only one thing, for in that case the irresponsible, the frivolous, the self-seeking, and the heterogeneous means would flow in between in confusing and corrupting fashion. Eternally speaking, there is only one means and there is only one end: the means and the end are one and the same thing. There is only one end: the genuine Good; and only one means: this, to be willing only to use those means which genuinely are good – but the genuine Good is precisely the end (*Purity of Heart*, p. 177).

Kierkegaard's point is substantially the same as Kant's remarks on the heteronomy of the will. But one does not have to go outside the present century to find a powerful attack on the alleged importance of the means–ends distinction for morality. I refer to the neglected, but important, writings of J. L. Stocks. Stocks questions, quite rightly, the adequacy of the Aristotelian notion of rational action as an account of morality. But he does not suggest that the distinctive contribution of morality to action consists in adding a further purpose to the action, or in superseding purposes already given. Morality operates as 'an additional principle of discrimination . . . by setting a differential value on features which to purpose were indifferent or equal in value'.[6] Once this is recognised, the inadequacies of the means–ends distinction are soon apparent.

The moral attitude is essentially a concern for the rightness of action . . . morality requires that all means shall be justified in some other way and by some other standard than their value for this or any end: that however magnificent is the prospect opened out by the proposed course of action, and however incontestable the power of the means chosen to bring this prospect nearer, there is still always another question to be asked: not a question whether in achieving this you will not perhaps diminish your chances of achieving something still more important; but a question of another kind. 'There is a decency required,' as Browning said; and this demand of decency is prepared to sacrifice, in the given case, any purpose whatever.[7]

Stocks illustrates his point with the simple example of someone who discovers a quick and legally admissible way of making money. The means are in his power, and the end in view is undeniably profitable. But morality says, 'Not that way'. Nothing is denied that the purposive outlook asserts: the relative lack of effort needed, the rich recompense expected, the calculation involved. But given the proposed action, morality sees in it a barrier which cannot be passed. To the observer who has eyes only for the end and the easiest methods of attaining it, the moral judgement will seem arbitrary, and close to madness. The judgement can only be understood by those who have a regard for decency, or, as Kierkegaard would have said, 'a love of the good'.

But what of those who wish to reconcile the purposive outlook with morality? Could they not say that the non-moral end of the above example is subordinated to a higher *moral* end? To this suggestion, Stocks has the final answer:

I know that there are many who will tell me that my difficulty is imaginary; that there is a moral aim and purpose, which is the ultimate overriding purpose of life; that this man, who rejects a safe and legally admissible means of enriching himself, rejects it because he is after something more important than that, with which in the given circumstances that conflicts. He is seeking, they will perhaps say, his own spiritual development and perfection. To which I might reply that the act must first be shown to be right now before it can be relied upon to build up righteousness in the future; and – more relevantly to our present enquiry – that there may well be such an aim, and it may well be considered more important than riches, but that it is after all only an end, like any other, a possible result of action, and that it falls, with all other ends, under the inflexible moral rule that it may not be pursued by any and every means. Morality may call on a man at any moment to surrender the most promising avenue to his own moral perfection ('The Limits Of Purpose', pp. 28–9).

It is to Mrs Foot's credit that there is little talk of the goal of moral perfection as the point of moral conduct in her writings. On the other hand, it is not at all clear to me that the profit she envisages as the result of just conduct is moral profit at all. Judging from the long passage from her paper which I have made the basis of my objections, the opposite seems to be the case. That being so, let us imagine a person who refused to take Mrs Foot's advice at the outset of life about the probability of profit being on the side of justice. Certainly, at that early time, he had good reason to choose justice rather than injustice, but, being a gambler by nature, he chose injustice. As it happened, things went well for him. He profited in every way he wished to profit. Now, on his death-bed, he looks back over his life with relish: 'It was certainly a lucky day for me when I gambled against the odds on lying, cheating, swindling, and betraying, paying off.' We want to say that what this man did was wrong. The fact that in facing death he shows no remorse is but an additional mark against him. But Mrs Foot can give no account of this judgement. She must admit that he has in fact lived the best life he could have. Her only consolation is that such a man, like everyone else, had good reason to choose justice rather than injustice. But he chose injustice!

The man who chooses justice may not profit as our rogue has done. None of the things that Mrs Foot envisages as probably coming his way may prove to be his lot. Nevertheless, since his regard for decency does not depend on such probabilities being realised, in the only sense relevant to morality, he has accomplished all.

10

In Search of the Moral 'Must': Mrs Foot's Fugitive Thought

Mrs Foot, in her recent writings, continues to be bothered by the character of the necessity we find associated with moral considerations.[1] Moral considerations, we want to say, *must* be taken into account. But what does this 'must' amount to? Many have thought that what is involved here can be brought out in terms of a distinction between hypothetical and categorical imperatives. Foot is suspicious of this distinction: 'That moral judgements cannot be hypothetical imperatives has come to seem an unquestionable truth. It will be argued here that it is not.'[2] As a matter of fact relatively little is said of the sense in which moral considerations are hypothetical imperatives. Most of Foot's efforts are devoted to showing that much of what is said of moral considerations as categorical imperatives will not bear close examination. While it will become obvious in this paper that I agree with much of what she has to say, I want to argue, nevertheless, that there is good reason for retaining the distinction between categorical and hypothetical imperatives in certain contexts, and that one misunderstands the character of moral considerations if this is not recognised.

In talking of the distinction between categorical and hypothetical imperatives it is natural that Foot should have Kant in mind. Yet what I believe is most important in the distinction Kant wishes to call our attention to can be found throughout the history of moral philosophy. J. L. Stocks points out that

> it is admitted by writers of widely different schools of thought that the claims of morality, as they operate in human life, present on the face of it a very different appearance from the claims of policy or purpose. They come as a recognized obliga-

125

tion to do or not to do, which is often seen to involve the temporary surrender or restriction of a desire in itself innocent, of a perfectly legitimate purpose. All serious moralists have had to recognize this very obvious and familiar contrast. Even the Greeks, in spite of their preoccupation with purpose, were unable wholly to deny the difference in kind between the moral and the purposive attitude. For Plato the virtue of the philosopher, who has passed beyond all calculation of profit and loss, is the only virtue which deserves the name. In Aristotle's *Ethics* the moral act is an act wholly inspired by love of itself: it is Greek characters, i.e., directed to its own beauty or nobility; and he makes no attempt whatever to show that this motive is merely an ultimate clarification of the motive operating in less deserving action. On the contrary, he speaks always as if it were a motive peculiar to the good man and different in kind from others. It is not necessary to multiply instances. Butler speaks of the magisterial exertions of conscience; Kant of the categorical, as opposed to the hypothetical imperative; and John Stuart Mill has to recognize as the most serious objection to the theory of utility, the apparently absolute and imperative character of the claims of justice. In explaining this absolute away as the socially salutary, but theoretically indefensible, conversion of a difference in degree into a difference in kind, he took the course which must I believe in the end be taken by all who believe that morality is purposive.[3]

The essential distinction which these writers wanted to make is to be found also in Kierkegaard when he marks off the demands which purposive interests and designs make on us from the demands of morality, speaking of the former as temporal and the latter as eternal;[4] it is found in Wittgenstein's distinction between absolute and conditional uses of 'ought';[5] and it is found in Stocks' own insistence that after all has been said about ends sought and the means necessary for their attainment, there remains 'an additional principle of discrimination'.[6] Foot concedes that the kind of distinction all these philosophers want to make has support in everyday language:

> for we find in our language two different uses of words such as 'should' and 'ought', apparently corresponding to Kant's hypothetical and categorical imperatives, and we find moral judge-

ments on the 'categorical' side. Suppose, for instance, we have advised a traveller that he should take a certain train, believing him to be journeying to his home. If we find that he has decided to go elsewhere, we will most likely have to take back what we said: the 'should' will now be unsupported and in need of support. Similarly, we must be prepared to withdraw our statement about what he should do if we find that the right relation does not hold between the action and the end in that it is either no way of getting what he wants (or doing what he wants to do) or not the most eligible among possible means. The use of 'should' and 'ought' in moral contexts is, however, quite different. When we say that a man should do something and intend a moral judgement we do not have to back up what we say by considerations about his interests or his desires; if no such connection can be found the 'should' need not be withdrawn. It follows that the agent cannot rebut an assertion about what, morally speaking, he should do by showing that the action is not ancillary to his interests or desires. Without such a connection the 'should' does not stand unsupported and in need of support; the support *it* requires is of another kind (pp. 307–8).

As I shall try to show, it is far easier to understand where Foot thinks the support cannot be found than to understand where she thinks it can be found.

Kant thought that the support which marks off moral 'oughts' and 'shoulds' can be found in formal considerations alone.

Now an action done from duty must wholly exclude the influence of inclination and with it every object of the will so that nothing remains which can determine the will except objectively the *law*, and subjectively *pure respect* for this practical law, and consequently the maxim that I should follow this law even to the thwarting of all my inclinations.[7]

Kant was right in saying that moral considerations do not have to be justified by appeal to an agent's interests, but when he elaborates on what respect for such considerations amounts to, we find it is nothing but respect for the form of law involved. But, although he sees that something distinctive can be said about the form of moral considerations, he fails to see that this is made possible by ways of behaviour and ways of living in which certain things come to be thought to have a special importance. It is the content of moral considerations which makes it possible to say the kind of thing that Kant and others have wanted to say about their form. It is instructive to note what Schiller had to say about Kant's attempt to derive the importance of moral considerations from the form of the categorical imperative:

> Moralists had laboured fruitlessly for ages to formulate a moral law which should be fool-proof and applicable to *all* cases, but had succeeded only in compiling systems of casuistry which were compendia of putrid immorality. So it struck Kant as a bright idea to conceive a Moral Law which simply abstracted from application altogether. Then it could never be corrupted, nor could any case, however hard, upset it. It could never be convicted of failure to work, because it could never be required to work at all. Nay, it could glory in its uselessness, and conceive it as the proof of its immaculate purity. So the Categorical Imperative was made inapplicable, to conceal a collapse of moral theory.[8]

Philosophers who want to speak of the inescapability of moral considerations, a way of talking which puzzles Foot, need not fall into Kant's confusions in this respect. They may refuse to say with Kant that 'even though there might never yet have been a sincere friend, yet not a whit the less is pure sincerity in friendship required of every man, because prior to all experience, this duty is involved as duty in the idea of a reason determining the will by *a priori* principles' (pp. 24–5). On the contrary, they may insist that were it not for the fact that friendships do develop among human beings it would make no sense to speak of the inescapable demands of friendship. Thus, if Kierkegaard and Wittgenstein, who draw their conclusions from *examples* of the inescapability of moral considerations, speak in this way, they can hardly be called followers of Kant. The same can be said of contemporary philosophers who argue in like fashion.[9] They too need not agree with Kant that the unconditional character of moral requirements can be derived from formal considerations alone, any more than they need agree with him that acting from a sense of duty is the only acceptable moral motive. They might want to argue that it is the content of moral considerations, although Kant would deny this, which gives what he says about the form of moral considerations its credibility.

Yet these conclusions do not take us very far. We have to ask what it is about moral considerations which gives them their special status. Here, again, Foot does not think an appeal to categorical imperatives is helpful. That appeal has sometimes amounted to saying that moral considerations, unlike other considerations, give a man a reason for acting. Mrs Foot wants to deny this:

> there is one version of the doctrine which seems to me to rise to the level of falsity. I mean the idea that moral judgements, unlike hypothetical imperatives, have an automatic reason-giving force. As Frankena puts it, quoting from G. C. Field, ' . . . it is "one of the most deeply recognized characteristics of the moral fact" that it is in itself and necessarily "a reason for acting"' (W. K. Frankena, 'Obligation and Motivation', in A. I. Melden (ed.), *Essays in Moral Philosophy*, Washington, Seattle, 1966). This is what I am denying when I deny that moral judgements are categorical imperatives.[10]

In saying this, Foot, as she admits, is departing radically from earlier judgements she has advanced in moral philosophy.[11] At that time she argued that any man, confronted by moral considerations, had a reason to heed them. The link between the moral considerations and the agent was found in his self-interest. She wanted to say that those who agree with Thrasymachus's premise, namely that injustice is more profitable than justice, and who nevertheless would condemn a man who was able to get away with injustice, were taking up an unsupportable position.[12] Her difficulties had been partly due to the fact that she thought she was faced with the following exclusive choice when trying to account for the absolute character of moral considerations. *Either* one must be able to show that moral considerations are necessarily connected with what is in a man's self-interest *or* one must be able to show that the moral 'must' has a magic force which resides in a feeling we have when we say the words. If one succumbs to criticisms of the first alternative[13] and continues to doubt the intelligibility of the second, it seems that one is at a loss to know where the 'must' of moral considerations can be located.

The reason why the second alternative continues to be unintelligible for Foot can be shown in the following quotation:

> The difficulty is obviously connected with the fact that without a special background there is no possibility of answering the question 'What's the point?'. It is no good saying that there would be a point in doing the action because the action was a morally good action: the question is how it can be given any such description if we cannot first speak about the point. And it is just as crazy to suppose that we can call anything the point of doing something without having to say what the point of *that* is.[14]

Thus, any appeal to self-authenticating feelings or attitudes as the justification for the force of the moral 'must' is unacceptable.

So far so good. But, then, when we turn back to the first alternative, that, by her own admission, will not do either.[15] It is not the case that a thousand tough characters who care for no one but themselves can be shown, on their own terms, that they have a reason to be just. A rogue is not a man who has miscalculated his self-interest. The indifferent cannot be made to care for moral considerations by showing the latter to be founded on what all men want. Foot says:

> I was in this difficulty because I had supposed . . . that the thought of a good action must be related to the choices of each individual in a very special way. It had not occurred to me to question the often repeated dictum that moral judgements give reasons for acting to each and every man. This view seems to me to be a mistake.[16]

So far I have agreed with Foot that the necessity we associate with moral considerations cannot be explained solely in terms of the formal characteristics of the categorical imperative or by appeal to the self-interest of the agent. I think she is also right in rejecting two other attempts at explanation. The first of these claims to show that there is some irrationality involved in disregarding moral 'oughts'. But, as Foot points out:

> The fact is that the man who rejects morality because he sees no reason to obey its rules can be convicted of villainy but not of inconsistency. Nor will his action necessarily be irrational.

Irrational actions are those in which a man in some way defeats his own purposes, doing what is calculated to be disadvantageous or to frustrate his ends. Immorality does not *necessarily* involve any such thing.[17]

The second attempt to explain why the indifferent man has a reason to heed moral considerations is that whatever other reasons for acting he may have, moral considerations always provide a reason from a moral point of view. In reply to this suggestion Foot wants to ask,

'Is a reason from a point of view a reason?' meaning 'Is the assertion that I have a reason from point of view P to do x inconsistent with the claim that I have no reason for doing it?'[18]

Clearly, if a man cares about the point of view in question there would be an inconsistency involved if he denied that he had *a* reason for doing it, but we are not thinking of such a man. We are thinking of men who are indifferent to moral considerations. If one insists that the mere existence of reasons from a point of view P makes it inconsistent to say that one has no reason for doing the action concerned, then, as Foot says,

it will be proper to some to deny that they have any reason from the point of view of etiquette to do 'what's done', and others will say that they do not have reason from the point of view of law to do what the law requires. The same will go for morality unless my challenge – to show how this is different – is met (p. 56).

There seems to be little point in calling moral considerations categorical imperatives since all our attempts so far to give this title any substance have failed. To say that moral considerations constitute a reason for the indifferent man because of their formal characteristics, because they are necessarily connected with his self-interest, because to ignore them involves one in irrationality, or because the existence of a moral point of view itself provides a reason for action, seems to have no substance. Since calling moral considerations categorical imperatives seems fraught with such difficulties, it is tempting to think one has no option but to call them hypothetical imperatives. If we accept this conclusion, what are we to make of Foot's admission, which we have already noted,[19] that 'we find in our language two different uses of words such as "should" and "ought", apparently corresponding to Kant's hypothetical and categorical imperatives, and we find moral judgements on the "categorical" side'?

Foot's answer to this question is to deny that this support in ordinary language achieves what Kant wanted it to achieve. Kant wanted to say that this distinction in usage reflects the special dignity and necessity which moral considerations have for us. Foot says that

> Modern philosophers follow Kant in talking, for example, about the 'unconditional requirements' expressed in moral judgements. These tell us what we have to do whatever our interests or desires, and by their inescapability they are distinguished from hypothetical imperatives. The problem is to find proof for this further feature of moral judgements.[20]

Why cannot the proof be found in the distinction between the uses of 'ought' already noted? Foot's answer to this is to point out that what we have called a categorical 'ought' does not belong exclusively to moral considerations. It also characterises considerations of other kinds, for example, etiquette. This being so, something other than these distinctions is needed to account for the dignity and inescapability associated with moral considerations. If moral considerations are more important than etiquette, but the 'oughts' involved in both contexts share the same characteristics, it follows that the importance of the moral considerations cannot follow from these characteristics alone. The alleged inescapability of this importance is, for Foot, a fugitive thought. It is hard to pin down. Her suspicion, however, is that this is not due to the complexity of the thought. It may be due to the fact that what we took to be a thought is in fact an illusion, an illusion which has an undesirable persistence in moral philosophy, but which is no less an illusion because of that. Foot's complaint against Holmes is that he has not taken up her challenge to show that talk of the unconditional requirements of morality is not an illusion by showing how moral considerations are different in kind from other considerations, say, those of etiquette:

> Indeed he is just as insistent that there are reasons from the point of view of etiquette to follow the rules of etiquette as he is

that there are reasons for acting morally from the moral point of view.[21]

It is now time to take up this challenge. Its terms of reference must be clear from the outset, however. I am not undertaking the task of showing that a man who does not care about moral considerations does have a reason to care about them.[22] That, I have agreed, is a futile undertaking. What can be shown is that caring for moral considerations is of such a kind that there remains a point in drawing a distinction between hypothetical and categorical imperatives and that this makes possible attitudes towards the person who cares and the person who does not care which would be inappropriate in other cases.

It may be thought that this admission on my part, namely, that what I say characterises a man who already cares for moral considerations, immediately makes any imperatives involved hypothetical. Is not the form of the imperative 'You ought to heed these considerations if you care or if you are interested'? This is not so. To think otherwise is to confuse the conditions under which a man has reasons for paying attention to moral considerations with his reasons for paying attention. He will not have such reasons unless he cares, but the fact that he cares is not his reason for caring. If, hurrying to the cinema, I stop to help the victim of an epileptic fit, while it is true that, in the absence of considerations of personal advantage, I should not have stopped unless I cared, it does not follow that my reason for helping him is because I care. The reason is to be found in the suffering of the epileptic. Speaking of an earlier age when I would not have stopped I say, 'And I *ought* to have stopped then', meaning 'The plight of this man is something I ought to have cared for then.' The fact that I did not care at that time, that I happened not to be interested, does not spare me from judgement. So though it is a fact that I must care in order that moral considerations can become reasons for acting for me, my reason for acting is not the fact that I care. Furthermore, caring for these considerations above all else is constitutive of what we mean by moral concern.

Foot thinks that there is just as much reason to call the use of 'should' connected with etiquette categorical as there is to call the use of 'should' connected with moral matters categorical. Considerations of etiquette are as 'inescapable' as moral considerations. Foot is wrong about this. She argues her case as follows:

we find this non-hypothetical use of 'should' in sentences enunciating rules of etiquette, as, for example, that an invitation in the third person should be answered in the third person, where the rule does not *fail to apply* to someone who has his own good reasons for ignoring this piece of nonsense, or who simply does not care about what, from the point of view of etiquette, he should do. Similarly, there is a non-hypothetical use of 'should' in contexts where something like a club rule is in question. The club secretary who has told a member that he should not bring ladies into the smoking room does not say 'Sorry, I was mistaken' when informed that this member is resigning tomorrow and cares nothing about his reputation in the club. Lacking a connection with the agent's desires or interests, this 'should' does not stand 'unsupported and in need of support'; it requires only the backing of the rule. The use of 'should' is therefore 'non-hypothetical' in the sense defined.

It follows that if a hypothetical use of 'should' gives a hypothetical imperative, and a non-hypothetical use of 'should' a categorical imperative, then 'should' statements based on rules of etiquette, or rules of a club, are categorical imperatives. Since this would not be accepted by defenders of the categorical imperative in ethics, who would insist that these other 'should' statements give hypothetical imperatives, they must be using this expression in some other sense.[23]

If we want to locate relevant differences between moral considerations and those of etiquette, we would do well to avoid those cases where they clearly overlap. Consider, for example, behaviour while eating food where gracelessness of sufficient extremity becomes the indecent and the gross. The censure due in such cases is certainly a moral censure. What can be said of the style of a man in such circumstances constitutes a comment on his moral character. Clearly, then, we do not have these examples in mind when we want to draw firm distinctions between moral considerations and considerations of etiquette. To draw these distinctions we must look elsewhere, to one of Foot's fugitive thoughts, in fact: to the inescapability of moral considerations. One can bring out what is involved by noting the way in which Foot says both too much and too little about considerations of etiquette.

First, she obscures the sense in which moral considerations are inescapable by claiming too much for certain rules of etiquette. As we saw, she wants to claim that 'there is someting like a non-hypothetical use of "should" in contexts where something like a club rule is in question' (p. 308). She has not established this. The citation of the example of the club rule is as irrelevant as the admitted irrelevance of such examples as 'when a nurse tells us that she has to make her rounds at a certain time, or we say that we have to run for a certain train'. The reason for the irrelevance is, as Foot says, that 'the acceptance condition can always be revoked' (p. 311). But the same is true of club rules. The 'necessity' of the obligation depends on whether someone is interested in joining the club. The conditional 'ought' may be expressed in this way: 'If you want to join the club, you must abide by the rules.' Moral rules cannot be made subject to any such conditions. Furthermore, there is an obvious sense in which I can escape from the club rules. I simply walk out of the club. What do I walk out of if I wish to escape moral rules? If I have been breaking the club rules again and again the steward may give me good advice: 'If they are that much of a burden to you, why don't you resign from the club, and then you needn't bother?' Let us suppose that I have been neglecting moral considerations again and again. What does it mean to say that I could be given advice such that taking it I needn't bother? 'I find it hard to abide by the club rules.' Reply: 'Then resign and you needn't bother.' 'I find it hard to treat him decently.' Reply?

On the other hand, the task of bringing out what is at stake in talking of the inescapability of moral considerations is made acute when we note that at times Foot claims too little for considerations of etiquette. She does so in drawing the following contrast:

> Law and etiquette require only that certain things are done or left undone, but no one is counted as charitable if he gives alms 'for the praise of men', and one who is honest only because it pays him to be honest does not have the virtue of honesty (pp. 312–13).

But etiquette may require more than Foot imagines. Within etiquette too there is the same distinction between genuine good manners and etiquette observed 'for the praise of men'. If someone were to doubt this, let him consider the following simple example: speaking of a man it may be said, 'He has a real concern for etiquette, for doing things properly'; but someone may reply, 'Don't be misled by that. He doesn't really care about such things.

If there were no one here he wouldn't bother. The man who really cares about etiquette would observe it even if he were the only one present.'[24] Because etiquette is, in an obvious sense, a convention, it does not follow that there is no difference between a man who is and a man who is not conventionally related to etiquette. On the contrary, the contrast marks the divide between someone who observes etiquette 'for the praise of men', from a need to belong, and someone who cares about the standards of etiquette. The former would adhere to *any* rules of etiquette as long as praise or acceptance followed in its wake. The latter might view a change in the procedures of etiquette as an advance or as a decline, adverse criticism or popular acclaim being of no concern to him. Foot herself observes (p. 314) that men are prepared to toil to dedicate themselves to matters other than morality. This certainly has been true of etiquette and, to a lesser extent, still is. Showing that more can be said for etiquette than Foot allows, however, seems to make the task facing us even more difficult, for now, even more than before, it seems that there is no essential difference between moral 'oughts' and the 'oughts' of etiquette. Even allowing for what has been said, this conclusion does not follow. Moral demands are unconditional in a way in which the demands of etiquette are not.

A man may be in no doubt about the economic superiority of certain measures which will rid him of his debt. These measures involve placing a friend in financial difficulties. He says, 'Not that way'. Here, although the end is not in dispute, nor the means needed to attain it, moral considerations constitute an additional principle of discrimination by which the means are put aside. So although the 'should' of financial policy does not stand in need of further support, it is overruled by moral considerations. So far, it may be said, the same could be said of etiquette. It may be admitted that the quickest and most effective way of cooling one's soup is to blow on it. Again, desirable ends and effective means cannot be denied. Nevertheless, etiquette says, 'Not that way'. Again, a 'should' that does not need support is overruled by considerations of another kind. So in each case it makes sense to say, 'I know that if I want to do X I ought to do Y, but I ought not to do Y.' The second 'ought' may be the 'ought' of morality or the 'ought' of etiquette. But this is insufficient to establish that the 'oughts' are unconditional. In order to establish this one needs to show that the 'ought' is such that it cannot be overridden by an 'ought' of any other kind.

Can the 'ought' of etiquette be overruled? Consider the following example. There may be a rule of etiquette governing the greeting of guests *in certain contexts* which stipulates when bowing or shaking hands is appropriate. Imagine a guest extending his hand when bowing is appropriate. In order not to upset him the host joins in the handshake. The host, as far as etiquette was concerned, was governed by the rule, 'You ought to bow in greeting your guests', which meant, by implication, that he ought not to have indulged in handshaking. Moral considerations overrule those of etiquette. The man concerned with etiquette may say, 'I know that etiquette says that I ought not to shake his hand, but I ought to shake his hand nevertheless.' We saw earlier that a man may care for the attainment of certain ends and yet say, for reasons of morality or etiquette, 'I ought not to pursue them by these means.' We have now seen that a man may care for standards of etiquette and still say in certain circumstances, 'I ought not to obey these rules.' This is not true of men's moral considerations. They cannot say, while caring for moral considerations, that they ought not to be fulfilled. There are of course limits to moral endeavour.[25] Some things we admire are beyond us. We may find in a moral dilemma that whatever we do we shall fail to meet an obligation. Here the alternatives are themselves moral alternatives. They are not evasions of moral considerations. A man may, of course, succumb to temptation and put other matters before his moral obligations. In that case, however, he feels remorse for what he has done. The demands which the fulfilment of his practical projects make on him are conditional, not only in the sense that if he happens to lose interest they do not remain obligatory, but also insofar as the efficacious means are answerable to considerations of another kind, those of etiquette or morality. The demands of etiquette are also conditional insofar as morality may ask us to put them aside. The demands of morality, however, are unconditional, in that they cannot be put aside for considerations of another kind. Of course, none of this will matter to a man who does not care for moral considerations. What we have seen, however, is that to care for moral considerations is to hold that they are more important than considerations of any other kind. The difference may be marked by saying that the demands of morality are categorical while all other demands are hypothetical.

Foot pays no attention to these considerations. At times she approximates intuitively to the point:

It is true that moral rules are often enforced much more strictly than the rules of etiquette, and our reluctance to press the non-hypothetical 'should' of etiquette may be one reason why we think of the rules of etiquette as hypothetical imperatives (p. 310).

We have seen that the enforcement has to do with the fact that moral considerations are, for the man who cares for them, the most important of all considerations. These conclusions, however, cannot be reached from a consideration of purely formal characteristics. They can only be appreciated by noting that we *do* say that moral considerations are all-important, that not hurting a person or humiliating him in public, for example, is more important than the formalities of greeting.

Foot has difficulties in seeing what we can be doing in insisting on the moral 'ought' when a man is clearly indifferent to the moral considerations involved. Having elucidated these considerations as best we can, we may be confronted by the persistent 'Why should I bother?' All we seem to say in return is 'You ought', or even 'Because you ought', which seems to offer a reason in the 'because' but one the nature of which is, to say the least, obscure. Foot says that if a person

> is a moral man then he cares about such things, but not 'because he ought'. If he is an amoral man he may deny that he has any reason to trouble his head over this or any other moral demand. Of course he may be mistaken, and his life as well as others' lives may be most sadly spoiled by his selfishness. But this is not what is urged by those who think they can close the matter by an emphatic use of 'ought'. My argument is that they are relying on an illusion, as if trying to give the moral 'ought' a magic force (p. 315).

Let us consider this matter in two contexts. First, consider the circumstances where I tell myself that I ought not to treat someone in a despicable way. I may be about to tell a lie which would suit my purposes, but which would cause others great distress, and I pull myself up in time saying, 'Come on now. You know you ought not to do that.' Does it follow that the reason why I should not do it is because I ought not to? Obviously not. The reason is because I should be lying and I would cause distress. The function of the 'ought not', the absolute 'ought not', is to remind me that such matters are not to be made subject to my plans and projects, but that my plans and projects are answerable to these considerations. A similar reminder may be given to another who has gone astray.

But what of the circumstances where the moral 'ought' is being administered not by oneself to oneself, nor to someone who cares but has been tempted to ignore moral considerations in this instance, but to someone who does not care? Foot is rather unfair in her depiction of the circumstances. As we have seen, she wants to say that the amoral man may be mistaken in thinking he need not care, since his life and the lives of others may be sadly spoiled by his selfishness. Here, she seems to be hankering after her earlier position of wanting to discover a reason for the amoral man which will show him why he should not be selfish. It seems one could appeal to a spoiled life as the proof. But this assumes that agreement could be reached on what is meant by a spoiled life. People may want to call a selfish man's life spoiled for reasons which would mean nothing to him. For example, someone might say that his life was spoiled because the promise of love and affection in it was strangled by his selfishness. The selfish man may refer to such promise as moments of weakness. In short, the absence of love and affection here determines what is meant by a spoiled life. Putting this criticism on one side, however, let us assume that the appeal is to such considerations as the harm selfishness can do. Foot says that 'this is not what is urged by those who think they can close the matter by an emphatic use of "ought"'. This is unfair. The situation one has in mind is where such considerations *have* been urged and are still met by 'But why should I bother?' The question is, what is a person doing if he replies with an emphatic 'You ought, that's all'? Foot can't see how he can be said to be doing very much more than reflecting 'the relative stringency of our moral teaching'. She believes

that this may have more to do with the matter than the defenders of the categorical imperative would like to admit. For if we look at the kind of thing that is said in its defence we may find ourselves puzzled about what the words can even mean unless we connect them with the feelings that this stringent teaching implants. People talk, for instance, about the 'binding force' of morality, but it is not clear what this means if not that we *feel* ourselves unable to escape (p. 310).

But why should the defenders of the categorical character of moral imperatives be reluctant to admit this? Is it not a fact that *one* element in determining what expressions mean may be the way and the context in which they were taught? In training young children they may be told they ought not to be selfish. The 'ought not' is administered even when selfishness pays the child handsomely. This being so, the child comes to see that this 'ought not' is not dependent on his own projects based on self-interest. That such projects are furthered seems irrelevant to the moral admonition. If this were all the child learned he would never come to despise selfishness for what it is. But it is a beginning. There are similarities with the amoral man and his persistent 'Why should I?' Of course, in asking such a question the amoral man may simply intend it as an expression of defiance. He may be asking, on the other hand, for a further elucidation of the moral views involved. If, however, after such elucidations, he still asks his question and thinks it deserves an answer, he is confused.[26] There is no more one can tell him. If one says, 'Well you ought, that's all!', at least one is indicating that the other 'oughts' to which he appeals are not sufficient to stop the adverse judgement and continued exhortation. The emphatic use of the moral 'ought', Foot claims, is thought to close the matter. She is dubious about this claim. But what matter does it close? It does indicate dogmatically that the moral judgement does not see itself as conditional on the other 'oughts' to which the amoral man appeals. If it does not give him a reason it shows him that *his* reasons are thought to be irrelevant to the issues in hand. It closes the appeal to such considerations. It is a way of saying, 'That's beside the point.' If that were all the amoral man came to see, he would never change his way of life. But it is a start. So 'You ought' said emphatically in these circumstances is, as far as appreciating moral considerations is concerned, not a way of closing matters, as Foot seems to think, but rather a continuing attempt to open matters up for the first time. There is an element of exhortation involved, since if the moral 'You ought' is said despite all the reasons advanced based on 'oughts' of other kinds, it at least asks one to consider whether there might not be considerations in relation to human conduct over and above the reasons based on 'oughts' of a non-moral kind. If a person comes to appreciate that there are, he will not have come to do so by finding that he has relevant reasons for heeding moral considerations, but by coming to see the moral considerations as constitutive of relevant reasons.[27] In that event he stops asking 'Why should I?' when confronted by moral considerations. He stops asking the question, however, not because he has found an answer to it, but because he has come to think it foolish to ask it.

Having tried to stress that moral considerations are absolute and unconditional in that they are given precedence over all other considerations, people may still be reluctant to conclude that there is therefore some importance in retaining the distinction between hypothetical and categorical imperatives. I believe Foot would share this reluctance. Why not say that people have many interests, among them moral interests? Why not say that among the varied hypothetical imperatives enjoined on man, the system of hypothetical imperatives which we call morality is the most important and leave it at that? The reason why it cannot be left at that is that it involves a falsification of the relation of moral considerations to human conduct. Foot's earlier position in moral philosophy involved such a falsification, but it is by no means certain that this is not also true of the new position she has now adopted.

In her earlier position Foot had said that a man could only have an interest in moral matters if those matters could be shown to be in his self-interest. Such a view created too many tensions for familiar ways in which we contrast moral considerations with self-interest. She located her mistake in equating a man's interests with what is in his self-interest. Once this mistake is cleared up she seems to think that her worst difficulties are over. All we need to stress is that

A moral man must be ready to go against his interests in the particular case, and if he has reason to act morally the reason will lie rather in what he wants than in what is to his advantage.[28]

Having done this we can simply say that a man has many interests, among them moral interests. But how are these interests to be characterised? Foot's answers to this question are rather brief and somewhat obscure. Here is one answer she offers:

Quite generally the reason why someone choosing an *A* may 'be expected' to choose good *A*s rather than bad *A*s is that our criteria of goodness for any class of things are related to certain interests that someone or other has in those things. When someone shares these interests he will have reason to choose the good *A*s; otherwise not. Since, in the case of actions, we distinguish between good and bad on account of the interest we take in the common good, someone who does not care a damn what happens to anyone but himself may truly say that he has no reason to be just. The rest of us, so long as we continue as we are, will try to impose good conduct on such a man, saying, 'you ought to be just', and there is much truth in the idea that there are categorical imperatives in morals.[29]

This makes it look as if there are different interest groups, among them groups with moral interests. The moral interest group simply advocates its interests as the most important in competition with the other groups who advocate theirs. Surely these implications cannot be allowed to go unchallenged.

Putting aside the difficulties inherent in the notion of the common good, the unitary conception of morality it involves, will it do to define a moral act as that act which leads to the common good? Foot may say 'No, since an action which contributes to the common good, but which was done "for the praise of men", does not count as a moral action.' But what of an action done out of interest for the common good which in fact contributes to the common good – is there any contradiction in the assumption that it could be an immoral action nevertheless? Surely not. Think of Ivan Karamazov's questions to Alyosha concerning this point. That being so, it follows that the morality of a means must be settled by something other than its likelihood of leading to any end, however desirable.

Foot does not seem to realise how far-reaching the criticisms are which can be made in this context. For her, the matter seems straightforward once we put Kant's theory of human action aside. 'Kant', she says, 'was a psychological hedonist in respect of all actions except those done for the sake of the moral law, and this faulty theory of human nature was one of the things preventing him from seeing that moral virtue might be compatible with the rejection of the categorical imperative.'[30] Whether this is fair to Kant or not need not concern us, since it does not bring us anywhere near the heart of the problem. It can be readily admitted that men engage in hosts of activities where it is obviously ludicrous to explain the ends sought or the means employed in terms of psychological hedonism. Many of these activities may be characterised by self-sacrifice, but the question of their morality remains. To recognise the question for what it is, what is needed is a radical change of direction. It is not a matter of asking how men's moral interests differ from their other interests, but of asking whether it is appropriate to speak of men having moral interests in this way at all. Does it not seem odd to include morality in the list if someone asks us to name those things we are interested in? Moral considerations are not themselves means or ends as such, but arise insofar as I am concerned about *the character* of the means and ends which are involved in my actions. I do not pursue honesty. Honesty may or may not be present in the activities I do pursue. As for pursuing humility – shall we know when we have arrived? Concern for the character of my activities, both means and ends, cannot itself be characterised adequately in terms of means and ends. We have already seen that for a means to be moral it is not sufficient or necessary for it to attain its end. Neither is morality characterised by distinctive purposes of its own. As Stocks says, 'The goodness of a good man does not depend on this, that he has a different end from the bad man, or a clearer view of the same end, or a single end where he has many. One or more of these superiorities he may well possess, but these by themselves do not constitute moral eminence. His distinctive gift and power must be sought elsewhere.'[31] I have suggested that it is to be found in a devotion to the moral character of one's actions, a concern which imposes itself on purposive actions, to which means and ends alike are answerable.

Foot, on the other hand, wants to retain the language of means and ends. For her, virtues are the means by which human good is attained. Sensing, perhaps, the difficulties involved in this suggestion, she claims that the connection between virtues and human good is not *contingent*: 'Honest action may happen to further a man's career; charitable actions do not *happen* to further the good of others' (p. 314). She thinks the same point can be made in relation to other virtues even when no one end is involved as in the case of charity: 'And why should the truly honest man not follow honesty for the sake of the good that honest dealings bring to men?' (p. 314). What these references to virtues as the means to human good amount to is extremely obscure. As they stand these remarks seem either circular or false.

What does Foot mean when she says that charitable actions do not *happen* to further the good of others? Suppose a widow wants some money in order to buy some decent clothes for her children. 'It would be an act of great charity', someone might say, 'if she were given the money by someone'. Yet that is insufficient, since even though we think the end good, that does not justify pursuing it by any means at one's disposal. Similarly, giving the money out of compassion need not in fact result in the good results that were sought due to accidents for which the agent is blameless. Of course he is bitterly disappointed for the woman and children's sake, since as Stocks reminds us,

> The concrete moral act must be the alteration of a situation, and that alteration must be intentional: the act must be purposive. This means that the agent must needs accept judgement by results. Failure is failure, and its bitterness is not diminished, rather increased, by the conviction that the energy spent fruitlessly in it had another justification.[32]

Failure due to accident, lack of knowledge, etc., if no carelessness is present, does not, however, turn the action into a morally bad action. If Foot is saying that the good of others which is internally related to charitable actions is the existence of charitable actions whether they achieve their results or not, what she says is circular. If she means by 'the good of others' what I have called the results, what she says is false. The results may not be achieved or, in one sense, may be achieved independently of charitable actions.

What Foot is saying is not circular insofar as she is pointing out that a charitable action must aim at the good of others. That is what we mean by a charitable act. But that must not be confused with the attempt to account for moral behaviour within the categories of means and ends. What can be said of charity alone, in any case, cannot be said of honesty. It is not at all clear that honesty *is* aimed at the good of men in this sense. The awkwardness of the sentence Foot has to devise in order to press it into this category partly bears witness to this fact. If we try to establish an internal relation between honesty and the good of others in the sense that the notion of charitable action allows such an internal relation to be established, then her claim is either circular or false in the ways I have tried to indicate.

As long as we remain within the language of means and ends all we are concerned with is the determination of which means will achieve the ends we desire with the greatest economy of expense and effort. Nothing we have in mind in this context is denied by moral considerations. Stocks argues that

Moral considerations do not arise upon further exploration of the causal nexus, or by the introduction of some wider and deeper purpose, or by the transference of the purposive problem from a purely individual to a social plane. Purpose must complete its own work, which includes all this; but when its work is completed, the problem of conduct is not yet solved. The moral consciousness supervenes with a further demand, which creates the specifically moral aspect of the problem (pp. 79–80).

The action as a whole, means and ends, has to answer to moral considerations in terms of which both are judged. The concern for the character of the action is brought to bear on means and ends alike, a concern the values of which, as Stocks says, are recognised as 'intrinsic and absolute, not relative and conditional like those of purpose' (p. 80). There is reason after all for these distinctions in everyday language. Morality is not a system of hypothetical imperatives.

Those embarking on any occupation must be able to come through the following test expressed in these questions by Kierkegaard:

What means do you use in order to carry out your occupation? Are the means as important to you as the end, wholly as important? Otherwise . . . the irresponsible, the frivolous, the self-seeking and the heterogeneous means would flow in between in confusing and corrupting fashion. Eternally speaking, there is only one means and there is only one end: the means and the end are one and the same thing. There is only one end: the genuine Good; and only one means: this, to be willing only to use those means which genuinely are good – but the genuine Good is precisely the end.[33]

We are now in a position to see what we felt intuitively was wrong with Foot's talk of moral interests and her depiction of them as if they were included as one group among many other interests. Moral considerations do not constitute an interest, but values to which the pursuit of any interest is answerable. For the same reason paying heed to moral considerations in one's life cannot be called an occupation. Moral values are not characteristics which belong to any distinctive interest or occupation, but may arise in any interest or occupation men engage in. They are not relative to an activity, but an absolute measure to which any activity is said to be answerable. Moral values run through the whole of life in this way. That is why, as we said earlier, there is no analogy between the rules of a club and moral rules. Morality is not an institution of any kind, but moral questions may arise in connection with institutions of various kinds. One can cancel one's membership of an institution and set oneself free from the obligations relative to it. But most moral obligations are not relative to any specific context in that way, a fact obviously relevant to what is meant by the inescapability of moral considerations. Any human activity has to answer to these considerations in the way Kierkegaard depicts.

From essentially the same considerations Stocks says that 'A project of action which survives this enquiry passes into action which can claim to be fully justified and to be morally justified, and to have a value in itself apart from its results' (p. 80).

Foot seems to be worried if the exercise of virtue does not bear fruit. Such an absence, she thinks, makes its justification problematic. And yet this feature of human life is by no means rare. Of course it would be perverse if the virtuous man did not hope to see the fruits of his labours. Yet, if this is not to be, are his labours in vain? The frequent occurrence of virtue's efforts being thwarted has led some to ask why the wicked prosper. It is rarer to see someone soldier on, not simply when he does not see the fruits of his labours, but when doing so involves great suffering and sacrifice for himself and others. When this happens we are stopped in our tracks. It is the exceptional that commands our attention. It is not something to wonder at and pass on. On the contrary, the moral purity it reveals casts its light on more familiar cases. We have to ask in moral philosophy whether we should devote our attention to the logic of the morally familiar, noting that what we say does not fit a few exceptional cases, or whether our attention should be devoted to the moral excellence revealed in the extreme, in the conviction that it is from this point that the familiar is best understood.

11

Do Moral Considerations Override Others?

In a paper called 'Are Moral Considerations Overriding?', in her published collection,[1] Philippa Foot replies to my criticisms[2] of her recent writings. She says, 'It is often said that in practical reasoning moral considerations must be overriding considerations; but I do not myself know of any good defence of this proposition, or even an exposition which makes the thesis clear. In my article 'Morality as a System of Hypothetical Imperatives' I said that there was nothing in this idea that could be used in defence of the doctrine of the categorical imperative, and that seems to me as true now as it seemed to me then' (p. 181).

I had suggested that one distinguishing mark of moral considerations is that if a person cares for them, he cannot, at the same time, say that they should be overridden by considerations of any other kind. Mrs Foot finds different senses of 'moral considerations' in my essay, but finds that my thesis is false no matter which sense one concentrates on. She offers counter-examples in an attempt to show that this thesis, in each context, is false. My aim, in the present essay, is not to quibble over the different senses of 'moral considerations' Mrs Foot detects, but, accepting her exposition of these senses, to show that none of her counter-examples work.

It ought to be obvious that I am not denying that men do, as a matter of fact, let other considerations override moral considerations. Only a madman could deny that. The question concerns what a man can say about the moral considerations which have been so overridden. Can he still say he cares for them? Well, he can if, after overriding them, he reacts in terms of remorse, regret, guilt, excuse, requests for understanding, reference to extenuating circumstances, etc. In other words, there must be some such story to tell; a story which recognises that he ought not to have done what he has done. But suppose that, in some cases, there is no

147

such story of regret for the overriding of moral considerations: can I still say, as I did in my paper, that 'the demands of morality are categorical while all other demands are hypothetical' (p. 137)? I think so. Let us now turn to a consideration of Mrs Foot's alleged counter-examples.

I had said that while a man could care for etiquette he could overrule such considerations for moral considerations, but that one cannot overrule moral considerations. Her first counter-example refers to the passage in my paper where I say, 'moral considerations are, for the man who cares for them, the most important of all considerations . . . we *do* say that moral considerations are all-important, that not hurting a person or humiliating him in public, for example, is more important than the formalities of greeting' (p. 138). Mrs Foot changes my example – of a host who shakes the hand a guest has extended, though bowing is required by etiquette, in order to save him embarrassment – by asking us to imagine that 'the price at which the hurt may be avoided is not the breaking of a rule of etiquette but rather the spending of a rather large sum of money; perhaps thousands of dollars or pounds. . . . We have, therefore, on one side the moral consideration about the hurt the other man will suffer, and on the other the non-moral consideration about the financial loss' (pp. 183–4). Mrs Foot argues that if my thesis were correct, 'anyone who "cared about" morality would have to spend the money if he were so placed' (p. 184). She counters this by saying, 'But of course no one expects him to. In face of a sizeable financial consideration a small moral consideration often slips quietly out of sight' (p. 184). But the question is not whether this happens, but what it makes sense to say if it does happen. Mrs Foot says that no one expects a man to suffer great financial loss in the circumstances described. What they expect is that the man will allow the other to be hurt. Similarly, and perhaps more realistically, it might be said that no one is surprised if someone rushing to the January sales does not stop to help an old lady to cross a road. But such expectations do not affect my thesis at all. We have these expectations because we know ourselves only too well. Money may well turn our heads away from major moral considerations, let alone minor ones. What this shows *is* that we do not care that much about such considerations, or that in some circumstances we ask for understanding: 'Don't be too hard on me. It was a lot of money', and so on. But we cannot have our cake and eat it. All the stories we tell are stories which explain why we ignore what is more important. They are not justifications for doing so.

More details than Mrs Foot provides could have been provided by examples such as the following.[3] Consider the case of someone who pays regular weekly visits to his hypochondriac mother. There is no hope of changing her and he thinks that this is the least he can do to make her happy. What if, on one particular week, he has an interview for an important job and attends it? Does this show that he had no moral consideration for his mother? Of course, one may say that he owed it to himself to attend the interview, and that there are moral obligations and rights involved here too. That being the case, the example would not be of the kind Mrs Foot needs. It can be changed, however, to meet the case. What if, instead of an interview, the son has to collect a large sum of money he has won that week? If he does not collect it, the prize passes to the contestant placed second. He is not in particular need of the money, but, still, it is a lot of money. If he collects the money are we forced to say that he did not care about the moral consideration involved? A number of different contexts spring to mind.

First, the man may collect the money and feel remorse for what he has done. Here, if he had his time over again, he would not collect the money. Clearly, this case does not threaten what I want to say. Second, the man may collect the money and feel sorry for hurting his mother, but not in the sense that, had he his time over again, he would not collect the money. I have argued elsewhere that there can be remorse without repudiation of the deed which occasioned it.[4] The same can be said of regret or feeling sorry. He does not regret *what* he has done, but *that* he had to do it. There are degrees of caring. True, he did not care enough about visiting his mother to renounce the money, but this is not to say that he did not care at all. His reaction of regret or feeling sorry gives us the conceptual foothold we need for saying that he cared about the moral consideration he neglected. But could we think of the case as one where there was no such reaction on the particular occasion and still say that the man cared for the moral considerations involved? I think so. A man may collect the money and not feel sorry that he had to do so. After all, he does see his mother every week. He may feel that it would be perverse to blame him for skipping this one occasion, and even more perverse to say on the basis of it that he did not care for his mother. It is, of course, the regularity of his visits which gives this reaction its point. What one can say here is that he cannot do such things too often and still say he cares. If he starts overlooking his obligations to his mother whenever he feels like it, we could not say that he cared about visiting her.

None of these cases shows that a man could overrule moral considerations without appropriate reactions or without an appropriate background against which the overruling is an exception, and still be said to care for these moral considerations. A man may regret that he has to give up non-moral considerations because of moral considerations, but if he does not, it would not follow that he did not care about them. He could be someone who did care, but who simply recognised the overriding claim of moral considerations. What cannot be said, though Mrs Foot seems to be trying to say it, is that we could claim that a man cared for moral considerations when he overrules them and shows none of the appropriate responses, varied though they may be, that I have indicated.

Mrs Foot thinks she strengthens her case by producing an example

> of a rule of etiquette which operates on most people so strongly that it takes precedence even over a rather weighty moral consideration. There is, for instance, a distinct resistance to the idea that a host or hostess might refuse to serve any more drinks when the guests have had as much as is good for them given that they must drive home. In spite of the fact that they might kill or injure someone, which is surely a moral consideration, the host is not expected to close the bar and refuse to serve more alcohol as soon as this point has been reached. A strong rule of etiquette forbids such a course of action, and it is the rule of etiquette that takes precedence in ninety-nine cases out of a hundred in circles familiar to many of us. But to say that no one in these circles 'cares about' morality would be a bit stiff (p. 184).

Again, the point is not to deny that such things happen. We might even agree that it happens in ninety-nine cases out of a hundred; that is, in parties and the like the host does not refuse guests drinks although he would know, if asked, that they have had more than enough given that they are going to drive home. I am not sure that it happens as Mrs Foot describes it. According to her 'a strong rule of etiquette forbids' refusing guests drinks in such circumstances. I suspect that in many of the ninety-nine cases the hosts do not intervene for different reasons. Though they recognise that a guest has had enough to drink, many feel that a man should be his own disciplinarian in these matters. They do not feel that they ought to impose this discipline on others. Here, one moral opinion overrules another. The host may even put the matter to his guest, but still give him a drink if he fails to persuade him. On the other hand, a host may not intervene because he believes it would simply be a waste of time. Of course, these are not the situations Mrs Foot has in mind, and they would not provide her with the counter-examples she needs. In fact, however, it is rather difficult to imagine many examples which would correspond to Mrs Foot's description. Remember, the person concerned is supposed to override the moral consideration in favour of the rule of etiquette. Surely the account which covers most of the cases Mrs Foot has in mind is one in terms of weakness or thoughtlessness. Imagine a conversation between a husband and wife when their guests have departed. The wife may say to her husband with some apprehension, 'Most of them had too much to drink.' Surely the most common replies are 'Yes, I know, but you don't like to push the matter, do you?', or 'Yes, I know, but you don't think about it when the party is in full swing.' In other words, it is admitted that the moral consideration ought to be overriding, but failure to observe this is explained, but not justified, in terms of weakness and thoughtlessness. This too cannot be the situation Mrs Foot has in mind, since it does not constitute a counter-example. In my thesis I allow that people who care about moral considerations do not always act on them. I insist that in such cases, a recognition of this in the form of remorse, regret, excuse, etc., accompanies the failure.

Mrs Foot asks us to imagine a host who actually plies his guests with drink because he thinks etiquette more important than the moral considerations involved. He is not even a man who could not care less about these moral considerations. On the contrary, Mrs Foot holds that to say he does not care about morality 'would be a bit stiff'. 'Care about morality' here is ambiguous. If interpreted generally Mrs Foot would be right. Obviously one cannot say that a man who ignores or overrides *one* moral obligation has no regard for *any* moral consideration. To say that would not be a bit stiff – it would be madness. That, of course, is not the thesis I hold. What I am saying, as applied to the present case, is that a man cannot be said to care for moral considerations, such as the disasters which may result from dangerous driving, and at the same time say that the rule of etiquette about supplying plenty of drinks for guests must take precedence. How would the care for moral considerations manifest itself? Where are the phenomena which would give us a conceptual foothold to speak of such care? Let us extend the example to illustrate the point. Suppose that on the next day the hosts hear that someone has been fatally injured by one of the drunken drivers. What are they supposed to say? Does it make sense to imagine them saying, 'Well, of course, we do care about this dreadful business, but you'll understand that a rule of etiquette had to take preference'? Surely not. If they cared about moral considerations they will have to recognise their share of responsibility. Failure to recognise it would mean that they did not care.

That my account is a more faithful one of the situation Mrs Foot has in mind is shown by the publicity given to it in trying to change people's attitudes. They are reminded of what they know ought to take precedence, but which may be ignored due to weakness, thoughtlessness, bravado, etc. We are told again and again, 'You know it makes sense.' I have not seen an anti-drink-and-drive film which asks us to reconsider whether we should drink and drive since etiquette may not, after all, be more important than the moral considerations involved.

So much for Mrs Foot's alleged counter-examples to my thesis where (what she calls) 'evidential' moral considerations are concerned. Mrs Foot now turns to the second sense of moral considerations she finds in my essay. She calls this the 'verdictive' sense of 'moral considerations', by which she means the consideration that something moral or immoral is being done. She says, 'Let us see whether these must be the most important considerations for anyone who cares about morality' (p. 184), and gives as a counter-example the conformity of the seconds in a duelling contest to the code of duelling, a code which, she says, is incompatible with the moral judgements of the community in which it existed. In *The Brothers Karamazov*, Dostoyevsky, in telling of the life of Father Zosima, recounts how as 'a young man Zosima had provoked another officer, simply because he was jealous of him, and forced him to issue a challenge. However, realizing that his conduct has been disgraceful he waits until the other man has shot at him and then, when it is his turn to shoot, throws away his pistol and apologizes' (p. 185).

The example does not show yet, as Mrs Foot thinks it does, that Zosima thinks his conduct disgraceful because of a clash between the duelling code and moral considerations. Duelling could and did involve genuine considerations of honour. What Zosima does is to *use* the code for his own ends – this is the disgrace he recognises. He does not say that the code itself is disgraceful. Having abused it, however, he does not feel entitled to proceed under it. And this does not show anything, one way or the other, about the angry reaction of the second: 'But you cannot apologize in the middle of a duel.' We are not told, however, what the second is supposed to think. Mrs Foot provides a number of questions rather than argument. First, she asks whether it will be suggested that 'the outraged second *couldn't* have recognized that an apology rather than a shot was what morality called for' (p. 185). No such thing would be suggested by me. I may know as a matter of fact that according to certain moral views I am called on to do a thousand things. Whether I care about what these moral views call on me to do is quite a different matter. But then Mrs Foot asks whether it will be said that the second *couldn't* have 'cared about' morality (p. 185). I am in no position to say any such thing until we know how the second reacts after his angry outburst. If it is consistent with everything he says later, then, obviously, he did not care about the moral considerations which moved Zosima. Mrs Foot asks, 'Are not these things being said simply to rescue the thesis, which is now in danger of becoming trivial?' (p. 185). On the contrary, the onus is on Mrs Foot to show what his caring amounts to. Can *anything* be called 'caring'? If not, what features of the second's behaviour merit this description? What does Mrs Foot offer us? More questions. 'Suppose the second did know perfectly well that, morally speaking, Zosima was right to apologize and refuse to shoot?' Does she mean that he knew that certain moral considerations do ask this of Zosima? If so, this, as we have seen, is quite consistent with his not caring about those considerations. But then Mrs Foot asks, 'And supposing he did care about morality?' (p. 185). But supposing *what*? Until she tells us, we do not know what 'caring' means here. Mrs Foot closes her treatment of this point with an example of how 'caring about morality' might manifest itself in the second's life: 'After all, duelling rules impinge rather little on most men's time and leave plenty left over for the pursuit of the moral life' (p. 185). According to this suggestion, caring about moral considerations is a matter of the timetable! If someone discovers that I have done something despicable and asks, 'But don't you care?', then it seems that I could always reply by saying, 'Of course I care about such things. What I did only took a short time and I now have plenty of time to pursue morality again.' Finally, the whole notion of 'pursuing morality', as if morality is listed among men's interests, itself obscures the ways moral considerations impinge on our activities. I argued this point towards the end of the previous chapter and Mrs Foot makes no attempt to answer these criticisms.

She suggests further, 'Perhaps it will be insisted that at least no one could actually *say* that an action was immoral and yet that it should be done' (p. 185). Perhaps, but not by me. As Mrs Foot says, 'a stronger word than "should" is often used: a man will say that although it is wrong to do a certain thing he "has to" or "must" do it in order to stave off disaster to himself, or his family, or his country' (p. 185). Again I am taking it for granted that such disasters do not constitute moral considerations for the people concerned, since such moral dilemmas would not provide the counter-examples Mrs Foot needs. If, however, moral consider-ations are put aside without remorse or regret, what are we to say of those who do this? And what are we to say of the many people Mrs Foot tells us of who 'are ready to do what they know and admit to be wrong for far less than this, as for instance in spending money on frivolities while other people starve'? (p. 185). Mrs Foot says that 'Professor Phillips will have to say . . . that such a man cannot *ipso facto* "care about" morality, in which case his thesis will once more become uninterestingly trivial' (p. 185). This is state-ment without argument. I ask again: what does the care consist in? Not apparently in the slightest expression of regret. Mrs Foot wonders that I have not noticed 'that it is quite common for people who do care about morality to admit that some of the things they do are morally indefensible and never lose a wink of sleep over it' (p. 186). Certainly I have noticed that many, myself included, often behave in such a way. We like to think that we care when we do not. In morality, as in other spheres where effort is required, indifference and mediocrity are the most common phenomena. Here, as elsewhere, the excellent is rare. That is why it stops us in our tracks.

Mrs Foot concludes that 'Only a philosopher could say the kinds of things that Professor Phillips says; and if the Martians take the writings of moral philosophers as a guide to what goes on on this planet they will get a shock when they arrive' (p. 186). The Martians will not get a shock, if they distinguish, as Mrs Foot does not, between the *character* of moral considerations for those who care about them, and the *factual* question of how many people in fact care for them. What would be dangerous would be if the Martians came armed with references supplied by Mrs Foot. Everyone seems to be called 'caring' where morality is concerned: those who sacrifice a great deal to help those who seek it from them; those who can be relied on to act decently in the numberless routine obligations of daily life; those who through weakness, ill-luck, etc., fail to do what they know they ought to do; those who observe the moral decencies for the sake of a respectable reputation; those who are always on the lookout for the main chance. All they need to say is that they care about morality, since such claims seem to be self-authenticating, not needing any evidence in moral behaviour. Of course, such claims for caring and deep concern are common in various quarters today. No matter what the evidence, people lay claim to a concern and seriousness 'deep down'. So deep down that it seems they rarely surface! Elsewhere I have stressed how important it is to distinguish between our recognition of the wonderful and what we care about. Speaking for myself, I should say that what is important is that I recognise that I do not care for that which I admire most. If I think of wonderful sacrifices or the way some people have given themselves to their subjects, is it the case that I have seriously considered doing these things, but decided in favour of some alternative? Not at all. It is important that I recognise that I have not the slightest intention of doing these things. Does it follow that I do not admire such things? No, but it would be a joke if a philosopher were to suggest that since I admire something I must care about it. As I have said elsewhere,[5] the moral relevance of what I admire but do not care about is that it prevents my over-estimating the limits within which I do care.

Mrs Foot offers an explanation to show why the thought that moral considerations are overriding is so persuasive. Concerning morality and etiquette she says, 'The fact is that there *is* a difference between the way the two codes are taught which is of just the right kind to explain why morality is supposed to be overriding in some significant way' (p. 186). Mrs Foot seems to have changed her mind about what the difference consists in. In her essay 'Morality as a System of Hypothetical Imperatives' she says, 'It is true that moral rules are often enforced much more strictly than the rules of etiquette, and our reluctance to press the non-hypothetical "should" of etiquette may be one reason why we think of the rules of etiquette as hypothetical imperatives' (p. 162). As compared with etiquette, the difference has to do with 'the relative stringency of our moral teaching' (p. 162). But by the time we come to her paper 'Are Moral Considerations Overriding?' the position seems to have changed:

> Etiquette, unlike morality, is taught as a rigid set of rules that are on occasion to be broken. We do not, as we might have done, incorporate the exceptions to rules about hand-shaking and so on into the code of etiquette. . . . And this is why children find the whole thing so confusing. They are taught that some things are 'not done' and then expected to *understand* that (of course) such rules may be ignored in an emergency, or even in the kind of case that Professor Phillips describes. We could have incorporated the exceptions into the rule of etiquette, but we do not do so. But morality we teach differently. Moral rules are not taught as rigid rules that it is sometimes right to ignore; rather we teach that it is sometimes *morally permissible* to tell lies (social lies), break promises (as, e.g., when ill on the day of an appointment) and refuse help (where the cost of giving it would be, as we say, disproportionate) (pp. 186–7).

All this being so, we can see why moral considerations are thought to be overriding:

> So we tend, in our teaching, to accommodate the exceptions *within* morality, and with this flexibility it is not surprising that morality can seem 'unconditional' and 'absolute'. In the official code of behaviour morality appears as strong because it takes care never to be on the losing side (p. 187).

These are somewhat startling conclusions. First, it should be obvious that some of them are blatantly untrue. Mrs Foot passes from the particular claim that *sometimes* we say that it is morally permissible to tell lies, to the claim that 'we accommodate the exceptions *within* morality'. On the basis of this it is said that 'morality appears as strong because it takes care never to be on the losing side'. Whatever we are to make of this last remark, it does not seem to be the case that moral considerations never yield or suffer. First, as Mrs Foot points out herself, people sometimes never lose a wink of sleep over their overriding of moral considerations. Unlike Mrs Foot, I do not know what is meant by saying that these people cared for those moral considerations nevertheless. People who ignore those who need them, flout their responsibilities, never give it a second thought – how can they be said to care for these considerations nevertheless? When this overriding happens, that is to say, moral considerations suffer. Second, sometimes moral considerations are overruled by other moral considerations. The moral priority is obvious. Mrs Foot seems to think that such priorities win for morality a pseudo-absoluteness. Yet, the pseudo-absoluteness would be the one that *denied* that some moral considerations can take precedence over others. A. I. Melden showed us in *Rights and Right Conduct*[6] that the absoluteness of a moral right consists in its demand to be *considered*, not in its demand to be *satisfied*. If locating a moral right entails that it ought to be satisfied, standing on one's right would be a superfluous activity and forfeiting one's rights (for example, in saying, 'Forget what you owe me') would be an immoral act. Third, in saying that sometimes one moral consideration takes precedence over another, I am not suggesting, like R. M. Hare, that establishing a set of exceptions to moral principles constitutes moral experience and maturity. To do so would take no account of difficult moral dilemmas and moral tragedies where, whatever one does, one is going to hurt someone. I have referred elsewhere to the failure of many moral philosophers who do not recognise such dilemmas and tragedies, who speak as if a moral precedence can always be established such that the agent need give no backward glance to the unfulfilled obligation. Many philosophers have argued that once one has done what one has to do in a moral dilemma, one may regret the unfulfilled obligation, but not feel remorse because of it. Remorse, however, may be felt even when the agent does not repudiate the action which occasions it. A failure to see this is born of the desire to tidy up our moral obligations, to think that any situation must present us with *the* right thing to do.[7] How could one speak here of 'accommodating exceptions within morality' or of 'morality taking care never to be on the losing side'? Doing what one has to do in a moral dilemma may still give one reason for remorse and penance.

12
An Argument From Extreme Cases?

William Davie does not want to adjudicate in the recent debate between Philippa Foot and myself, but he does want to comment on it.[1] The debate concerns whether moral 'musts' are categorical or hypothetical. Davie would like to drop this terminology altogether in favour of a consideration of examples piecemeal. First, however, it is as well to be clear about the character of the dispute between Foot and myself.

Davie's description does not quite grasp Foot's new position in moral philosophy. He says,

> Foot's idea is that we understand the reason for a would-be moral action as soon as, but not before, we know what benefit or profit resides in the action. The benefit need not be for the agent himself; it may be for someone the agent happens to care about. In either case, though, a moral reason works by making a connection between an action and some desirable thing to be achieved. Foot's view is that such a connection always can be found (p. 2).

This obscures the shift which has taken place in Foot's arguments. In her earlier papers, 'Moral Beliefs' and 'Moral Arguments', she wanted to say that what distinguished moral imperatives from imperatives of other kinds is that they give *every* man a reason for heeding to them. I argued against this view, claiming that it was impossible to show a rogue *on his own terms* why he should be just. Foot no longer holds that moral imperatives provide reasons for action for all men. Morality, in her new position, seems to be representative of an interest group, a group which has the common good as its concern. If you are interested in the common good, certain appeals can be made to you. If not, they will be ineffective. Yet, because the common good is so important to them, those who pursue it will keep trying to make the un-interested interested, but they realise that this can only be done by a change of interests, by coming to care for something different. Those engaged in moral endeavour seem to make up a voluntary association.

I have many misgivings with this new position. I doubt whether the means–ends distinction which it retains can be central in moral matters, since means and ends come under a common moral scrutiny.[2] I have difficulties with the notion of the common good[3] and of morality as making up a set of interests among my other interests. It would not occur to me to list morality as one of my interests. Rather, moral considerations constitute a demand for decency in various forms which, when effective, is brought to bear on the interests I have.

Yet, it is not difficult to see how Foot has reached her new position. Let us suppose you want to say that someone ought to be, or must be, decent in certain respects towards another. On her earlier view, there were only two ways in which the moral impera-tive in this context was to be understood: either it had its force from the fact that it was in every man's interest to obey it, or its force was magical and immediate in some sense or other. Foot, in her earlier and later positions can make no sense of the second alternative, and, in her later position, she has abandoned the first. Where is she to turn to now? She retains the link between the agent and his interest in explaining the force of the moral impera-tive, but now his interest is not his self-interest. It is, in fact, interest in the common good. The radically different alternative, the so-called magical moral 'must' remains as unintelligible for Foot as it has ever been. Thus, it is not surprising that much, if not most, of her time in the later papers is spent denying that any clear sense can be given to talk of a categorical imperative in morality, rather than elucidating at any length what is involved in calling these imperatives hypothetical. My aim, in criticising this new position is not to defend a Kantian position in ethics. I deny that explicitly. Rather, I am endeavouring to get at what it is about moral concerns that made people speak of a moral 'ought' as categorical. Davie dislikes this language because it is a philos-opher's invention. What I am interested in are the features of morality which occasioned or lay behind the philosophical inven-tion. All I mean by saying that there may well be a point in not abolishing the distinction between categorical and hypothetical imperatives altogether is that it may be a useful reminder of some central features of moral concern.

In my replies to Foot, I try to bring out the character of these central features in two contexts: (a) the character of moral concern when operative in a person's conduct, and (b) the character of a reminder of such concern addressed to a person who does not possess it. Davie's view of my strategy is rather different. He thinks that I try to show the character of moral concern by citing what he calls extreme cases. If we cite the example of Socrates refusing to escape from his cell, an extreme case, we may get people to see that 'not only Socrates, but also ordinary people, are capable of pure moral action' (p. 2). Davie does not make it clear whether these cases would, in that event, also be extreme. I suppose they would. If they are not to be so regarded, then the conclusion would be that extreme cases can throw light on the character of moral action in non-extreme cases. The character of the examples as moral would not, then, depend on their being extreme cases. I was not talking of extreme cases in the way Davie assumes I was at all. True, reference to them is made at the end of my paper, 'In Search of the Moral "Must"', the significance of which I shall return to later. But my main thesis applies as much to helping an old lady cross the street as to Socrates refusing to escape from prison. The so-called extremity of the example, at this stage, is neither here nor there as far as my thesis is concerned.

What is this thesis? I said that one distinct mark of moral considerations is that a person could not be said to be concerned about them and be prepared to overrule them with considerations of another kind. Of course, moral considerations do get overruled by others or ignored in favour of others. I am not denying the obvious. What I want to claim is that if we want to say that a person cares despite this fact, there must be some story to tell in terms of regret, remorse, slips, or exceptional circumstances which enable us to so describe him. In the absence of any such story, how could we say that a person cares for moral considerations while allowing other considerations to override them? Notice, this thesis does not depend on extreme cases. It claims to call attention to a feature of moral considerations not shared by others, such as considerations of etiquette, for example. My caring for etiquette is not rendered problematic if such considerations are overruled by moral considerations. What I am saying is that caring

for moral considerations is rendered problematic if other considerations are allowed to override them with no expression of regret,
remorse, or an appeal to very exceptional circumstances. Davie
says that someone favouring Foot might say that:

> Foot brings to light a problem which is endemic to morality – the
> problem of why a person should be moral. It is both a theoretical
> and practical problem. The practical problem arises because
> people are at times tempted not to be moral; the theoretical
> problem arises because it is not self-evident that being moral is
> always a good thing for every agent. Phillips has done nothing
> towards solving the problem at either level. He merely observes
> that there have existed a few rare persons for whom there was
> no such problem, persons who apparently valued moral good-
> ness above all else. Nothing is settled by these cases. The mere
> fact that such an attitude is possible does not show that it is an
> attitude that people should have. That is what Phillips would
> have to prove (p. 2).

I do not see that I have to prove any such thing, and neither, by
now, does Foot. Both of us now agree that moral considerations do
not automatically give every man a reason for pursuing them. That
they did was the position which Foot held once, but does not hold
now. I have never thought that there could be a universal method
to show all men why they should be just. So here what I am asked
to prove does not make sense. Further, as I have said, my argument does not depend on the citation of rare cases. It is supposed
to apply to all cases of caring for moral considerations. So Davie is
wrong when he says that I recommend, *in this context*, 'that we
begin . . . with exceptional cases, with cases of moral excellence
revealed in the extreme' (p. 3). Davie then says that not all people
regard moral considerations as absolute and overriding. There are
degrees of caring and some people care more for other things.
Presumably these are meant as factual observations and I agree
with them. How could I do otherwise? Given that such things
happen, my thesis concerns what we have to say subsequently
about the person's 'caring'. Foot in her reply to the paper Davie
discusses, and Davie too, seems to think that I deny that such
things happen. In 'Do Moral Considerations Override Others?'[4] I
gave the following example:

no one is surprised if someone rushing to the January sales does
not stop to help an old lady to cross a road. But such expectations do not affect my thesis at all. We have these expectations
because we know ourselves only too well. Money may well turn
our heads away from major moral considerations, let alone
minor ones. What this shows *is* that we do not care that much
about such considerations, or that in some circumstances we ask
for understanding: 'Don't be too hard on me. It was a lot of
money', and so on. But we cannot have our cake and eat it. All
the stories we tell are stories which explain why we ignore what
is more important. They are not justifications for doing so.

Davie imagines a philosopher favouring Foot saying that all I have
done is to show that 'there are a few cases, rare cases, where her
account will not fit'. This is not so. In my reply 'Do Moral Considerations Override Others?' I consider a range of cases, ordinary
cases, which Foot in 'Are Moral Considerations Overriding?' in
Virtues and Vices thinks contradicts my thesis. In 'Do Moral Considerations Override Others?' I try to show that none of her
counter-examples work. It is not my intention to rehearse those
arguments here, but they do serve as evidence that my thesis is not
meant to apply simply to some rare, exceptional cases.

Davie too wants to say that my thesis does not work, except he
wants to say that it does not work where all *rare* cases are concerned. So, as with Foot, what I want to do now is to see whether
his counter-examples are counter-examples to my thesis, since, if
he cannot find counter-examples, my thesis stands. His examples
adapt Dostoyevsky's characterisation of Dmitri in *The Brothers
Karamazov*. In Davie's example, Dmitri is condemned for the murder of his father which he had desired in his heart, but which he
did not commit. The first two examples which make use of this
incident are not meant to be counter-examples. In the first, though
legally innocent, Dmitri embraces the judgement of the court as a
just judgement because of the base desires for his father's death
which he has entertained. In the second example he has the same
attitude, but succumbs to the temptation of allowing his friends to
engineer his escape. But, Davie tells us, 'To the end of his days
Dmitri is haunted by the thought of what he might have done, of
what he should have done. He is full of remorse and his friends are
unable to console him' (p. 7). Davie agrees with me that this is not
a counter-example when he says 'The "must" can still be thought

of as categorical. Its continued presence is confirmed by Dmitri's lingering sense of guilt and his remorse later in life' (p. 8). So far, so good. Davie now produces examples three and four which *are* supposed to be counter-examples to my thesis. Do they work? Here is the third example. Dmitri is again going to embrace the court's decision. Davie tells us that 'Dmitri thinks of himself as a Christ figure. He must suffer for the sins of mankind. His life will be a symbol of sin and redemption' (p. 8). Now, is this a moral perspective or not? Well, it may or may not be. I must confess that the language suggests a case of self-deception born of romantic indulgence. What is more I have evidence for this, for, Davie goes on to tell us, when Dmitri's friends at the last moment before his transportation to Siberia arrange his escape, 'Dmitri agrees to co-operate with them' (p. 8). What! Just like that? If so, his romanticism is revealed. But let us waive my objections and say that his perspective is a moral one and that he succumbs to the temptation to escape. My thesis is that we can only say he still cares if he shows regret or remorse for what he has done. But in this example, we are told, 'He feels no guilt, no remorse' (p. 8). But is he still supposed to care? Apparently, since we are also told that 'He derives constant inspiration and consolation from the thought of that other Dmitri, the innocent Christlike one who would have undergone endless suffering and humiliation in the salt mines' (p. 8). But what purchase are we to give this inspiration and consolation in his life? We sometimes can see the point of perspectives other than our own, while not thinking that they are for us. Some aspects of Davie's example seem like that: what he remembers is 'that other Dmitri', one, by the way, which he feels happier than. But, then, how is he consoled or inspired by a perspective he has failed to make his own? He feels no guilt or remorse. 'He is happier than he would have thought possible' (p. 8). Davie even tells us that 'Dmitri forgives himself for not having found the strength to face such suffering' (p. 8). What this comes to is difficult to imagine. Maybe he is not obsessive about it. Fine. But how does the forgiveness fit with the constant inspiration? The example, to say the least, is not a clear one. Either Dmitri does not care any more, in which case the example is not a counter-example or he does care, in which case we look in vain for some foothold in his life to give this description a point.

Commenting on the example, Davie says,

Do we still have the moral 'must' in this example, or has it disappeared? The fact that Dmitri feels no remorse may trouble us. Our idea was that if a person does not do what he morally must do, he will inevitably feel bad about it. Dmitri does not display the lingering sense of guilt we expect. Still I hesitate to draw the conclusion that his 'must' was not in this case the moral 'must' (p. 8).

But why should anyone hesitate? The case is perfectly straightforward. A moral 'must' is overruled. My thesis is that if the person who does this is said to care about the moral consideration, the overruling must be accompanied by remorse or regret or some very exceptional story. Here, these accompaniments are ruled out. So Davie does not give an example of a person who *still* cares but has no remorse or regret. His is a picture of one who no longer cares, but who remembers the other Dmitri who did care. How that memory is a consolation or an inspiration is an obscurantism which Davie's example does nothing to resolve. Indeed, it is the example which generates the obscurity.

What of Davie's fourth example which is an elaboration of the one we have just discussed? Here, Dmitri looks back on his perspective before he decided to cooperate with those who engineered his escape: 'I was entranced with the idea of moral perfection; I looked forward to the ultimate humiliation of digging salt in the company of thieves and murderers. I would overcome my pride, I would fill my heart with love and forgiveness – that is what I thought' (p. 9). This time we do not have to wonder about the status of these desires. The judgement comes from Dmitri's own mouth: 'What a romantic I was! Thank goodness Alyosha came to me and urged me to escape' (p. 9). So far, there is no problem. Alyosha is urging him to escape from romantic illusions. Thus far there is no counter-example either, since there is no moral perspective in evidence in the first place. But then, as Dmitri's speech progresses it seems that Davie does want to characterise it as a moral perspective after all. 'For a Karamazov, escape from suffering requires great strength and humility. I had to forsake the idea of meaningful suffering and put ordinary happiness in its place. I had to accept my own limitations and imperfections' (p. 9). I have difficulty, as before with the internal consistency of the argument. Sometimes this man seems to be faced with a moral dilemma, and sometimes he seems to be settling for less. If, of course, his situation is in any sense a dilemma, it is not a counter-example to my thesis which concerns whether a person can be said to care for moral considerations if he overrides these considerations with concerns of *another kind*. In a moral dilemma, no such overriding takes place; one moral perspective overrules another, or a person may do what he has to without talking of one perspective overruling another.[5] As Davie puts it, 'He had a hard choice to make. Was he to follow the stern demands of moral perfection or rather accept the less stringent life of ordinary good deeds, decency, and happiness?' (p. 9).

But, if we do not look on Dmitri's problem as a 'hard choice', a moral dilemma, but as an instance of settling for less, what can be said about it? Dmitri admires the wonderful possibility, but he cannot go through with it. On this view, to speak of strength and humility in his choice jars. He recognises he does not have it in him, that's all. But what of his admiration of that which he cannot attain? We only get into trouble here if we think that we must care, in the sense of aspire to, that which we admire. In both my papers on Foot's later position, I stress the importance of distinguishing between what is wonderful and what we care about. It is in this context, and not as a consideration at the centre of all my arguments, that the appeal to extreme cases in ethics is important. Here, I simply repeat my comments in 'Do Moral Considerations Override Others?'

Speaking for myself, I should say that what is important is that I recognise that I do not care for what I admire most. If I think of wonderful sacrifices or the way some people have given themselves to their subjects, is it the case that I have seriously considered doing these things, but decided in favour of some alternative? Not at all. It is important that I recognise that I have not the slightest intention of doing these things. Does it follow that I do not admire such things? No, but it would be a joke if a philosopher were to suggest that since I admire something I must care about it. As I have said elsewhere,[6] the moral relevance of what I admire but do not care about is that it prevents my over-estimating the limits within which I do care.

My thesis all along has been that one cannot say that a man cares for moral considerations if he is prepared to override those considerations with considerations of another kind and show no regret or remorse or appeal to very exceptional circumstances. As Davie says, 'The categorical character of the moral "must" is not compromised by the observation that only certain people and not others, would acknowledge its presence in a given case' (p. 9). Yet, Davie says, this thesis falls to counter-examples. These may be extreme and rare, but they are counter-examples nevertheless. They are examples three and four of Davie's paper. What I have tried to show, however, is that Davie does not succeed in showing that these are counter-examples. Thus, although my thesis may be false, Davie, so far, has not shown this to be the case.

13

Morality and Purpose

I was fortunate enough to be introduced to J. L. Stocks's writings on moral philosophy when I was an undergraduate. Ever since I have been puzzled by the lack of attention given to his work by contemporary moral philosophers. Stocks was interested in the difference moral considerations make to human action. How do moral questions enter into our assessment of actions? Stocks could say at the time he wrote these papers, and the same could be said today, that 'From the time of Aristotle to the present day it has been more or less common form among philosophers to regard purposive action as the summit of human achievement on the practical side. Man was the rational animal, and in the field of conduct he proved his rationality so far as he made his action a well-conceived step towards a clearly-defined end'.[1] Stocks argued, however, that the importance of moral considerations, or of artistic and religious considerations for that matter, cannot be understood or accounted for in terms of purposive action. The distinction between means and ends is central in purposive action. The means are the 'well-conceived step towards a clearly-defined end'. In themselves the means are relatively unimportant. They are important only insofar as they lead to the proposed end. A purposive view of action, then, involves taking an abstract view of action: one element in the situation is abstracted from it, namely, the end in view, and all else is made subordinate to it. This implies that the importance of the means is not only assessed by whether in fact it does lead to the proposed end, but also by the economy and amount of effort and energy it involves. If alternative means can be found which achieve the same end with greater economy and less effort and energy, the former means are cast aside without remorse or regret (see p. 38). If someone wanted to account for moral considerations in terms of purposive action, while wanting at the same time to preserve some kind of distinctiveness for moral considerations, he might argue that morality brings to action purposes of its own, or a clearer view of the purposes in hand. This Stocks will not allow: 'The goodness

167

of a good man does not depend on this, that he has a different end from a bad man, or a clearer view of the same end, or a single end where he has many' (p. 58). What, then, does Stocks take the distinctive contribution of morality to action to be?

Consider the following example. A man may discover a brilliant and legally admissible way of making money. The prospects are great and the profit envisaged sure. Yet morality says, 'Not that way'. Perhaps the proposed way of making money involves betraying a friend. For someone with eyes only for the end and the best means for attaining it, the moral prohibition will seem arbitrary and close to madness. But what if he asked the person involved to justify his conviction that it was wrong to betray his friend? Is it not 'difficult to get beyond the simple formula that one recoils from the thought of so acting in the given situation'? (p. 28). We see that the moral contribution to the action 'At a certain point, without rhyme or reason, . . . makes a man see a barrier he cannot pass; he can only say that he does not consider himself free to improve the situation in just that way' (p. 28).

The above example illustrates why it will not do to think of moral considerations as providing purposes of their own, or a clearer view of purposes already given. What they do is to give attention to details which are unimportant from the point of view of purposive action.

The moral attitude is essentially a concern for the rightness of action. A true instinct exhibits it as interfering with the execution of purpose in stigmatising as immoral the doctrine that the end justifies the means. The phrase implies that morality requires that all means shall be justified in some other way and by some other standard than their value for this or any end: that however magnificent is the prospect opened out by the proposed course of action, and however incontestable the power of the means chosen to bring this prospect nearer, there is still always another question to be asked: not a question whether in achieving this you will not perhaps diminish your chances of achieving something still more important; but a question of another kind. 'There is a decency required', as Browning said; and this demand of decency is prepared to sacrifice, in the given case, any purpose whatever (p. 77).

Purpose was concerned only with the end in view and the most economic means of realising it. But there are other elements in the situation which the purposive view takes no account of. While men are engaged in various activities they develop a regard, not only for specific ends and the surest ways of attaining them, but also for character in action, ideals of behaviour, ways of doing things, which cannot themselves be explained in terms of the distinction between means and ends. If one asks why men should have a regard for such ideals and standards of behaviour, one can only reply that they do, that is all.

But many philosophers have not been content with this answer. They have wanted an answer to the question, Why should I be moral? Stocks discusses some of them, like Green and Bradley, who, it must be remembered, were searching for an alternative to Utilitarianism. They thought they could overcome the main objections to thinking of morality in terms of the distinction between means and ends, and yet retain an account of morality which is essentially purposive. They agreed that a purposive interpretation of moral action which involves a *contingent* relation between means and ends must be rejected. But if the end of moral action is self-affirmation or self-realisation, they suggested, a purposive interpretation of morality can be endorsed. My present state, as exemplified in the moral actions I now perform, is not a mere means, since it is itself part of the greater whole which is the end of my actions, namely, self-realisation. On the other hand, insofar as this 'greater self' (conceived of in different ways by different philosophers) has not yet been attained, a reference to future results is still justified. The development of character thus breaks down the externality of the means–ends relation.

The above attempt to establish an internal relation between means and ends does not escape Stocks's criticisms. He points out that no single end, including that of one's own moral development, can guarantee the rightness of one's actions, and that among the many ends men aim for, one's own moral perfection is not the highest (see p. 78). To those who think that Stocks' worries about these matters are unnecessary, and that obviously the man who spurns a legally admissible way of making money *is* seeking a higher purpose, namely, his own moral perfection, Stocks replies:

that the act must first be shown to be right now before it can be relied upon to build up righteousness in the future; and – more relevantly to our present enquiry – that there may well be such an aim, and it may well be considered more important than riches, but that it is after all only an end, like any other, a possible result of action, and that it falls with all other ends, under the inflexible moral rule that it may not be pursued by any and every means. Morality may call on a man at any moment to surrender the most promising avenue to his own moral perfection (p. 29).

Stocks does not give as many examples to illustrate his points as he might have done, and the examples he does give sometimes lack force. Perhaps the following example will serve to bring out the force of his reply. Consider a case of two friends who want to break with their way of life as prostitutes. Only one of them has the resolution to do so. She knows that to stay means going to pieces sooner or later. But she also knows that her going means that her friend would lose the little genuine affection and worth her life possesses. Her friend begs her not to go. There is little hope that things will change, that her friend will muster enough resolution to leave one day. On the contrary, it is pretty certain that if she stays, they will both be dragged down. Yet, she decides to stay. It might be said that she rejected the most promising avenue to her own moral perfection, but many would find her decision admirable nevertheless.

Some philosophers today, while differing from Green and Bradley in other respects, also look for an alternative to Utilitarianism while wanting to retain an account of moral considerations in terms of purpose. They too want an answer to the question, Why should I be moral? They suggest that an answer to this question can be found by showing how the virtues constitute a good to the just man, or by showing how what are regarded as virtues are connected to the needs of man. What is hoped for is a positive theory of human nature.[2] Just as a plant needs certain things in order to flourish, might it not be the case that man needs certain things in order to flourish too? The actions which would satisfy those needs would be actions which men *ought* to perform. Thus, a perfect marriage between morality and rationality is brought about. The positive theory of human nature is thought of as essentially descriptive, and to say that something ought to be done would be to state an obvious fact. The troublesome barrier between facts and values would be broken down. Indeed, advocates of this view tend to deny that there is any reason to speak of *moral* obligation or of *moral* goodness. What needs elucidation is the way in which certain kinds of actions are in men's interests and others not. These philosophers are contemporary examples of the kind of moral philosophers Stocks refers to as adherents to the principle of Aristotle's Golden Mean. In relation to conduct, Stocks sees the principle as implying that:

> desires and emotions are neither good nor bad, but are material, in itself neutral, out of which, by certain different arrangements and adjustments to environment, what we call goodness and badness is made: that the positive achievement which we call goodness comes, not by elimination of certain elements as bad, or by the introduction of some new factor which is the soul of goodness, but simply by the right arrangement and adjustment of these materials (p. 87).

Why do philosophers find the doctrine of the Golden Mean so attractive? Stocks remarks that 'In ethics it seems to hold out the promise of fairly meeting two demands which I think we are most of us nowadays inclined and entitled to make of an ethical theory; that it shall exhibit virtue or goodness as a positive achievement, and not as a mere negation, and that it shall offer an escape from the dualism of the moral and the natural which unsystematic reflection on the problem of conduct is apt to fall into, not without support from ethical writers' (p. 89). Today we speak in terms of the dualism between facts and values. It is significant that those contemporary moral philosophers who advocate a revival of ethical naturalism do so, partly, because of a desire to avoid talk about 'evaluative meaning' and the 'commendatory force' of moral utterances.[3] They deny that there is any need to appeal to any realm of evaluative meaning beyond the realm of facts. Stocks would agree with this. Where he would disagree with them is in their assumption that the only alternative to talking of a special kind of meaning called evaluative meaning, is to give an account of morality in terms of purposive action. Stocks stressed that it is wrong to think of moral considerations as being independent of purposive action. Insofar as the action has an end in view, moral action is purposive. But the moral importance of the action will be explained by reference to features of the action for which the agent has a regard. These ideals in action cannot be accounted for in terms of adjusting or arranging men's interests into some kind of hierarchy, a hierarchy which perhaps reflects the 'true' interests of the agent. Stocks brings out these facts very clearly.

First, the reference to the self in moral considerations is purely contingent. Whether there is any such reference at all will depend on the circumstances in which moral action and moral judgement are called for. If we insist that every moral action must be justified in terms of the agent's interests, we shall find that self-denial and self-sacrifice have been reduced 'by some spurious arithmetic to cases of self-seeking' (p. 95).[4] But no such justification is satisfactory or called for.

Are we to think, as some moralists have thought, that it is the fear of the pains of self-reproach or the love of the delights of self-approbation that makes men moral? Every unsophisticated mind will be against us here, and will agree rather with Marcus Aurelius in preferring the man who 'has no conception that he has done anything whatever, but may be compared to the vine that bears her grapes and seeks nothing more when once she has done her work and ripened her fruit' (p. 68).

Nevertheless, Stocks is not suggesting that the self has no part in moral deliberation. Insofar as one is dissatisfied with oneself, one is being called on all the time to try to be more decent. But this call cannot be described as egoism or altruism, since it is the call of morality itself. It is connected with what Spinoza called 'the effort to persevere in one's own being' (p. 69).

Second, the reference to the ideals of human action cannot be explained in terms of organising the chaos of human interests, since the picture it creates of the agent confronted by a range of commensurable goods is alien to many situations in which we are called upon to fulfil important moral obligations. For Stocks, all theories based on such explanations stop short at the frontiers of morality. In terms of such theories, moral deliberation and calculation come to much the same thing. The only question of ultimate importance is whether some actions affect the agent's interests more or less than others. In other words, moral considerations on this view can be explained in terms of *desire*.

For desire what is significant is the general character which enables a given individual to provide the appropriate satisfaction, the eatability of the roll of bread, the drinkability of the glass of wine. The object of desire is the mere vehicle of a motion which ends in the organism in which it begins. This means that any individual object offered for use in the satisfaction of desire may be replaced without loss or disturbance by some other individual object possessing the same general character. Discrimination between one instance and another is at most a matter of degree: this is more eatable or drinkable than that. The impulse at once fastens, without remorse or regret, on that which is placed higher in the scale. Desire is essentially transferable or vagrant as between individuals of the appropriate kind, and its valuations are necessarily relative (p. 38).

But, clearly, desire does not account for all the important features of life.

If this were a complete account of human nature the world would be a very different place from what it actually is. If desire and its service were the whole of life there would be no fondness for places and buildings, no contemplative enjoyment of sights and sounds, no ties of affection and friendship, but only the continual grasping calculation of something to be got from men and things as they served a more or less transient need. The convenience of a utensil would be the highest form of praise (pp. 39–40).

Desire is not the only principle at work in human nature. There is also the principle of *affection*. Affection concentrates on the individual and the particular. 'The wife or mother, good or bad, is an individual significant by her individuality' (p. 38). Desire, on the other hand, abstracts and generalises. The notion of commensurable goods is alien to affection. Affection recognises special obligations born of special relationships. Unless this is recognised a great many moral dilemmas will be distorted and not understood. Consider the following example which Wittgenstein discussed on one occasion. The example concerns a man who has come to the conclusion that he must either leave his wife or abandon his work in cancer research. Wittgenstein said something like this about the problem:

Such a man's attitude will vary at different times. Suppose I am his friend, and I say to him, 'Look, you've taken this girl out of her home, and now, by God, you've got to stick to her'. This would be called taking up an ethical attitude. He may reply, 'But

what of suffering humanity? how can I abandon my research?'
In saying this he may be making it easy for himself: he wants to
carry on that work anyway. (I may have reminded him that there
are others who can carry it on if he gives up.) And he may be
inclined to view the effect on his wife relatively easily: 'It probably won't be fatal for her. She'll get over it, probably marry
again', and so on. On the other hand it may not be this way. It
may be that he has a deep love for her. And yet he may think
that if he were to give up his work he would be no husband for
her. That is his life, and if he gives that up he will drag her
down. Here we may say that we have all the materials of a
tragedy; and we could only say: 'Well, God help you'.[5]

How perverse it would be if someone confused desire and affection in Wittgenstein's latter description of the husband's dilemma!
If one thinks it is a matter of deciding what one wants most, one
cannot begin to see what the difficulty is. Imagine someone saying,
'Get another job', or 'Get another wife who'll be prepared to accept
the situation.' What has he missed? Is it not the fact that the
dilemma is inexplicable apart from *this* woman and *this* vocation
involved in it? The reference to the husband is incidental in what
has to be decided. His love of his wife and his love of his work are
the important factors.

What Stocks stresses again and again is that the moral values for
which people have a regard cannot be explained satisfactorily in
terms of a scale of interests or in terms of basic human needs. The
values are adhered to for their own sakes, because they are what
they are. People often think otherwise because in a moral dispute
what is stressed are details, consequences, which each party thinks
the other might have overlooked. This emphasis on consequences
leads one to suppose that 'the whole dispute can be reduced to a
question of means and ends' (p. 81). But these details and consequences once brought to light await evaluation in terms of values
and conceptions of importance which cannot themselves be explained in terms of them. For Stocks, judgements made in terms of
these values are intuitive and cannot be argued. Stocks saw that
the philosophers of his day who were prepared to account for moral
considerations in terms of purposive action, were influenced, not
merely by Utilitarianism, but by Aristotle, who regarded action as
being essentially purposive, and recognised no higher practical
category than that of the good to which an action is the means. The

same influences are to be seen in much contemporary moral philosophy. Stocks contrasts his own view with them, describing it as a non-utilitarian and intuitive ethic. The latter description has traditional difficulties, but I do not see that Stocks inherits them. As far as I can see, he called his ethics intuitive because he refuses to seek 'ultimate' justifications, rationalisations, or explanations in non-moral terms, of moral beliefs. It is this which contrasts his views with recent movements in ethics. Reading him, for me, was like discovering a reinstatement of morality in philosophy.

Stocks also raises the question of the relation between moral philosophy and the ways in which moral considerations enter people's lives. He says that people have no right to expect philosophers to legislate on moral matters. Stocks compares the relation of the philosopher to the moral agent with the relation of the philosopher to the scientist. Philosophy cannot legislate for science. If science trespasses in the realm of metaphysics, that is another matter, but 'in practice the fact is evident that the scientific world is self governing and will not submit to the dictation of philosophy' (p. 108). Similarly, Stocks claims, it is not the business of philosophy to exhort on moral matters. If the philosopher does exhort or advocate, his philosophy becomes impure. Often, in doing so, the philosopher falsifies the facts. There is an enormous gap between the diversity of people's moral beliefs 'and the tidy ethical systems which philosophers offer us as the result of their reflection upon it. The philosopher does not trouble much to show the steps by which from that starting-point he arrived at this result. It often seems as though he had been content to generalise from his own limited practical experience, assuming that it was typical or authoritative' (p. 124).

While one might agree with the main point Stocks is making, there is reason to doubt whether moral practice and philosophical reflection can be held apart so completely as Stocks suggests. While it may not be the purpose of ethics to influence conduct, the fact remains that many moral theories have had such an effect. Moral beliefs may be based on conceptual presuppositions, for example, on presuppositions concerning the common good. A criticism or refutation of such presuppositions may lead to a change in moral beliefs. Once it is admitted that conceptual confusion can have moral consequences, one can see how practice and reflection may be interwoven, how moral and conceptual clarification may come to much the same thing in this context.

Stocks' remarks on the positive contribution of philosophy to practical affairs are less happy. The task of social philosophy is to make explicit the fundamental principles which, according to Stocks, underlie moral action:

> The only sense in which philosophy can be said to determine what is ethically or politically valuable is this, that in its critical examination of the practice and in its exposition of its principles it is attempting to make explicit and evident assumptions as to the nature of good which are for the practitioner largely concealed within the concrete detail of his judgements and decisions (p. 128).

Stocks claims that it is important to remind men of the principles underlying human conduct. 'The man of action has little leisure or inclination to discuss the principles on which he acts. . . . When men do not know the faith by which they live, they will be apt inadvertently to betray it' (p. 115). In all this, however, philosophy is not legislative, since the principles made explicit are said to be those which are in fact implicit in conduct. They are not the creation of philosophers. If men cared little for the consistency of their principles, the philosopher's indication of whether they are deviating or not from such principles would matter little. But since men do care about the consistency of their conduct, the philosopher's exposition can have an enormous influence.

Stocks' hopes for a philosophical exposition of the fundamental moral principles are based on a falsification of the facts. They seem to depend on viewing the vast variety of ways in which moral considerations enter people's lives as manifestations of a greater whole called 'moral action'. According to Stocks:

> the would-be theorist of conduct has to face the mass of material above described and attempt to reduce it to some degree of order. He has to show that this multiplicity is at bottom a unity, that this unorganized sequence of decisions and judgements has none the less its own inner organization and can be plausibly regarded as the expression of a single principle or of a few fundamental ideas which are in intelligible relation to one another (p. 125).

In this task the philosopher 'will be telling the practical man what he really is aiming at all the time' (p. 123). As a result Stocks thinks it will be possible to show men their moral confusions. For example, adherents to Marxism can be shown to be wrong, not by offering them a rival utopia, 'but by showing them on the evidence of the actual achievements of humanity what man's fundamental beliefs really are' (p. 116). But we need to stress, as against Stocks, that the different moral beliefs people hold are not parts of something called Morality; they are what they are. There may be points of contact between the moral views of Genghis Khan, St Paul, Nietzsche, or James Joyce, insofar as one calls them *moral* views at all, but the differences are likely to be far greater than the similarities. Any hope of reducing their views to an 'underlying unity' is futile, and the supposition that anything they may have in common is therefore fundamental in their beliefs, is unfounded. The diversity and multiplicity of people's moral beliefs, instead of leading Stocks to look for an underlying unity in them, should have prevented him from thinking that such a unity exists. Stocks seems to be guilty of introducing the desire for tidiness and the kind of impurity into moral philosophy which he himself deplored.

What is obscure and perhaps mistaken in J. L. Stocks's moral philosophy is far outweighed by his observations on the role of morality in action, his criticisms of the means–ends distinction and accounts of morality in terms of purpose, and his important distinction between ethics and advocacy.

J. L. Stocks speaks directly and penetratingly on many of the problems being discussed at present in ethics. Not only does he give illuminating answers to these problems, but he asks us to reconsider whether certain issues, which contemporary philosophers think important, are the fundamental questions of moral philosophy. In doing so, I believe, he stands as one of the most important writers on ethics since 1900.

14

How Lucky Can You Get?

In their symposium on 'Moral Luck', Bernard Williams and Thomas Nagel argue against some of the basic assumptions of an influential Kantian tradition in ethics. According to this tradition, 'there is one basic form of value, moral value, which is immune to luck'.[1] It is clear to Williams and Nagel that this is not the case. They differ, however, in what they take the consequences of the involvement of luck with morality to be.[2] For Nagel, they lead to our living with a number of unresolvable contradictions. When we *argue*, it seems to him irrational to condemn or praise people for features of their character, or for consequences of their actions, if those features and consequences are not within their control. On the other hand, when we *act*, we find moral judgements occurring involuntarily in just these contexts. For Nagel, it seems that we simply live with these tensions between rational reflection and moral practice. Williams's conclusion is very different. His main conclusion seems to be that once we have recognised that morality is inextricably bound up with luck, we can see how, in certain circumstances, luck can make us immune to moral considerations. In seeing this, Williams argues, we attack the assumption that morality has an unconditional claim on our interests and desires. According to Williams, we are glad that we live in a world where we allow certain interests and desires to overrule moral considerations. The difference between Nagel and Williams might be put like this: Nagel claims to recognise the place moral considerations have in our lives, but is puzzled by the fact that, philosophically, that place seems irrational. Williams, reacting to what Kantians have said, wants to put morality in its place, a place far less exalted than the one philosophers would give it.

In this paper I shall argue that Nagel and Williams are both wrong: Nagel in thinking that when we make moral judgements we are turning a blind eye to the irrationality of doing so; Williams in thinking that he has put morality in its place.

I

Nagel discusses three contexts in which moral considerations are not immune to luck: the consequences of our actions, constitutive luck, and circumstances. In all three Nagel suggests that in making moral judgements we are often not behaving rationally. It is difficult to see what this appeal to rationality amounts to. What is important is that we *do* make moral judgements in the contexts Nagel finds suspect. In elucidating what these judgements may involve, I am not endeavouring to establish their rationality to meet Nagel's charge of irrationality. Rather, in bringing out the character of the judgements, we see that talk of rationality and irrationality adds nothing, but only serves to hide from us the character of our practices.

In the first context he is concerned with, Nagel points out that *the consequences of our actions*, and other factors not under our control, affect the character of these actions when seen from the perspective of either agent or spectator. For example, as Nagel says, whether there are pedestrians in the path of a drunken driver whose lorry runs out of control is a matter of luck. Yet, what the driver has to face, morally, and what he can be said to be responsible for, will depend on this luck. It also seems puzzling to Nagel that 'the penalty for attempted murder is less than that for successful murder – however similar the intentions and motives of the assailant may be in the two cases. His degree of culpability can depend, it would seem, on whether the victim happened to be wearing a bullet-proof vest, or whether a bird flew into the path of the bullet – matters beyond his control' (p. 141). Again, Nagel points to the innumerable examples in history where luck plays a major part in determining what agents can be said to have done, the descriptions they and others give of their deeds, and the assessments they and others arrive at:

If the Decembrists had succeeded in overthrowing Nicholas I in 1825 and establishing a constitutional regime, they would be heroes. As it is, not only did they fail and pay for it, but they bore some responsibility for the terrible punishments meted out to the troops who had been persuaded to follow them. If the American Revolution had been a bloody failure resulting in greater repression, then Jefferson, Franklin and Washington would still have made a noble attempt, and might not even have regretted it on their way to the scaffold, but they would also have had to blame themselves for what they had helped to bring on their compatriots. (Perhaps peaceful efforts at reform would eventually have succeeded.) If Hitler had not overrun Europe and exterminated millions, but instead had died of a heart attack after occupying the Sudetenland, Chamberlain's action at Munich would still have utterly betrayed the Czechs, but it would not be the great moral disaster that has made his name a household word (p. 142).[3]

When Nagel looks at these moral assessments in the light of philosophical reflection, they seem irrational to him:

From the point of view which makes responsibility dependent on control, all this seems absurd. How is it possible to be more or less culpable depending on whether a child gets into the path of one's car, or a bird into the path of one's bullet? Perhaps it is true that what is done depends on more than the agent's state of mind or intention. The problem then is, why is it not irrational to base moral assessment on what people do, in this broad sense? It amounts to holding them responsible for the contributions of fate as well as for their own – provided they have made some contribution to begin with. . . . But here too it seems rational to subtract the effects of occurrences subsequent to the choice, that were merely possible at the time, and concentrate moral assessment on the actual decision in the light of the probabilities. . . . The result of such a line of thought is to pare down each act to its morally essential core, an inner act of pure will assessed by motive and intention (pp. 143–4).

Bernard Williams's reaction to the involvement of luck in morality is very different. He considers the case of a lorry-driver, who, through no fault of his own, runs over a child, and observes, rightly, that the driver is likely to feel differently about what he has done from the way any spectator is likely to feel. He may well feel that he is to blame. Williams says that others will attempt to persuade him to feel differently about the matter, although, he says, 'some doubt would be felt about a driver who too blandly or readily moved to that position' (p. 124). Why should this be so? Is it not because such over-readiness would reveal an insensitivity to the terribleness of what has happened, a terribleness for which he is unintentionally responsible? The driver is likely to want to make reparation, even if someone else has seen to the insurance payments. Where there is no room for reparation, then, as Williams says, 'only the desire to make reparation remains, with the painful consciousness that nothing can be done about it; some other action, perhaps less directed to the victims, may come to express this' (p. 125). No doubt there will be disagreements about the extent to which an agent's feelings should be engaged by what he has unintentionally done. Where some see depth, others may see excess. But, as Williams says, 'it would be a kind of insanity never to experience sentiments of this kind towards anyone' (p. 125). He goes on to say, however, that 'it would be an insane conception of rationality which insisted that a rational person never would' (p. 125). But the moral reactions Williams refers to are neither rational nor irrational. They simply *are* moral reactions which very many people share. Calling them 'rational' does not add to our understanding of them.

Williams says that to insist on a conception of rationality which excludes these moral reactions 'would, apart from other kinds of absurdity, suggest a large falsehood, that we might, if we conducted ourselves clear-headedly enough, entirely detach ourselves from the unintentional aspects of our actions, relegating their costs to, so to speak, the insurance fund, and yet still retain our identity and character as agents' (p. 125). But, for Nagel, this identity and character is hard to find: 'The effect of concentrating on the influence of what is not under his control is to make this responsible self seem to disappear, swallowed up by the order of mere events' (p. 148).

The source of many of Nagel's difficulties rests in his conception of the relation of willing to action, a conception which, Wittgenstein says, leads us to think of 'doing' as seeming 'not to have any volume of experience' and to be like 'an extensionless point'.[4] It seems that Nagel regards his problem as insoluble 'because something in the idea of agency is incompatible with actions being events, or people being things' (p. 148). The difficulty is that once these events and things are recognised, 'nothing remains which can be ascribed to the responsible self' (p. 148). But a sign that not all is well with his problem is shown in Nagel's admission that he 'cannot define the idea of the active self that is thus undermined' (p. 149). Winch has given an account of similar difficulties which Wittgenstein worked through:

A man, considered as a moral being, is an active centre of consciousness. As such, he is not really in the world at all: the world, that is, in which actions in the ordinary sense and their consequences occur. This is something which he contemplates and, in a way which on this whole view must remain essentially mysterious, may sometimes causally affect. The mysteriousness of this causal relation is brought out in Wittgenstein's difficulties with the concept of will in the *Tractatus* and *Notebooks 1914–16*[5] . . . Thus Wittgenstein argued with himself, anything which brings about changes in the world must itself be in the world and, if we speak of the will in this connection, it must be a *phenomenon* of which we speak. But if the occurrence of a volition is a phenomenon then it occurs subject to the same sorts of conditions (conditions in the world) as does any other phenomenon. But as the 'willing subject' is not 'in the world', then *it* cannot be the cause of this (or any other) phenomenon. 'I am completely powerless.'[6] So if the willing subject is to be spoken of as in any way ethically responsible, this must be in respect of a 'will' in quite a different sense: 'the will as the subject of ethical attributes', which has no special relation to anything in particular that happens in the world but only a relation to 'the world as a whole'. On the other hand . . . Wittgenstein was unable to give any account of how ethical attributes could attach to the will in this sense without supposing (what he thought he had shown to be impossible) that the willing subject could make a difference to what happens in the world.[7]

Wittgenstein overcame these difficulties in a way very different from Nagel's resting-point. Nagel's view, as we have seen, is that when we philosophise, the ways in which we actually speak of actions and the agent's responsibility for them seem irrational. Wittgenstein's procedure is the reverse: he asks us to reflect on the ways in which we actually do speak about these matters and see how we have been misled in our philosophisings. Nagel says, 'The account of moral luck cannot be understood without an account of the internal conception of agency' (p. 150), an account Nagel admits he does not have. But, on Wittgenstein's view, it is this very conception of internal agency which creates the problem in the first place. Wittgenstein says, 'Willing, if it is not to be a sort of wishing, must be the action itself. It cannot be allowed to stop anywhere short of the action. If it is the action, then it is so in the ordinary sense of the word; so it is speaking, writing, walking, lifting a thing, imagining something. But it is also trying, attempting, making an effort – to speak, to write, to lift a thing, to imagine something, etc.'[8] Nagel thinks of 'trying' or 'deciding' as forms of 'willing' conceived of as essentially internal events prior to action. The agent is responsible only for these 'willings'. Once we see that willing is internally related to action, we are brought back to responsibility for our actions, for what we do, in the sense with which we are familiar in actual practice. Since 'trying' is a form of willing, to be responsible for what we try to do is to be responsible for our actions under a certain description. As Peter Heath says, 'to talk of trying is not to describe anything, but is merely a way of setting actions in a certain context, or construing them in a certain light. The context in question is that of success or failure, and more especially the risks, obstacles or difficulties, real or apprehended, that are faced or overcome by the agent, or by which he is defeated, and which may mitigate or excuse his failure, or enhance the merit of his success.'[9] Once this is recognised, we can discuss, as Winch proceeds to do, how trying to do something, as distinct from actually doing that something, may be related to the agent's responsibility. Winch stresses the feature of these situations which tends to get lost in Nagel's analysis, namely, that in both instances we are discussing what an agent has *done*. The fact that an *action* has occurred is central even when luck intervenes to thwart the terrible consequences of a foul deed. 'For example', Winch says, 'a man may betray a friend to his friend's enemies and the enemies may then be prevented through further circumstances from harming the betrayed one. That does not alter the fact that the betrayal was a terrible thing to have done. And notice that we are still speaking of what was *done* and not merely of what was attempted.'[10] In considering the difference between committing a murder and attempting to commit a murder, Nagel is puzzled as to why luck should be able to determine the degree of culpability involved. Yet, if we embrace the solution he offers, separating from the original intention everything which is not under the agent's control, what a man has to face who has attempted murder turns out to be the same as that which has to be faced by the successful murderer. Winch shows why this will not do. He states his conclusion in general terms as follows:

If a man tries to do something evil and fails, then he does not become what his success would have made him and thereby the possibilities of moral assessment of him are different. It is not that the man who fails has nothing to condemn himself for or to be condemned for; but he does not have that to condemn himself for which he would have had if successful. He can later thank God he failed. What he is then thanking God for is that he did not become what he had it in him, and was ready, to become. What was 'within him' was not realized.[11]

As Nagel says, the murder may be prevented by luck, by the fact that the intended victim was wearing a bullet-proof vest, or the fact that a bird flew in the path of the bullet. The fact remains that a murder was attempted; the attempt was *made*. As such, it enters into the network of moral relations Winch describes.

In this network, an individual stands in a unique relation to his own actions, to what he has actually *done*. As we saw, Williams emphasises that when a lorry-driver kills a child, accidentally, it is extremely difficult for any sensitive person, so placed to dissociate himself from the action. Although it was an accident, he has killed a child. It is far worse, of course, when negligence has been involved. Winch quotes remarks by Molly Parkin in an article on drinking and driving, where she 'quotes the words of a man who once while drunk knocked down and killed a youth with his car. "He has changed dramatically", she comments and quotes him as saying: "It's as if I'd been involved in one of the major mysteries of Life, as to Who gives it, and Who takes it away. To end another human being's life is a shocking thing. The most profoundly disturbing experience that can happen to anyone."' But even when negligence is not involved, one's involvement in bringing about what is terrible makes admission of responsibility by the agent readily intelligible. As Williams points out, such admission is central in tragedy:

> When Oedipus says 'I did not do it' (Sophocles *OC* 539) he speaks as one whose exile proclaims that he did do it, and to persons who treat him as quite special because he did. Could we have, and do we want, a concept of agency by which what Oedipus said would simply be true, and by which he would be seeing things rightly if for him it was straight off as though he had no part in it? (pp. 134–5; n. 2).[12]

It is unclear whether Williams is saying that he could understand why Oedipus, as well as feeling responsible for what he has done, would want to blame himself for what he has done. Perhaps he would take the same view here as he does in the case of the lorry-driver who accidentally kills a child. While condemning a driver who feels no responsibility, he says that spectators, rightly, would try to get the driver to stop blaming himself; try to get him to take up something more akin to a spectator's view of his action. But Oedipus *does* blame himself for killing his father and marrying his mother, though he had no way of knowing that he was doing these actions. Had he known what he was doing, he would have undoubtedly refrained from doing so. There are people who think it wrong for Oedipus to blame himself. Winch has no philosophical objection to anyone taking this view. He objects only to those who advance a philosophical thesis which states that it is incoherent for Oedipus to blame himself. Winch says,

> Well, there is one important feature of the situation which we should not lose sight of, namely that Oedipus has *done* those things – married his mother and killed his father, even if he had not intended them. For this reason his perspective on these happenings was quite different from that of an onlooker on natural happenings. I do not find it at all difficult to understand that he should blame himself in these circumstances; neither do I feel inclined to say that it was irrational for him to do so.[13]

Williams and Winch appeal to the spectators' understanding of the unique relationship in which an agent stands to a terrible deed he has done unintentionally, but in Williams's case the understanding is of the naturalness of an admission of responsibility, whereas in Winch's case the understanding is of the naturalness of self-reproach. Williams says,

> Doubtless, and rightly, people will try, in comforting him, to move the driver from this state of feeling, [i.e. blame] move him, indeed from where he is to something more like the place of a spectator. . . . We feel sorry for the driver, but that sentiment co-exists with, indeed presupposes, that there is something special about his relation to this happening, something which cannot merely be eliminated by the consideration that it was not his fault. It may be still more so in cases where agency is fuller than in such an accident, though still involuntary through ignorance (p. 124).

Winch says,

> If Oedipus had intended what he did, I might indeed think it
> appropriate for me to blame him. As it is, the appropriate
> reaction is surely one of pity, the attitude which Sophocles' play
> invites from us. But for what are we invited to pity him? Not, I
> think, just for the terrible consequences which befall him when
> his deeds are discovered, for though we could indeed pity
> another man to whom, for quite different reasons, such things
> happened, it would not be the same sort of pity. The pity we feel
> for Oedipus is inextricably connected with our realisation of
> what he has *done* and with our understanding that these are
> actions for which he could not help blaming himself. What
> makes the consequences so terrible is precisely *what* they are
> consequences *of*; they are, as it were, the vehicle which carries
> our understanding of what Oedipus is by virtue of what he has
> done. But the moral character of Oedipus's situation would have
> been the same, even if there had been no such consequences;
> and we could still have pitied him.[14]

The point of relevance for our discussion is to note that in either
event, whether we agree with Williams or Winch, the involvement
of luck does not place the unintended action outside the scope of
moral assessment. To reach the conclusion that the driver or
Oedipus should not blame themselves is not to place their actions
beyond moral judgements. On the contrary, that is the moral
judgement reached on them. The crucial involvement of luck in the
determination of the nature of the actions performed, in the determination of what it is the agent has to face, and in the influencing
of the reaction of the agent and spectators to the actions, does not,
as Nagel thinks, make irrational the exercise of moral judgements
and assessments in these contexts. I have not been demonstrating
the rationality of these judgements and assessments, but simply
exhibiting their character.

The second context in which Nagel and Williams consider the
involvement of luck in morality is what they call *the role of constitutive luck* in the character of the agent. As in the previous context,
Nagel argues that we simply live with a tension between rationality and moral practice. He notes that 'Kant was particularly insistent on the moral irrelevance of qualities of temperament and
personality that are not under the control of the will' (p. 144). Yet

we undoubtedly do praise people for such qualities, for example, for possessing a generous nature. So we seem to praise people while being convinced at the same time of the irrationality of doing so. Nagel expresses what he takes to be the unresolvable tension as follows:

> One may want to have a generous spirit, or regret not having one, but it makes no sense to condemn oneself or anyone else for a quality which is not within the control of the will. Condemnation implies that you shouldn't be like that, not that it's unfortunate that you are. Nevertheless, Kant's conclusion remains intuitively unacceptable. We may be persuaded that these moral judgements are irrational, but they reappear involuntarily as soon as the argument is over. This is the pattern throughout the subject (p. 145).

Williams mentions constitutive luck but does not discuss it at any length. He says that 'the dispositions of morality, however far back they are placed in the area of intention and motive, are as "conditioned" as anything else' (p. 116). It is not clear how being 'conditioned ' differs from being conditioned, but clearly Williams wants to draw a contrast with the Kantian tradition. Of that tradition, he says:

> Anything which is the product of happy or unhappy contingency is no proper object of moral assessment, and no proper determinant of it either. Just as in the realm of character it is motive, not style, or powers, or endowment, that counts, so in action, it is not changes actually effected in the world, but intention. With these considerations there is supposed to disappear even that constitutive luck which the ancient sages were happy to benefit from; the capacity for moral agency is supposedly present to any rational agent whatever, to anyone for whom the question can even present itself. The successful moral life, removed from considerations of birth, lucky upbringing, or indeed of the incomprehensible Grace of a non-Pelagian God, is presented as a career open not merely to the talents, but to a talent which all rational creatures necessarily possess in the same degree. Such a conception has an ultimate form of justice at its heart, and that is its allure. Kantianism is only superficially repulsive – despite appearances, it offers an inducement, solace to a sense of the world's unfairness (pp. 115–16).

We cannot escape the questions Nagel and Williams pose, by trying to argue that all moral dispositions are, in the sense they require, under our control. For example, contrast generosity of spirit with, say, that equanimity of spirit said to be attainable in face of the twists and turns of fortune. Williams argues that while 'the sage was immune to the impact of incident luck, it was a matter of . . . constitutive luck that one was a sage, or capable of becoming one: for the many and the vulgar this was not (on the prevailing view) an available course' (p. 115). Whatever of this, let us assume that the equanimity of spirit in face of incident luck being offered *is* some kind of teachable technique of control. Suppose we are asked to reflect that when we buy an earthenware pot, we understand that it may break. When, as bad luck would have it, it does break, we can use that understanding in such a way that it rescues us from undue distress. Again, when we marry, we are told that we realise that the loved one will die one day and that it is possible that death may come sooner rather than later. Understanding this, and adapting it appropriately, it is said, when earthly death does come we are not unduly distressed. But everything depends on the *use* of these understandings. The person distressed at the destruction of a cherished object or torn apart by the death of a loved one, understood that these calamities were possible. Where equanimity of spirit is concerned, it looks as if it is not the understanding which determines the character of the love and attachment, but the character of the love and attachment involved which makes someone content with that equanimity and with that understanding. But the kind of natural generosity Nagel and Williams have in mind would not exhibit that kind of control and could not be taught by some kind of technique.[15] So their original question remains: why do we praise people for moral dispositions which are not under their control?

Once again, Nagel's difficulties in this respect come from his assumptions about the relations between 'willing' and 'acting'. If 'willing' is thought of as 'being in control', then, if generosity of spirit is said not to be 'under one's control', it follows that generosity of spirit cannot be willed. But if this disposition is not willed by the agent, it cannot be said to be *his*. If the disposition is not his, how can the agent be praised for possessing it or blamed for not possessing it? So runs the argument.

Nagel has observed, as many of us have, someone acting with a marvellous spontaneous generosity of action or thought. We admire it. It is effortless. Indeed, that is partly why we admire it. But then we are tempted to think that if there has been no effort there has been no willing either. If something not willed cannot be his action, our reflections open up a gap between the agent and his action which is so wide that the action is characterised as an event which befalls him. Once again, Winch's reflections on 'willing' are extremely relevant to Nagel's predicament. Winch says,

> It is because, besides doing a thing, our talk about action also includes reference to trying, choosing, deciding, intending, etc., to do a thing, that it is possible to drive a wedge between acting and willing. Or, more generally, this possibility arises because the concept of acting requires that agents should have a concept of what they are doing, that there could be such a thing as talking about and discussing one's actions. But the possibility of such a wedge in some cases does *not* mean that it can *always* be driven. There are cases, many standard cases, where no distinction at all can be drawn between willing and acting.[16]

Wittgenstein says,

> When I raise my arm I do not usually try to raise it.
> 'At all costs I will get to that house.' – But if there is no difficulty about it – *can* I try at all costs to get to the house?[17]

If there are standard non-moral cases, there are standard moral cases too. Winch considers the case of someone being required to pay a bill. Where there are no difficulties or complicating factors involved the person, often enough, simply pays the bill. He does not *try* to pay the bill and yet paying it is something he *does*. No doubt the simple act of paying a bill does not capture the spirit of the dispositions Nagel and Williams have in mind. On the other hand, it is instructive to remember that when questioned as to a person's honesty when people want to know whether he will pay his bills, etc., we can often answer, 'Of course he will. There's no question about it.' If we said that such a man would try to pay his bills or had his bill-paying under his control, we would be giving entirely the wrong impression of him, suggesting that obstacles, difficulties and temptations are present where none exist. An example of a natural disposition nearer to what Nagel and Williams may have in mind, can be found in Simone Weil's example of a father absorbed in play with his child. She offers this as an example of a pure action. Winch asks us to 'consider the case of a man who finds himself unable to enjoy himself spontaneously with his child; though he goes out of his way to entertain the child out of duty as a father. May he not quite well regard his relative lack of spontaneity, *vis-à-vis* the father in Simone Weil's example, as a *moral* failing? Can he not, without confusion, regard himself as a "worse man" than the other?'[18] The father he admires is not playing with the child out of a sense of duty. He is not playing with the child for its own sake, if by that is meant playing because he regards the play as something having value in itself. He is not trying to play with the child. He does not have his playing with the child under his control (which does not mean that it was out of his control). Any such description would fail to capture the purity of the father's action. He does not play with the child *for* anything. He is absorbed in play. If the essence of constitutive luck is the absence of effort or striving in arriving at the disposition the father possesses, this in no way places such dispositions beyond the scope of moral assessment. These dispositions are possessed in a world where it is all too easy not to possess them. When possessed they are manifest in people's actions.

The third context in which luck is involved in morality, which Nagel considers, briefly, is *the nature of one's circumstances*. He says,

> The things we are called on to do, the moral tests we face, are completely determined by factors beyond our control. It may be true of someone that in a dangerous situation he would behave in a cowardly or heroic fashion, but if the situation never arises, he will never have the chance to distinguish or disgrace himself in this way, and his moral record will be different (p. 145).

In this third context, too, Nagel finds a tension between rationality and moral practice:

> Here again one is morally at the mercy of fate, and it may seem irrational upon reflection, but our ordinary moral attitudes would be unrecognisable without it. We judge people for what they actually do or fail to do, not just for what they would have done if circumstances had been different (p. 146).

Nagel recognises, but does not give sufficient weight to the fact that the moral concern is with what is actually *done*. The fact that luck can affect what is done, so far from being necessarily at variance with moral assessment, often plays an important part in shaping its character. How it is shaped depends on the character of the moral reactions involved. I simply offer some examples. We have already seen that the pity Sophocles invites us to feel for Oedipus is inextricably bound up with the recognition of the part fate had played in his life. Further, Sophocles is suggesting that failure to give fate its due is a case of *hubris*, the *hubris* of which Oedipus is guilty when he says that it is unthinkable that he, of all people, should be cursed among men.[19] To speculate about what one would do if certain circumstances arose, to *want* to be put to the test, has sometimes been praised, sometimes condemned. When condemned, it has been described as 'tempting fate' or 'tempting God'. One is told to refrain from doing so because 'sufficient unto the day is the evil thereof'. The failure to recognise constitutive luck is central in some forms of religious judgement. The pharasaism involved in thanking God that one is not as other men are is a standard form of such failure. The opposite attitude is found in the reaction to another's moral failure: 'But for the grace of God there go I.' Where others speak of luck, the religious believer may speak of grace, a grace which informs his very conception of endeavour. Simone Weil locates Peter's denial of Christ illuminatingly, not in the breaking of his promise, but in the making of it: 'Denial of Saint Peter. To say to Christ: "I will never deny Thee" was to deny him already, for it was supposing the source of faithfulness to be in himself and not in grace.'[20] In endeavour, so understood, Nagel's necessary tension between moral judgement and luck becomes an internal conceptual relation between them.

The fourth context where luck is involved with morality, which Nagel considers, concerns *freedom of the will*. His conclusions, however, depend on the conception of the relation of willing to acting which we have already considered and rejected. We do not need to repeat these arguments.[21] Our conclusion is that in the three contexts we have considered, consequences, constitutive luck and circumstances, the involvement of luck in morality need not lead to placing what is actually done in such contexts beyond the scope of moral assessment. Neither does it involve, as Nagel claims, living with an unresolvable tension between philosophical reflection and our moral practices.

II

The case which occupies Williams for most of his paper is, as Nagel rightly observes, very different from those which we have considered. Williams, like Nagel, has insisted that morality cannot be made immune to luck. But even if this could have been shown, he insists, moral values would still be one kind of value among others. It would not show that 'moral values possessed some special, indeed supreme, kind of dignity or importance' (p. 116). The concern about whether moral values are supreme values is a curious one. One wonders what it has to do with those moral considerations which may go deep with a person. Do they go deep because they are supreme? Insofar as Williams is concerned to question such matters, all well and good. The difficulty is that he wants to oppose one generality with another. Objecting to the place Kantians have given to morality, he too wants to accord it a place. Williams wants to say that we often prefer other values to moral values and are glad that we live in a world where this is so. But the generality of this reaction simply serves to obscure different cases. I may have promised to repay the five pounds I have borrowed from you next Monday. It becomes inconvenient for me to do so and I break my promise. No doubt I am blameworthy, but, as it stands, such an example is hardly likely to throw light on those situations where a person says, 'I just can't do that', where what is envisaged is, for example, breaking a promise by a parent to stand by a young person when he appears in court. What is involved in the two promises is very different. No doubt it is the conviction that here are things one *can't* do, that those who speak of moral values as supreme values are trying to capture in their characterisation. What these things are, are not the same for everyone. In discussing Williams's example my purpose is to attack the generalities he wants to base on it. To his credit, he chooses an example which does go deep with many people, namely, how one treats one's family. On the other hand, his claim is that good luck can make a person immune to the moral considerations involved, considerations to which he would have been answerable if bad luck had been his lot. I shall first present the example Williams asks us to consider and then show how the issues involved cannot be separated from the question of the place they have in people's lives. Appreciating this may dissuade philosophers from thinking that they can determine, in some impersonal way, the place which moral considerations should have.

Williams's example concerns a painter called Gauguin in thinking of whom we are not meant to be limited by historical facts. He wants to realise himself as a painter and, in order to do so, deserts his family. From his new life, his best paintings come. As a result, he is glad he made the decision he did, and feels no remorse for what he has done. In reaching his decision, we are told, Gauguin was not indifferent to moral considerations. On the contrary, Williams says that he cares about the claims his family have on him and the distress he will cause in hurting them. Williams describes the effects on the deserted family as 'grim'. Had Gauguin failed as a painter, he would have had much to answer for. What are we to make of this example?

Our initial response might be to say that Gauguin is faced by a *moral dilemma* or a *moral problem*. Williams mocks attempts by moral theorists to accommodate the choice Gauguin has to make within moral rules:

> What could that rule be? It could not be that one is morally justified in deciding to neglect other claims if one is a great creative artist: apart from basic doubts about its moral content, that saving clause begs the question which at the relevant time one is in no position to answer. On the other hand, '. . . if one is convinced that one is a creative artist' will serve to make obstinacy and fatuous self-delusion conditions of justification; while '. . . if one is reasonably convinced that one is a great creative artist' is, if anything, worse. What is reasonable conviction supposed to be in such a case? Should Gauguin consult professors of art? The absurdity of such riders surely express an absurdity in the whole enterprise of trying to find a place for such cases within the rules (p. 119).

The trouble is that this talk of 'accommodation within moral rules' is itself highly artificial and gives no real sense of what a moral dilemma or a moral problem could be. If we want some grasp of what a moral problem is, we need examples of real ones. As Rush Rhees has said, these would be 'problems by which people are faced when they may feel like saying "I wish to God I knew what I ought to do". Treatises on ethics sometimes talk about "conflicts of duties". But that phraseology is already making the matter pretty artificial, I think.'[22] But Williams's Gauguin does not wish to God that he knew what he ought to do. He knows perfectly well what he is going to do. He is going to leave the family he says he cares about, despite the fact that the consequences for them are going to be grim, in order to do what he wants. So Williams's Gauguin is not faced with a moral dilemma or a moral problem.

Coming to this conclusion, it may seem natural to assume that the alternative is to say that Gauguin is faced by a *moral temptation*. We are speaking here, as Williams does, of how the agent thinks of his situation. It is clear, however, that he does not see his wanting to be an artist as a temptation to ignore his moral obligations to his family. If he did see his decision as succumbing to temptation, he would have been ashamed of it, felt remorse, and have wanted to make reparation. But Williams's Gauguin does not say he is tempted by or ashamed of what he has done. When successful, he says he has done the right thing, although it is not morally the right thing.

Coming to this conclusion may tempt us to offer a third description of what Gauguin has done: he does not succumb to temptation; he *repudiates the moral*. But talk about 'repudiating the moral' can itself be pretty slippery talk. Rush Rhees has noted why:

> 'Philosophers often speak of "morality" – as though it were plain what is meant by this. It seems that there are those who care about morality, and those who wish to opt out of morality – almost as though "morality" were a term comparable to "military service" or "membership of the National Union of Railwaymen". But there are various people who might be said to care about morality, although they (a) use the term in very different ways, and (b) have very different ways of showing that they "care".'[23] Therefore, as Rhees says, 'It always muddles the discussion when someone speaks as though there were some all-embracing morality – some *general* moral principle or ultimate standard, of which the standards the people of . . . various communities recognise are so many different expressions.'[24] He goes on to say: 'So if someone tries: "The Stoics and Cynics were opting out of the morality of the Roman burghers – but they were not opting out of *Morality*" – I can only say that I am not impressed. I do not say that someone who said this would not have anything which could be discussed. But he has not made it clear what this is. Part of what he means, I suppose, is that the

reaction of the Stoic or the Beatnik is not simply negative: he is making a positive move in another direction. I agree that this is important. But can "repudiating morality" be understood in some way which does not include this? or is this part of what we should *mean* by repudiating morality?'[25]

But Williams's Gauguin does not include this and so nothing like this could be meant by his alleged repudiation of morality. True, Gauguin's reaction is not a negative one. He too makes a positive move in another direction. But the other direction is not another *moral* direction. Rhees says immediately after the remarks quoted above: 'What Kierkegaard called "the aesthetic view of life" was still a view of life. But he did not call it *ethical* on that account.'[26] Williams's Gauguin does not reject one moral perspective for the sake of another.

The difficulty is to see what moral considerations come to for Williams's Gauguin. According to Williams, the example shows the proper place morality should have. But, clearly, from certain moral perspectives, Gauguin can be seen as *someone for whom moral considerations do not go deep*. As we have seen, Williams tells us that Gauguin is faced with 'definite and pressing human claims on him' (p. 117). We are told that he 'is concerned about these claims and what is involved in their being neglected (we may suppose this to be grim)' (p. 118). But how much does Gauguin care? How urgent are those moral claims for him? Does he see the *kind* of importance they can have for some people? Of course, the moral claims do create problems for him, but when they are deep problems for some people, then, as Rhees says, 'they are unlike problems relating to success or failure in one's vocation'.[27] But Gauguin turns away from his moral obligations in pursuit precisely of this kind of success. In that case, how urgent can the moral claims be said to be for him? Rhees stresses the distinctive relations in which we may stand to moral considerations:

'If I cannot find some answer, I cannot carry on in business at all.' 'If I cannot find some way out, I shall have to give up teaching.' But then what about the moral problem? 'If I cannot find some way . . .' What is the urgency here?

'I shall never be any better in music, I can see now that I shall never be a musician.' 'Well, you'll have to take up something else.'

But: 'I just never get any better (morally). With every failure, I have found the courage to go on only with the thought that by trying I shall gradually get better. And I have only to look at the record now, to know that I never shall.' Well? Tell him to take up something else?

'If you're not a first-rate teacher, then you'll just have to learn to live with the fact that you are a second-rate or a third-rate teacher.'

'If you find that you just are never going to be decent even to the people that you love, then you'll just have to . . .'. Hell.[28]

But according to Williams, when success comes to Gauguin, he does not regret what he has done. He *can* live with it. In fact, his success is sufficient for him to justify what he has done to himself, to think that he did the right thing. But this is not because his moral perspective differs from those who may criticise his actions, a perspective akin to Nietzsche's, for example. No, we are told that his moral values overlap those of his critics. For example, he accepts that 'The reproaches of others he may never have an answer to, in the sense of having a right that they accept or even listen to what he has to say' (Williams, pp. 118–19). As far as those who have suffered at his hands are concerned, 'There is no ground . . . for demanding that they drop their resentment' (Williams, p. 133). Neither is there any reason why they should be impressed by his success.

Normally, to say that one has no answer to the moral reproaches of others is to admit one's answerability to them. It is to say something about one's own moral state. Not so in Gauguin's case. He is not answerable to them in his own eyes. Recognising the reproaches of others, for him, simply means, we are told, that he has no right to expect them to listen to *him*. He is not responding to the reproaches. This is part of what is meant in saying that the reproaches do not go deep with him.

It may be thought that there is a lack of depth in Gauguin's conception of his vocation. If he is successful, he will not regret his decision, whereas if he is unsuccessful the whole venture will have been in vain. Contrast this with Rhees's discussion of Wittgenstein's remark, 'Go the bloody *hard* way.' Rhees says, 'Philosophy, as he practised it, was "the bloody *hard* way" in the sense of being opposed to looking for consolation or for stimulus. And it was not only a way of thinking and working, but a way of living as well.

And the "hardness" was really a criterion of the sort of life that was worth while. Perhaps I should add "for him".'[29] But Rhees goes on to say, 'I do not mean that if you cannot do philosophy *as well* as Wittgenstein did – or even if you cannot have the same measure of seriousness that he had – you should leave it alone. But I do mean that if you want to pursue philosophy as something in which you can take it easy, then you should leave it alone. (Or in other words, if you try to do anything that way, you will not be doing philosophy.)'[30] The emphasis is not on success or failure, but on the spirit, the seriousness, which informs the enquiry.

There is something of an analogy here with the way in which Gauguin thinks of his moral obligations. These obligations do not inform his conception of what he has done; they are not constitutive of his perspective. On the contrary, the position they occupy is subordinate to the success or otherwise of his artistic endeavours. This is another way of saying that moral considerations do not go deep with him. In the case of studying philosophy, Rhees asks us to consider the following:

> Suppose someone said: 'I know you cannot do it really well without going the hard way. But I am going to achieve what I can in it – even though I cannot bring myself to go the hard way.'
> I do not find this hard to imagine; *mea culpa*.[31]

The necessity of the hard way is not that of a means which happens to lead to a goal specifiable independently of it. The hard way *is* the way of studying and living. In saying what he says, Gauguin is already outside *that* way. But it is not his moral failure alone which determines that. Williams recognises that a person may feel basic moral regret for what he has done, even though he would have to do the same if the circumstances repeated themselves. He has in mind those moral dilemmas where, whatever one does, one is going to hurt someone. But the same point can be made about basic moral regret in other circumstances: situations which limit what can be done; limitations of character which make certain moral possibilities unrealisable; circumstances in which life has dealt too harshly with a person.[32] Such situations are ignored by those moral theorists who think that the moral house can always be put in order. Yet, even the character that they unwittingly portray 'as he goes on his orderly way, needs to recognize . . . how much luck, good fortune, and external circumstances need to

favour him in order that he might enjoy his modicum of success'.[33]
So it is not failure which marks what may be thought of as
Gauguin's lack of moral seriousness. Even in the various failures I
have outlined, the outcomes, with all their limitations, are seen
under a moral aspect. What marks out Gauguin is the feature
which Williams makes central to his case: the absence of Gauguin's
mea culpa. His success, we are told, frees him from its necessity.
Contrast this with another who achieves greatness in his art.
Thomas Mann's Adrian Leverkühn[34] achieves great music by selling his soul to the Devil. But success does not make him immune
to moral considerations. So far from being glad of what he has
done, he goes mad.

Wittgenstein discusses a case with which it is instructive to
contrast Gauguin. Although Rhees says that moral problems are
unlike problems relating to success or failure in one's vocation, he
also recognises that 'such questions run into one another often'.[35]
The depth a moral problem has for a person will be shown *in* the
way these questions affect one another. Wittgenstein discussed a
case, suggested to him by Rhees, of 'the problem facing a man who
has come to the conclusion that he must either leave his wife or
abandon his work of cancer research'.[36] Rhees wrote down the
following recollections of Wittgenstein's comments a few hours
after their conversation:

> Such a man's attitude will vary at different times. Suppose I am
> his friend, and I say to him, 'Look, you've taken this girl out of
> her home, and now, by God, you've got to stick to her.' This
> would be called taking up an ethical attitude. He may reply, 'But
> what of suffering humanity? How can I abandon my research?'
> In saying this he may be making it easy for himself: he wants to
> carry out that work anyway (I may have reminded him that there
> are others who can carry it on if he gives up). And he may be
> inclined to view the effect on his wife relatively easily: 'It prob-
> ably won't be fatal for her. She'll get over it, probably marry
> again,' and so on. On the other hand it may not be this way. It
> may be that he has a deep love for her. And yet he may think
> that if he were to give up his work he would be no husband for
> her. That is his life, and if he gives that up he will drag her
> down. Here we may say that we have all the materials of a
> tragedy; and we could only say: 'Well, God help you.'

Whatever he finally does, the way things then turn out may

affect his attitude. He may say, 'Well, thank God I left her: it was better all around.' Or maybe, 'Thank God I stuck to her.' Or he may not be able to say 'thank God' at all, but just the opposite.[37]

Whatever the outcome, moral considerations are not subordinated to success as they are in Williams's example, although prospects of success may enter into the person's moral deliberations. Does Gauguin make it easy for himself? Does he want to do his work anyway? Of course, another person may not have the problem Wittgenstein discusses. Wittgenstein says, 'If he has, say, the Christian ethics, then he may say it is absolutely clear: he has got to stick to her come what may. And then his problem is different. It is: how to make the best of this situation, what he should do in order to be a decent husband in these greatly altered circumstances, and so forth. The question "Should I leave her or not?" is not a problem here.'[38] Wittgenstein says this is so because the person already has an ethics. In Williams's example, his Gauguin is going to leave come what may, and if he turns out to be a successful artist will have no basic moral regret about doing so. He does not have an ethics which prevents him from having a problem, since the problem he has is not a moral one. Moral considerations are not constitutive of his problem. For this reason, one *possible* judgement which can be made of Williams's Gauguin is that moral considerations do not go deep with him.

Williams can readily admit that his Gauguin is not faced with a moral dilemma or a moral problem. He can also admit that he is not faced by a temptation, that he is not repudiating one moral perspective for another. That Gauguin is not describable in any of these ways is an essential part of Williams's case. But can he admit the *possibility* of the depiction of Gauguin as someone for whom moral considerations do not go deep? I do not see that he can. There are two reasons for my thinking so. The first is that Williams seems opposed to those moral perspectives from within which the judgement of lack of depth comes.

Williams, quite rightly, does not want us to gloss over the fact that we often turn our backs on moral demands with little regret. We often put other considerations above moral considerations. But from the fact that this happens, it does not follow that a morality must be embraced which accommodates these facts by changing my idea of what is required of me. Of course, such a morality may be embraced and Williams may want to recommend it. But his recommendation would be one among others, not *the* rational product of reflection in moral philosophy. Let us examine Williams's recommendations with respect to third-person judgements of Gauguin's conduct.

According to Williams, since Gauguin gives a good to the world in his paintings, if we are glad to have them, we must salute the project which led to them and be glad that Gauguin put moral considerations in second place. But Williams has not earned the right to speak so confidently of what *'we'* have to say. There is nothing confused, for example, in being glad to have Gauguin's paintings while saying, at the same time, what a pity it was that he had to treat his family in such a grim way. For some, his treatment of his family will affect the way they see his paintings. Some will undoubtedly blame Gauguin for what he did, while others, regretting what he did, may not blame him, conscious as they are of how difficult such situations can be. What is to count as a moral possibility cannot be determined by an appeal to 'our common psychology' or 'the world we want'. These appeals depend on a commonality which does not exist. People will differ in what they think is important. As we have seen, from certain moral perspectives, Gauguin will be seen as someone for whom moral considerations do not go deep. In emphasising this, one need not advocate this view. But we need to protest against a moral philosophy which can give no account of it. What Williams has succeeded in doing is not to put moral considerations in their place, but to show the place they have for his Gauguin.

There is a second reason, however, why Williams would find it difficult to accommodate the moral reaction to Gauguin I have tried to elucidate. There are times when Williams speaks as though his philosophical project is more ambitious than anything I have mentioned so far. On the view I have in mind, Williams could not be content with recommending one moral view among others. This is because the more ambitious claim is that he is *showing what moral considerations already are for us.* He is not saying: be like Gauguin, but, rather: you are already like him. Even though we may not realise it, it seems, we give moral considerations a place in our lives similar to that which Gauguin gives them.

Once again, however, such matters cannot be determined with the degree of generality Williams seeks for. Let us consider the issue in the context of how a person stands to his own moral obligations. If it were suggested to some people that certain of these obligations should be put aside, they would respond by saying, 'I just can't do that.' Treating one's family in the grim way which Gauguin's decision involved, may constitute such a moral limit for many people. For others, it may not be such a limit. But, as Owen Flanagan admits, those who see a moral limit here are not going to be put off by the fact that others think differently. Their assessment is not going to be determined by 'how high or low we have in fact set our moral sights'. But Flanagan objects to this attitude by saying 'that deep-seated and widespread feelings cannot be irrelevant to our considered judgements of morality – that a reasonable moral conception should not be deeply psychologically unrealizable.'[39] But the man who says, 'I just can't do it' is not judging morality; if anything, morality is judging him. Williams, too, asks us not 'to evade the basic and connected questions of what one really wants the world to be like and what human dispositions are involved in its being like that' (p. 134). But from where is this Aristotelian question supposed to come? Our questions about what we want will, if they are morally serious, *already* be informed by moral considerations. Even so, they cannot be settled in the impersonal kind of language in which Williams presents them.

Admittedly, it would be odd if moral values were never realisable. One would wonder how human beings came to have a regard for them in the first place. But the cases we have discussed with reference to Rhees, Winch and Wittgenstein are not extravagant in that sense. On the contrary, they simply exhibit different moral possibilities and reactions from those we find in Williams's Gauguin.

Faced with circumstances similar to those which faced Gauguin, some will say, when tempted to cause grim distress to their families, 'I just can't do it.' If they find that, after all, they had it in them to do it, they may well feel the shame of having done so for the rest of their lives. This may be so even if they are convinced that the break had to be made. If, telling them the story of Gauguin, Williams were to say 'that if we believe in any other values at all, then it is likely that at some point we shall have reason to be glad that moral values . . . have been treated as one value among others, and not as unquestionably supreme' (p. 133), they may wonder what this has to do with how they see things. Causing the distress is something they simply cannot do, but not because of any philosophical view about which values are supreme. Alternatively, if they have caused the distress, the shame of having done so is something they simply cannot put aside. If others cannot understand them, they may think them guilty of what Kierkegaard called 'ethical forgetfulness'. The task of re-educating others about the nature of their moral stand will be rendered all the more difficult if philosophers come on the scene to tell them that, no matter what they think, their real attitude is one they share with Williams's Gauguin. In this way, moral philosophy can contribute to the decline of the possibility of certain moral stands.[40]

According to Williams, if luck is on Gauguin's side, he is someone who can put aside his moral obligations. On the other hand, if he is unsuccessful as a painter, he has to answer for his moral neglect, for the distress he has caused his family. Williams concludes, 'This is one way – only one of many – in which an agent's moral view of his life can depend on luck' (p. 134). In the collection *Moral Luck*, the revised version of the paper has a slightly different emphasis. There, Williams concludes that when we see the limits of morality's demands on us, we are left with 'a concept of morality, but one less important, certainly, than ours is usually taken to be; and that will not be ours, since one thing that is particularly important about ours is how important it is taken to be' (*Moral Luck*, p. 39).

If Williams is saying that there is a view of the importance of moral considerations which he wants to overthrow, then he is simply presenting and advocating a rival conception of moral considerations which we may or may not want to support. I suspect, however, that he wants to say that the view he opposes is a confused moralism. He would see his work as revealing this confusion and as an attempt to free those who are in its grip.

I am arguing that nothing Williams has said shows that the moral reactions I have instanced, which differ from his own, are in any way confused. Of course, they may be and are opposed, morally, from different points of view, but that is another matter. From the moral perspective I have in mind, if Williams's Gauguin can look back on the distress he has caused without thinking that he has a great deal to answer for, this shows that moral considerations do not go deep with him. For Williams, luck may allow Gauguin to give moral considerations concerning the distress he has caused, a secondary importance. On the opposing view, no one can be said to be that lucky.[41]

15

Some Limits to Moral Endeavour

I

The question of the ways in which moral considerations place limits on human action is one which can never be far away from central issues in moral philosophy. It is generally agreed that some account must be given of the limiting role of moral considerations, since, without one, one is left with a mere caricature of human action. That caricature would consist, roughly, of a picture of human action as the calculation of the most efficient means of attaining predetermined ends. Within this context, of course, there is legitimate talk of limits. If a man has a purpose in mind, the very character of that purpose rules certain means out of consideration. It does so, not only by showing that some means are more effective than others in securing the desired end, but also by circumscribing a certain area of relevance so that courses of action which fall outside it would not even arise for consideration. Thus, if what I want to do is to add to the money I have in the bank, various suggestions may be made to me. I may be told to leave it where it is, buy a business with it, invest it, gamble with it, or a thousand other things. People would differ over the effectiveness of the means proposed, but not anything could count as possible advice. If someone told me to give all I had away or to go for a long walk, I might take this as a way of telling me to forget the purpose I had in mind, but I could not take it as possible means of attaining that end.

Purposive activities must not be ignored in an account of human behaviour. It would be foolish to do so, since it is hard to see how one can speak of human activities as rational or irrational without ever mentioning the purposes of those activities and the means which lead to them. Seeing the bearing which one thing has on another is often a matter of seeing how one thing leads to another.

The point to stress, however, is that this is often, but not always, the case. This is why J. L. Stocks spoke of 'the limits of purpose'; he wanted to deny that purposive action exhausted the character of human actions. Indeed, if that were all there were to tell, things would be very different from what we know them to be.

If this were a complete account of human nature the world would be a very different place from what it actually is. If desire and its service were the whole of life there would be no fondness for places and buildings, no contemplative enjoyment of sights and sounds, no ties of affection and friendship, but only the continual grasping calculation of something to be got from men and things as they served a more or less transient need. The convenience of a utensil would be the highest form of praise.[1]

We know, however, that things are not like this; that there is such a thing as moral praise and blame; that there is a concern, not simply with working out the best ways of getting what we want, but with the character of our wants and the nature of our strivings to satisfy them. Here we have a limit placed on human action which is different in kind from the limits which our purposes place on the means we employ. The limits set by moral considerations constitute what Stocks calls 'an additional principle of discrimination', since more is taken into account than our purposes and the best ways of achieving them. When purpose and its execution have said all there is to say, there remains the question of whether such a course of action can be undertaken in the name of decency.

It is very tempting to minimise the differences between the limits which purpose imposes on action and those limits determined by moral considerations. It is tempting to suggest that morality is an additional guide to human conduct which gives men, not concerns which are different in kind, but purposes which are higher on the scale of human desires, purposes which constitute what a man really wants in the end. In this way, morality, like any other means, would be concerned with the attainment of human purposes and with removing or minimising any difficulties which stand in the way. I have been suggesting that this misrepresents the ways in which moral considerations place limits on human conduct. Peter Winch makes the same point in his inaugural lecture when he says that, of course, men try to attain goals and they encounter obstacles in their way: lack of money, lack of various kinds of natural ability, lack of friends, opposition by other men, to name just a few. But morality has nothing much to do with helping people to overcome any of these. On the contrary, were it not for morality, they would often be a great deal easier to overcome. . . . Morality, we are told, is a guide which helps him round his difficulty. But were it not for morality, there would be no difficulty!²

Moral considerations impose a limit on our purposes and their execution which the distinction between means and ends cannot account for, since means and ends alike come under moral scrutiny. Yet, in passing, it should be said that to say that such scrutiny imposes limits on our conduct, though correct, may mislead if talk of limits is conceived too narrowly. It may give the impression that moral considerations play a purely negative part, namely, that of preventing men from doing what they want to do and pronouncing vetoes from time to time on their plans and aspirations. While it is true that moral considerations limit our actions in this way, they also constitute a limit in another sense. To appreciate it, one must not think of the limit simply as a boundary which curtails expansion, but also as the boundary of a territory which has riches to offer to those who pass over into it which cannot be found elsewhere. If moral considerations condemn meanness, they also extol generosity; if they condemn lying, they have a regard for truthfulness. Generosity, truthfulness, kindness, loyalty, etc. are not mere negations or restrictions, but positive virtues and ideals in human life which for many make that life worth living. Morality is as much a discovery of the worthwhile as a condemnation of the worthless.

Instead of pursuing the above point further, I want to take a brief look at some recent accounts of the relations between moral considerations and human actions. I want to suggest that if there are dangers of presenting a caricature of human action if one neglects to take account of the limits imposed on it by moral considerations, there are also dangers of caricature involved in attempting to give an account of these limits. I shall take a brief look at three accounts presented in recent moral philosophy.³

II

According to the first account of moral values I want to consider, such values do constitute a limit on human actions. Moral values are the product of our commendations, evaluations and prescriptions. Men decide their ultimate moral principles and, in theory, anything could count as a moral principle. On the other hand, moral principles are also the product of reason and are therefore universalisable. Thus, we expect our moral judgements to win the assent of any reasonable man placed in similar circumstances. Granted that a fanatic could hold that one should be free to kill anyone one dislikes as long as he accords this right to anyone who wishes to kill him for the same reason, we do, nevertheless, call such a man a fanatic, and his kind make up a very small minority. Normally we find a general agreement in the things men prescribe because of an agreement in the kinds of things men want and need. Furthermore, the commendations and prescriptions which men make form a rough-and-ready hierarchy in their eyes. Moral maturity consists in recognising this hierarchy; recognising when one moral rule takes precedence over another; always being alive to circumstances which present exceptions to our present rules. To tell the truth blindly, without considering whether the principle applies to the given case, is the very antithesis of moral sensitivity. Thus, corresponding to a hierarchy in our purposes and methods of attainment, we have a hierarchy of commendations and prescriptions. The morally mature man not only puts aside his previous purposes when moral considerations demand that he should do so, but also puts aside some moral considerations in deference to others once he begins to appreciate the relations between moral rules and their exceptions. The discrimination of moral maturity is matched by its sincerity. The moral man's actions are as good as his word. What he believes is to be found in what he does; and failure to act in accordance with professed belief is generally a sign of insincerity.

In the second account I want to present to you, moral beliefs are not conceived as limits on human purposes. They cannot be so conceived since, according to this view, they constitute the best means of attaining those purposes. There are certain things which all men want, things which make up human good. Similarly there are things which all men want to avoid, things which make up human harm. Acting according to moral beliefs is the way to attain human good and to avoid human harm. A man needs the virtues in order to flourish just as a plant needs water in order to grow. Sometimes men do not realise this; they think they want other things. This is the case when men ignore moral considerations or disagree about them. Such disagreement and lack of attention are understandable, since the appreciation of what constitutes human good and harm often requires experience and imagination. Once all the facts were known, however, such shortsightedness and disagreement would be rectified, since the facts would reveal human good and harm. Since all men appeal to such facts in deciding what is good and bad, ideally, though often not realised in fact, moral values would commend themselves to all men in an agreed hierarchy of priorities.

The third account of moral beliefs I want to consider denies that alleged facts concerning human good and harm could somehow establish for us what is good and what is evil. On the contrary, it is argued, men come to have a regard for certain ways of doing things, come to extol a certain character in human actions and relationships, but this concern does not depend on anything external to itself which is meant to demonstrate its validity. Furthermore, no one thing can be accepted as a definition of such concern, since there is a complex of varied moral beliefs within most societies. Different institutions and movements are characterised by different ideals, different rights and obligations. On many occasions, not all the rights involved can be satisfied, not all the obligations can be fulfilled. What is important, however, it is argued, is that all the moral factors involved in the situation are considered. There will always be exceptions to rules which state that certain rights should be fulfilled or that certain obligations should be met. There is no exception to the rule that rights and obligations should be considered when they are involved in a situation in which a moral decision is called for. Given that such consideration has taken place, the people involved will recognise the procedure by which a decision is reached as being characteristic of a not uncommon moral wisdom. Within an institution such as the family, for example, decisions are accepted even when they do not satisfy all the rights involved. In this way, it is argued, the family is maintained as a moral community. Similarly, when the claims of a man's family conflict with the claims of his work, the decision which a man makes after due consideration and which is accepted, sustains the wider moral community of which family and work form a part. In this way, within something called the total moral community, a hierarchy of decisions can be agreed on and progress made.

What are we to say of these three accounts of the relations which are said to hold between moral beliefs on the one hand and human purposes and methods for attaining them on the other? They represent views which, though different in ways which it would be important to bring out in other contexts, can be said to have three characteristics in common, namely – order, progress and optimism. While they see that moral beliefs place limits on human conduct, they characterise those limits as ordered in some kind of hierarchy of importance, so that a man will know where his allegiance lies without too much difficulty.

I said at the outset that if moral considerations are left out of an account of human activities one has a mere caricature of those activities. Man is represented simply as calculating the best ways to get what he wants, whereas we know that he also cares about ideals, rights and obligations, with all that entails. Nevertheless, it is also possible to present a caricature of men's moral concerns, and I suggest that our three accounts have come close to doing so. We are asked to accept that men aim for certain things, but that above these considerations of efficiency and attainment are moral considerations to which the former must always be subordinated. The method and order of this subordination is something which reasonable men will agree about. Purposive activities afford the opportunity for a rich moral harvest, and if the reapers are few that is only because men lack experience and imagination and are sometimes mistaken about what they really want. Once these shortcomings are removed, moral considerations, already in a system of priorities, will bring order to the range of human desires. Thus ethics and rationality are made to coincide: the moral thing to do is also the reasonable thing to do. A man learns to put first things first, not only in his purposive activities, but in his moral concerns as well. Ideally, what is important in a man's life is seen in the orderly subjection of his purposes and methods of attainment to an already ordered set of moral values. These values are brought to bear on his actions as a hierarchical system which commends itself to him as being what he really wants or as the values of a community he wants to perpetuate. If the ideal were realised in practice, a man would go about his business choosing which goals he favours, which human relationships he enters into, which decisions he makes, all in accordance with his hierarchical system of moral beliefs. The picture is one of order, progress and optimism. It constitutes what I mean by the second caricature of human activity.

III

When we turn from these tidy philosophical accounts of the ways in which moral beliefs place limits on human actions to look at actual situations, do we not want to accuse these accounts of an over-simplification and falsification of the facts? If asked what accounts for these distortions, I think much of the answer would be found in the neglect of the sense in which I want to speak of the limits to moral endeavour. The sense I have in mind is not that in which moral considerations place limits on human actions, but that in which moral endeavour itself is often subjected to limits. The three accounts we have considered give little, if any, hint of these. On the contrary, they speak as if the subjection of human wants and desires to moral considerations were an orderly progressive procedure. But is this the case? Is there a blueprint by which a moral order, agreed on by everyone or almost everyone, is imposed on our activities? What is one to make of remorse, helplessness, the impossible good, the unanswerable difficulty, the restricted sphere of action, and countless other barriers to moral endeavour? These are what constitute the limits to moral endeavour, and when we take account of them, we begin to recognise the three outlines I have presented as attempts to account for moral considerations in human activities, but as caricatures of those activities nevertheless. This conclusion can be underlined by considering four contexts in which one would want to speak of limits to moral endeavour.

Since I have spoken of the first limit to moral endeavour I want to mention elsewhere, I shall not dwell on it for very long here.[4] I refer to moral dilemmas. If one accepts the reality of such dilemmas, one can see how the optimistic progressive picture of the relations between moral considerations and human conduct becomes less plausible. When one finds oneself in situations where, whatever one does, one is going to hurt someone, talk of arranging goods in an order of priority often seems out of place. The discovery of what is morally possible for one in such situations is not the elevation of a good in an order of priority such that once the order is established one does not have to worry about the lower reaches of the scale. On the contrary, as I have argued elsewhere, even after a person has decided what he must do in these situations, he may still feel remorse for having committed the evil which his decision inevitably involved. When one lies to save a friend further suffering despite the fact that one's whole relationship with him has been characterised by absolute straightforwardness and honesty; when one has to go against the wishes of parents who have sacrificed a great deal for one in deciding to marry a certain woman or to take up a certain job; when a man is forced to kill another person in order to save a child's life; talk about establishing an order of goods would be a vulgar falsification for many people. They did what they had to do, but they did not glory in it. In the cases I have mentioned, a trust in truthfulness has been betrayed, great sacrifice has been counted an insufficient reason, a life has been taken: all these are considered to be terrible, and the decisions which brought them about and had to be taken were terrible decisions nevertheless. It is essential to recognise that in moral dilemmas, the discovery of what must be done often involves one in evil, pain and suffering.

The above account of moral dilemmas is unacceptable to those who think that moral decisions establish or reflect an ordered hierarchical system of goods. It can be no part of the philosopher's intention to deny that there are such people, people who in one way or another can describe their activities as putting first things first. What can be said is that such people, from the very nature of the case, cannot be faced with dilemmas such as those I have described. For them, there are no such dilemmas. If they present philosophical accounts of moral endeavour which allow no place for these moral dilemmas, they can be accused of falsifying the facts and obscuring moral possibilities. Within the variety of moral attitudes and responses one finds the man who sees his life as the establishing of a moral order which reaches out for higher and higher achievements. One also finds the man who morally does not know where to turn, and in making his decisions hopes that he will not hurt too many people. One thanks God that he is getting better all the time; the other thanks God if he finds he is no worse. Philosophical accounts of moral endeavour must not deny the first his heights, but neither must they deny the second his limits. I have been insisting on the recognition of these limits by philosophers, and on the fact that moral decisions often carry with them measures of guilt almost equal to any good achieved.

In the moral dilemmas we have considered, the limits to moral endeavour come from the fact that not all the moral beliefs involved can be acted on. Yet, in resolving the dilemma a person discovers what he must do. In making his decision he discovers something about himself; he discovers what was possible for him. In the second context of some limits to moral endeavour I want to consider, however, there is often no difficulty in seeing what the outcome of a situation ought to be; no difficulty in appreciating what morality requires. The trouble is that all this is thwarted by the situations themselves; the situations themselves limit the possibilities of moral endeavour.

In William Faulkner's novel, *Sanctuary*, Benbow, a city lawyer, accidentally falls into the company of a group of liquor pedlars, one of whom, Popeye, is a killer. He has to spend a night in the company of these men. Later, when one of the gang is killed, Benbow has no doubt that Popeye has murdered him. The local leader of the liquor pedlars, Goodwin, is accused of the crime. Benbow feels that he must do something to help. After all, it was quite clear that Goodwin was being accused unjustly, that Popeye was going to get away with a murder, and that Goodwin's mistress and their ailing child needed his help and protection. He believes unquestioningly that he can help because he believes that justice and truth will prevail. When he fails to get Goodwin to testify against Popeye, he pursues his enquiries further until he persuades Temple, a college girl who witnessed the murder and who has since been abducted by the murderer, to give evidence. The results are disastrous. Temple gives false evidence which damns Goodwin who meets his death at the hands of an infuriated mob.

We might agree with Benbow that Goodwin was accused unjustly and that he ought to be acquitted; we might agree that Popeye was guilty and that he ought to pay for his crime; we might also agree that a false conviction would be disastrous for the accused's mistress and child. It seems to follow inevitably that something should be done about these things. But this conclusion does not follow. As we have seen, all Benbow's attempts at making things better, made things infinitely worse. What Benbow lacked was psychological insight into the character of the people with whom he was dealing. He was an outsider who did not appreciate the forces and counter-forces at work in the situation in which he found himself. To have psychological insight one must have a knowledge of men and the lives they lead. One must be acquainted with their different ideas of what is worthwhile in life and with how they would react to various circumstances. In short, one's knowledge must extend beyond one's immediate circles. Benbow's knowledge does not extend thus, and therefore he has no knowledge of the liquor pedlars who are social outcasts. He cannot appreciate their way of thinking, their sentiments and their fears. Goodwin knows how useless it would be to give evidence against Popeye. As soon as he did so his days would be numbered. One way or another Popeye would claim his revenge. This is what Benbow cannot understand. His thoughts are governed by ideas of justice prevailing and the security of the law. These ideas meant little to Goodwin. He had been in jail, struggled for existence, and risked his life many times. He knows that it is better to take his chance in a trial without saying a word about Popeye, than to ensure his own death by testifying against him. Benbow has no idea of the influence the murderer has had on the young college girl plunged into what for her was a world of nightmares.

No doubt Goodwin would have agreed with Benbow that justice, truth and fairness are fine things, but he might well have asked, 'What has that to do with the situation I find myself in?' Benbow failed to recognise the limits which the situation placed on the pursuance of his moral ideals. He was convinced that he ought to help, whereas he should have seen that there was little, if anything, he could have done to help.

I have emphasised one example in order to show that it is just as important to recognise that there are situations in which one should not try to help, as it is to recognise situations where help is called for. The conviction that one *must* help to relieve distress, and that it *must* be possible to help, is a tempting but mistaken doctrine. There are plenty of examples other than the one we have considered which illustrate this truth, but one more will suffice. A man may feel that he must try to help to keep his friend's marriage from breaking up. It might well be the case, however, that nothing can be done from the outside, that the difficulties are such that there is no solution to them. To interfere in such circumstances is usually to court disaster and to make matters worse than they were before. Once again, there may be no disagreement about the things one should strive for in marriage, or about what an ideal outcome of present difficulties would be. Nevertheless, it is recognised that, in the case in question, these things are not possible. The difficulties place limits on moral endeavour and limit the moral possibilities open to would-be helpers.

A persistent optimistic moral theorist would try to avoid the conclusions of this chapter, conclusions which he would find extremely distasteful. He might suggest that the realisation that nothing can be done to help in various situations is itself a moral realisation. Even if this is so, however, it can in no way obscure the limits to moral endeavour which those situations illustrate. Recognising that one can do nothing to help in certain situations may be the product of moral or psychological insight, but one could hardly call it a moral achievement. The insight in question, far from being a source of moral satisfaction, is one of the reasons for that sense of helplessness which sees that there are limits to moral endeavour, and that often the morally admirable action is simply not possible.

The third context in which some limits to moral endeavour can be found is related to the examples we have just considered. In those examples I referred to situations which limited the possibility of moral endeavour in various ways. In the examples I want to consider now, moral endeavour is limited, not by the situations in which it is called for, but by the people it is required of. We have just seen how mistaken it is to assume that in all situations where help is needed it makes sense to think of providing it; to assume that where morally satisfactory outcomes can be thought of abstractly, it must be possible to implement them in actual situations. It is equally mistaken to assume that if we can think of something morally finer and more admirable than we have attained, we should, if that description is correct, aim for those ideals. It is easy to accept that a man's attempts to be better may fail, but it is harder to see that sometimes a man should not try to be better. Yet, to recognise the third context of some limits to moral endeavour is to accept this conclusion. This can be shown by considering three examples.

A minister of religion may have no doubt that a fellow minister who works in the city slums has a deeper sense of vocation than himself. Let us assume that his judgement is correct. It certainly does not follow that he too should go to work in the slums. He knows only too well that if he did he would make a complete mess of things. He may also recognise that more often than not the question does not even arise for him; that his sense of vocation is not deep enough for such a commitment. He concludes, rightly, that it would be foolish of him to endeavour to be like his fellow minister. He accepts his limitations.

Or again, consider a married couple who start off their marriage with certain ideal conceptions of what married life ought to be like. They may know of marriages where these ideals are realised to a large extent. Very soon, however, they have to accept the fact that their marriage is not going to be like that. This does not mean that their relationship is devoid of any integrity, but it is not what they thought it might be. They conclude, rightly, that it would be foolish of them to try to emulate or seek after the kind of relationship they believe is deeper. They settle for less.

In Dostoyevsky's *A Nasty Story*, Ivan Ilyich Pralinsky is full of ideas of social reform and equality, although a sense of his own social superiority is never absent from his presentation of these ideas. One evening he discusses his views with a colleague and his superior in government service.

'And I persist in the idea, and put it forward on every occasion, that humanity, and specifically humanity to inferiors, of the official to the clerk, the clerk to the porter, the porter to the lowest peasant – humanity, I say, may serve, so to speak, as the corner-stone of the coming reforms and generally of our regenerated society. Why? Because. Take the syllogism: I am humane, therefore I am loved. I am loved, consequently they feel confidence. They feel confidence, consequently they believe in me; they believe in me, consequently they love me . . . no, what I mean to say is that if they believe in me, they will believe in the reforms as well, they will understand, so to speak, the very essence of the matter, so to speak, they will morally embrace one another and settle the whole thing amicably and fundamentally.'⁵

His colleague comments, 'We shan't be able to stand it', but Ivan does not understand what he means. On leaving his host and having to walk home Ivan passes the house of one of his minor clerks whose wedding supper is taking place. The scene is one of great merriment and jollity. Ivan sees a chance of putting his love of humanity into practice. He is sure that after an initial bewilderment and surprise at his arrival he will be welcomed as an example of the reformed society to come. In this spirit he enters the wedding-feast. The results are disastrous. The guests cannot forget his official status and are extremely uncomfortable in his presence. Champagne is brought to him although the household cannot afford it. Ivan realises that he is ruining the occasion. Later, when the party regains its liveliness, Ivan, eating and drinking too much, can see that his intrusion has been put down to drunkenness. His plans for preaching fellowship and equality are shattered and becoming drunker and drunker he is reduced to seeking reassurances that he has not disgraced himself. In the end he is so ill that he has to be put to bed. He is given the best bed, the bridal bed. Ivan is ill for eight days. When he returns to the office he cannot face anyone. He is relieved to find that the clerk has put in for a transfer to another department. Ivan's love of humanity is replaced by very different conclusions:

> 'No; severity, severity, nothing but severity!' he almost unconsciously whispered to himself, and suddenly his face was suffused with bright red. He felt ashamed and oppressed as he had never done in the most unbearable moments of his eight-day illness. 'I wasn't able to stand it!' he said to himself, sinking helplessly into his chair.[6]

No doubt in Dostoyevsky's story the social situation limits the possibilities of moral endeavour as much as do the limitations in Ivan's character. Nevertheless, the story does show how nasty the consequences can be sometimes when a man attempts to do what is morally beyond him or what is morally misconceived. I do not deny that others in Ivan's position might improve as a result of greater moral endeavour. The same point could be made of the other two examples I have mentioned. I am also taking for granted that self-deception is absent in these cases; that people are not appealing to assumed limitations in themselves to get out of doing what they could if only they tried. What I am insisting on is that people can come to the conclusion, rightly, that it would be foolish of them to try to be better than they are in certain respects. I am insisting that these pessimistic conclusions cannot be ruled out as signs of moral seriousness.

It may be argued that having given up trying to be better, people will no longer see any worth in the qualities and ideals they have failed to achieve. Cynicism may result from such failure, but it is not a necessary consequence of it. Pessimism about oneself is not incompatible with moral seriousness. This is difficult to accept if, like some moral philosophers, one holds that what a man believes to be decent is shown only in what he achieves. The unattainable good, for a serious person, is a constant comment on the little he has achieved. In the first example I considered, the minister of religion may see his fellow minister's sense of vocation as a judgement on his own. In that way, the life he admires becomes a source of humility in his own. The unattainable good, so far from being a moral irrelevance, is often, when recognised, the occasion for understanding, pity and compassion.

In many of the examples I have considered, it makes sense to say that but for certain limitations things might have been different. A lot of distress could be avoided if people had more moral or psychological insight. Things would be different in many relationships and vocations but for the limitations of the people involved. In the fourth and final context I want to consider, however, one cannot point to a limitation of character which accounts for things going in a certain way. I have in mind situations in which we say, 'They didn't stand a chance', 'Life became too difficult for them', 'Things went against them', where our reason for saying so is not any moral defect in those whom life has made its victims. I shall simply remind you of one striking example: Hardy's *Tess of the D'Urbervilles*. There is nothing in Tess's character which shows why she should end up being executed for murder. The interest of her parents in their likely descent from the D'Urbervilles, a noble family; the fact that she is sent to claim kin to a nearby family who had simply appropriated the D'Urberville name and is seduced by Alec D'Urberville; the early death of her illegitimate child: all these are things which happen to her despite herself. Her misfortunes continue when, after her marriage to Angel Clare, he cannot forgive her for what has happened, despite the fact that she has forgiven him a worse fault. Separated from her husband who leaves the country, her path crosses that of Alec D'Urberville again. After long persistence on his part and his assurances that her husband would never return, she agrees to live with him. Her sense of the wrong which has been done to her had made her indifferent to what happens to her in the future. When, however, Angel Clare does return, ready to admit that he has wronged her deeply, it is too much for her to bear. The course of her life seems to rise before her in mockery, and in anguished torment she kills Alec D'Urberville.

We want to say that life has been too cruel to Tess; that it was too much to expect anyone to bear. We have no hesitation in giving assent to Hardy's choice of subtitle, *A Pure Woman*. The limits which life placed on Tess's endeavours occasion the following reflections by Hardy early in the novel: 'Nature does not often say "See!" to her poor creature at a time when seeing can lead to happy doing; or reply "Here!" to a body's cry of "Where?" till the hide-and-seek has become an irksome, outworn game. We may wonder whether at the acme and summit of the human progress these anachronisms will be corrected by a finer intuition, a closer interaction of the social machinery than that which now jolts us round and along; but such completeness is not to be prophesied, or even conceived as possible'.[7]

There is something approaching an attempt at such completeness in the three theories in contemporary moral philosophy that I outlined earlier. They present a picture of ordered moral priorities and optimism. There is little indication of 'the social machinery which jolts us round and along'. I have sought to correct this picture by providing reminders of some limits to moral endeavour. It may well be true that where paying attention to moral considerations is concerned, the reapers are relatively few, but it should not be assumed that a readymade harvest awaits those who attempt to reap, that success inevitably crowns the endeavours of men of good will.

IV

In this chapter I have mentioned four contexts in which some limits to moral endeavour can be found: moral dilemmas, situations which limit what is morally possible, limitations in character which curtail moral endeavour, and circumstances in which life's burden has become too heavy for a person to bear. What if these contexts are ignored by moral philosophers and others who may write on such subjects? The consequences may be far-reaching. By ignoring such cases the very notion of moral endeavour has new limits set on it; the concept of moral endeavour is itself changed. One might want to say that ignoring such cases brings about a decline in our conceptions of moral endeavour. Yet, even without making any moral judgement one can speak of a limiting of our conceptions. If certain ways of regarding moral problems and difficulties are constantly ignored, misunderstood or misrepresented, those ways will sooner or later cease to be part of our conceptions of moral problems and difficulties. The contexts I have mentioned can be considered in the light of this conclusion.

If the kinds of moral dilemma I mentioned are not taken into account, people will fail to see why anyone should regard such dilemmas as tragic; why anyone should feel, even after arriving at a decision, acting on it and not wanting to repudiate it, that he still has blood on his hands. The idea of a dilemma would gradually change to what it has already become for some, namely, a question of establishing priorities among competing claims, and of going forward with confidence and without a backward glance once that priority has been established. To continue to feel remorse in such situations, it will be said, is to be in the grip of what some psychologists have condemned as 'unproductive guilt'. The moral house can always be put in order.

Consider what might happen in a society where, increasingly, the limitations of character and the situations which limit moral endeavour which I have mentioned are not recognised. It is probable that the idea that there must be a solution to every difficulty would become even more prevalent than it is already in certain circles today. If this were to happen, the very idea of what a difficulty is would have changed in important respects. Difficulties would now be regarded as signs that something had gone wrong, in much the same way as a flaw in a product shows that there is something wrong in the techniques of production. In a society where difficulties are thought of in this way, there is also likely to be much talk of 'success' in personal relationships, and many formulas offered to ensure such success. In such a context, it is not hard to see how friendship, for example, could become a commodity and the provision of it a skill. Even now a social worker can give the advice 'that it is the duty of a social worker to establish a relationship of friendship with her clients; but that she must never forget that her first duty is to the policy of the agency by which she is employed'.[8] It is also easy to see in such contexts how the cardinal sin would be a refusal to be helped, since this would be described as pride or anti-social behaviour.

Furthermore, in a society where 'success' is the key word, the notion of living with insuperable difficulties is likely to decline. This is seen most clearly in changing conceptions of marriage. I deliberately emphasise extreme cases. When marriage vows are thought of as eternal and unbreakable, difficulties, when they arise, must be met in terms of them and, if needs be, lived with despite the cost. When such difficulties are regarded as things to be helped, coped with, ironed out, their persistence might well be regarded as proof that an experiment in co-habitation has failed. The vows which once were eternal may become, as they have for some, the tentative terms of reference for a trial period.[9] Similarly, if success and achievement are emphasised to the exclusion of all else, a sense of tragic inevitability such as that depicted by Hardy is likely to diminish. Life can only be too difficult, it will be said, for those who fail to take advantage of the services and help at hand. It is not hard to see how such ideas would have a direct effect on what people think of pity and compassion.

The changes in moral beliefs I have noted are simply some of those one would expect if the ignoring of the limits to moral endeavour, already present in our society, became more widespread. It is not the task of a philosopher to make moral judgements on such changes. It is his task, however, to take account of the variety of moral beliefs people hold, since recognition of, or failure to recognise, this variety can affect one's understanding of the nature of moral beliefs. For example, emphasising this variety would be one way of bringing out the confusion involved in the fashionable practice of describing newly-acquired moral views as freedom from inhibition and the casting off of old taboos.

My complaint in this chapter has been that the varieties of moral endeavour have not been paid enough attention in contemporary theories of ethics. These theories have attempted to be altogether too tidy and all-embracing. The character they have unwittingly portrayed is that of a moderately decent man, fairly content and at home in his world, whose achievements are solid enough if not particularly inspired. Yet, even such a man, as he goes on his orderly way, needs to recognise more than he or his philosophical creators realise at the moment, namely, how much luck, good fortune and external circumstances need to favour him in order that he might enjoy his modicum of success. It might be argued that even where a man is favoured with freedom from the kind of limits to moral endeavour we have discussed in this paper, he needs to be aware of the possibility of such limits in order to understand the endeavours of others, and in order to have a proper sense of his own. There may come a time when moral ideas are such that this will no longer be true, but such a time has not come yet. Therefore, a conceptual analysis of the relations between moral considerations and human conduct must take account of the limits to moral endeavour. This chapter has tried to make a contribution to this end.

Hardy, referring to the limits which circumstances placed on Tess's moral endeavours, complains ironically that 'why so often the coarse appropriates the finer . . . the wrong man the woman, the wrong woman the man, many thousand years of analytical philosophy have failed to explain to our sense of order'.[10] Hardy, of course, was not looking for explanations. Any sense of order which would have been satisfied with one would be defective just for that reason. It is certainly not the task of philosophy to explain away the limits to moral endeavour, but to display them in all their variety and to bring out their character. I have suggested that philosophy itself has a responsibility in doing this, since, as I have tried to show, failure to do so can itself contribute to a limiting of our understanding of moral beliefs. Philosophy often speaks of things which have a reality independent of philosophy. This is certainly true of moral philosophy. Thus, limitations within philosophy can lead to limitations in our ideas of things which are outside philosophy, not least among them being our ideas of moral endeavour.

16

Self-Knowledge and Pessimism

To achieve self-knowledge, Ilham Dilman tells us, is to 'emerge from naivety, innocence, falsity, a purely habitual existence, or one in which we are largely what others expect us to be, to "become" authentic or true' (p. 205).[1] This knowledge of oneself is not there, readymade, waiting to be discovered. On the contrary, it can only emerge as a result of the development Dilman refers to. What he means by self-knowledge, however, is *more* than knowing the kind of person one is. He says, 'It goes beyond recognizing one's capacities, inclinations and vulnerabilities. It involves taking an attitude towards them and determining one's course in life' (p. 206). What does such an attitude and determination involve? First, it involves being realistic about oneself, about one's capacities and limitations, the claims of one's past, one's present commitments and one's future possibilities. Second, it involves a form of self-acceptance which is different from being resigned to what one is like:

> It is a recognition and acceptance of what are possibilities for one, as these are delimited by one's sex, the accidents of one's birth, one's early experiences, one's physical make-up, health and innate talents, the choices one has already made and commitments one has undertaken. To recognize and, if need be, to reconcile oneself to these, to develop one's interests within the limits set by them, to make one's own the obligations they create for one within the parameters of one's convictions, is for a person to accept himself (p. 207).

Dilman argues that self-knowledge does not develop in isolation from knowledge of others. He says 'one has to be able to relate to them as real people, capable of good and evil, with dreams of their own, ideals, ambitions, concerns and passions' (p. 210). In these

221

two contexts, knowledge of oneself and knowledge of others, Dilman asks whether 'self-knowledge is the prerogative of those we would call virtuous' (p. 211). I am not going to comment on the different cases he discusses, for example, his claim that a selfish person cannot be said to know himself. Rather, I want to comment on the way Dilman characterises the self-knowledge he admires and seems to advocate. He claims that 'a person's capacity to act as a fully intentional agent and take charge of his life and his capacity to know good and evil are interrelated' and that 'He comes to acquire these capacities in his relation to the moral norms which form part of the culture to which he belongs and in his relationships with other people. These relationships too are interrelated and, indeed, interdependent' (p. 213).

The overall impression I have in reading Dilman's paper is one of optimism. The person who has self-knowledge is said 'to take charge of his life'. As we have seen, Dilman emphasises the importance of realism, of being aware of one's capacities and limitations. He also speaks of being aware of the possibilities open to one, possibilities which are limited by a number of factors. He emphasises the importance of developing one's interests and facing one's obligations within these limits. Dilman does not give examples of what he has in mind, but the following occur naturally to one. If I have failed morally, in certain respects, over and over again, to think that one *further* failure would make no difference, is to deepen my self-deception. Again, moral failure in certain contexts, must not be dwelt on to the exclusion of those obligations I can fulfil in others. Yet again, my failures must not poison my capacity to rejoice in the success of others. In all these cases, and in others related to them, it is important that limitations do not become distorting influences. If this is the kind of thing Dilman means by saying that, despite one's limitations, one should take charge of one's life, develop one's interests, I have no philosophical quarrel with him.

Difficulties begin to arise when we notice what is missing from Dilman's paper. Despite referring to moral limitations, he seldom mentions *the price they exact*. His emphasis is very much on what we can achieve despite them. It is in this context, for example, that Dilman speaks of a person taking charge of his life. But when a person reflects on his limitations, he may find that he cannot speak of himself in this way. Coming to know himself has been, for him, deeply discouraging. When he looks at his relationship with others, his children, say, the record drives him to despair. I am not thinking, of course, of a person who couldn't care less about his children since, for such a person, there would be no despair. No, I am thinking of a person whose love for his children is precisely what has created the problem. These possibilities play little part in Dilman's deliberations. He emphasises, rightly, that love, caring, a regard for values, are the conditions which make moral achievement possible. What he does not pay anything like enough attention to is that love, caring, a regard for values, are *also* the conditions which make possible moral censure and despair. Again, I want to insist that the difficulties I have in mind are created by caring, not by the lack of it. Dilman has a tendency to speak of love and caring as means of coping with difficulties, but says little of them as the creator and source of difficulties in human lives. Again I do not mean difficulties created by someone loving in a way he ought not to love. I have in mind difficulties created by the ways in which people *do* love. The deeper the love, the deeper the difficulties may be. Love can be wonderful, but it can also be terrible, where the terribleness is not something apart from the wonder of it. Failure in this context does not excuse one from doing what one can elsewhere in one's life. But the achievements may not be seen as compensation for the failure. The failure may be such that a person would not dream of speaking of his being in charge of his life. He knows himself too well to speak in this way. Dilman, on the other hand, argues that to know oneself *is* to be in charge of one's life. There seems to be no justification for saying this.

There is one way in which Dilman might try to keep his thesis intact. He might argue that autonomy and control of one's life are achieved by knowing what one is like. That being so, whatever one comes to know, one has, by doing so, achieved autonomy and control. The trouble is that Dilman's thesis has now become tautological. It still takes no account of *what* one comes to know, and the effect this may have in one's life. The price of knowledge may be high. In parenthesis, it must be said that the view that a person is *always* better off if he sees what he really is, cannot be sustained. A person's delusions about himself may, in certain circumstances, be sustained by those who are convinced that he would be utterly destroyed by the truth.

If one is deeply discouraged about what is central in one's life, one can be said to be discouraged about the way most of one's life has gone. In such circumstances, it would be even more strained to speak of autonomy or of being in charge of one's life. Yet, one would have come to self-knowledge. As a result, a person may become resigned to his failures, recognising that nothing can be done.

It is unclear whether Dilman will allow this conclusion. He seems reluctant to allow that moral pessimism may be the fruit of self-knowledge. Perhaps this is because Dilman thinks that resignation to what one is like is a form of bad faith – *pace* Sartre (see p. 207). He contrasts resignation with self-acceptance. By the latter he means 'recognition and acceptance of what are possibilities for one' (p. 207). But what if, in certain respects, *there are no possibilities*? A person, seeing how he is, and how the others involved are, comes to the conclusion that *nothing* can be done. The knowledge makes him deeply pessimistic. Other things in his life, his religion maybe, may sustain him in his pessimism, but they need not revise it. He sees that in some respects he is not going to change.

Dilman may think that these conclusions have unwarranted metaphysical implications. If a person says that he *cannot* change, it may seem to Dilman that he is claiming to have access to something called 'the essence' of his self. This 'essence' shows that certain possibilities are ruled out. But Dilman has argued that the notion of such an essence is confused. He says, 'there is no such pre-existent self, nor any pre-formed pattern particular to a person, pre-dating him as an individual' (p. 205). If the person who says that, in certain respects, he cannot change, or that nothing can be done, *were* making any such philosophical appeal, Dilman would be right to point out his confusion. But why on earth should we suppose that a philosophical appeal is being made? He is making remarks we are well acquainted with in the normal course of human life. Surely, it is *our* philosophical assumptions which are leading us astray if we want to deny or explain away these ordinary reactions. In fact, we may be in the grip of the very philosophical assumptions we attributed to the speaker. We are assuming that the ordinary use of 'I cannot change', 'I don't have it in me', 'There's nothing to be done', *could* only have sense if there *were* the kind of essence of the self to which Dilman is objecting!

The person who says he cannot change may say so with *good reason*. After all, he has tried again and again, but the catastrophic results cannot be denied. If someone, despite this record, says, 'He can change' or 'There is always the possibility of change', the *a priori* tendency seems to be on his side, since he seems to need *no reason* for his reaction. If it is said that if a person changes, his claim that he could not change will have been shown to be wrong, it can also be said that, if he does not change, his claim will have been shown to be right. If, outside any such context, someone says, 'It is *always* possible for someone to change', what sort of thesis is that? If not overtly metaphysical, it is certainly abstracted from the realities of the life of the person about whom the remark is made.

In certain circumstances, the remark, 'You can do it if you want to' may be used as a kind of encouraging slogan. Sometimes the words of encouragement themselves help to create the conditions which make improvement possible. We say, in that event, that a little encouragement goes a long way. It would be foolish to deny such cases. It would be equally foolish, however, to think that such a remark could have application in all circumstances. In some it would be romantically indulgent or pretty silly. For example, think of circumstances where, though a father loves his children deeply, the very love he is capable of is what creates difficulties. He sees that his love is destroying his children and his marriage. Dilman admits that commitments make more determinate the directions in which a man can find authenticity. But the *same* commitments may also make more determinate the directions in which it *cannot* be found. Dilman fails to recognise this because he continues to link 'authenticity' with 'taking charge of one's life', 'being in control of one's life' and 'determining the course of one's life'. To say to the man I have described, 'Keep on trying. You can do it', is silly and indulgent. It trivialises the harm that he sees he is causing others.

In a further paper, 'Self-Knowledge and the Possibility of Change'[2] in which Dilman tries to meet some of these objections, he wants to insist that in face of moral pessimism or even despair, one should always say, 'Keep on trying'. His reasons for this insistence seem to me to be confused. I shall comment on the ones which have a direct bearing on my arguments. Dilman denies that he is optimistic in the way I have described. But he says of the man who is deeply pessimistic about certain relationships, that telling him that he can change is a reminder to him. What kind of reminder? Dilman argues that 'an unfavourable prognosis is only an unfavourable prognosis; where human life is concerned the possibility of change cannot be finally ruled out'. But this is not an expression of optimism. It says: even when you can see no ground for hope, you should not despair. In any case, a person may give up his desire to change and find that he has changed in a way that had never entered his mind before. There may be certain things in one's past, for instance, which can never be undone. But one may find a way of bearing them without going to pieces. One may indeed. I would not dream of denying this possibility. But why does Dilman deny examples where his account would be grotesque? The father who sees that his love is destroying his children and his marriage may come to the conclusion that he has to leave them, leave the family that means everything to him. He says that he *has* to withdraw, although he may go to pieces as a result. I think it is morally and philosophically presumptuous to say to such a man: 'even when you can see no ground for hope, you should not despair'.

Dilman wants to revise the language of my arguments: 'Phillips would say: "He saw the record of his past failures and this made him see – in the proper sense applicable here, an inductive one – that there was no way ahead for him, that he could not, or would not ever change." I would put it differently: "He could not see a way ahead for him, he lost all hope of changing, and he gave up"'. Whatever Dilman is putting differently, it is not what I said. The judgement a person may come to, regarding what is possible for him, is not based on inductive arguments. Because he does not appreciate this, Dilman sees such a person as arriving at 'a counsel of despair [which] goes well beyond what knowledge of his own past justifies'. The judgement I am talking about is different. The person does not speculate, abstractly, 'How can I ever know that the fact that I have done something a number of times gives me reason for thinking that I shall keep doing it?' Rather, he may react to what he has done with disgust, disgust at what it shows about him. He faces the fact that he has it in him to do these things; a realisation which may include acceptance of the likelihood of his doing so again. Think of a child molester who comes to these conclusions. He kills himself, determined that no other children shall become his victims. Dilman has to deny that such a person has achieved self-knowledge. This is because he thinks that self-knowledge 'involves authenticity, emotional learning and growth, and that includes the resolution of inner conflicts, the achievement of greater unity of self'. If we have either to deny such examples or deny Dilman's definition, is it not clear that it is the definition that has to go? Dilman claims that 'coming to see the catalogue of one's failures without understanding the inner conflicts which lie at their source, and so without being able to work through them, is *not* coming to self-knowledge'. What he never acknowledges is the possibility of a person coming to see his inner conflicts and concluding that they *cannot* be worked through. In short, Dilman fails to recognise that despair, with respect to some things, *is* a form of moral self-knowledge. Elsewhere, Dilman wrote and repeats here: 'There is nothing final about failure. If one cannot make a go of what one has tried time and again, one can at least turn in a different direction, succeed at something else, learn to accept and live with failure.'[3] But contrast the tenor of those remarks with the following:

'I shall never be any better in music, I can see now that I shall never be a musician.' 'Well, you'll have to take up something else.'

But: 'I just never get any better (morally). With every failure, I have found the courage to go on only with the thought that by trying I shall gradually get better. And I have only to look at the record now, to know that I never shall.' Well? Tell him to take up something else?

'If you're not a first-rate teacher, then you'll just have to learn to live with the fact that you are a second-rate or a third-rate teacher.'

'If you find that you just are never going to be decent, even to the people that you love, then you'll just have to . . .' Hell.[4]

The emphasis in much of what Dilman has said is on what an individual can achieve: autonomy, self-control, self-knowledge and the rest. If we are not careful, the contexts in which we engage with others will be seen as mere means for this personal achievement. The harm often caused to others as a result of one's moral endeavours, cannot be seen simply as the occasion on which an individual strives for autonomy. Neither can he be urged to keep on trying, or to try something else, as though that harm has no price to exact. Aware of what he has done, a person may have to withdraw from what he cares for most. To speak of such a withdrawal in terms of his being reconciled to his limitations, of developing new interests within these parameters, and determining the course of his life, may often be sadly misplaced.

If we accept these conclusions, we can see that Dilman has failed to establish internal relations between 'self-knowledge', 'autonomy', 'being in control of one's life', 'determining the course of one's life' and 'acceptance of one's life'. There is more than one reason for this failure. I have simply drawn attention to what I take to be one of the more obvious reasons: Dilman's neglect of possible connections between self-knowledge and pessimism. To make up for this neglect, he would have to pay attention to possibilities he ignores; differences in the relations in which people stand to their moral subjects. Dilman, at times, seems to say: 'If the subject has failed you, change it'. But some people cannot act in this way. The subject absorbs them. Their concern is not with the fact that the subject has failed them, but with the fact that they have failed the subject. They may judge themselves in the light of this failure. Indeed, if the failure is serious enough, their judgement on themselves may be a kind of last judgement, one which cannot be deflected by advice to regard it as the last judgement but one.

17

My Neighbour and My Neighbours

In his excellent collection, *Trying to Make Sense*, Peter Winch juxtaposes two papers, 'Eine Einstellung zur Seele' and 'Who is My Neighbour?'.[1] In the former, he discusses what is involved in Wittgenstein's remark, 'My attitude toward him is an attitude towards a soul. I am not of the *opinion* that he has a soul' (*Investigations* II, iv). In the second, he discusses the reaction of the Good Samaritan to the man who had fallen among thieves. Winch argues that what Wittgenstein says about an attitude towards a soul throws considerable light on the Samaritan's reaction. But what exactly does this involve? The more carefully we try to answer this question, the more doubtful Winch's claim becomes. In fact, one may conclude that very little light is shed on the Samaritan's reaction by Wittgenstein's notion of an attitude towards a soul. That is the conclusion for which I shall argue in this paper.

I

There are countless questions I may have reason to ask concerning people who surround me in different circumstances, every day of my life. I may wonder whether a person in a cluster of people walking towards me, is the one I have come to meet. I may wonder whether the people walking in the same direction as myself are going to the same meeting as I am. I may wonder how many in a crowd are supporters of a visiting team. And so we could go on for example after example. But among these examples, there is one I do not expect to come across, unless a special context is provided: I do not expect to hear of someone wondering, in the kinds of situation I have described, whether the beings who surround him are human beings. As with the rest of us, the question simply does not arise for him. We do not question the fact that we live in a

229

human neighbourhood. We do not entertain the possibility that we are surrounded by automata. It was the obviousness of all this that Wittgenstein tried to capture in his remark.

Once we ask what this obviousness amounts to, the matter can seem extremely puzzling. It has certainly seemed so to me. There seems to be an obvious generality involved in our attitude to others as human beings, but it is not at all easy to say what this generality amounts to.

Part of the difficulty surrounds the use of 'attitude' in 'my attitude to others as human beings'. Sometimes, we use the word 'attitude' as we use 'belief'. Wittgenstein gives the following example: 'I tell someone I am in pain. His attitude to me will be that of belief, disbelief; suspicion; and so on' (*Investigations* I, 310). Here the different attitudes we display on particular occasions, take the form of belief and disbelief. But, clearly, this use of 'attitude' is to be contrasted with Wittgenstein's use when he speaks of his attitude towards a soul, his attitude to another as a human being. This latter attitude, unlike our attitudes to pain, is not entertained on some occasions and not others. It is tempting to conclude, therefore, that the latter attitude is more general than our attitudes to people's pains. In fact, it *is* more general, but what does the greater generality consist in? What Wittgenstein is saying is that it is not a more general form of *belief*: he is not of the *opinion* that the other has a soul.

In the context of our attitude to others as human beings, the use of 'attitude' is being contrasted with our use of 'belief'. This attitude is immediate and unreflective. But how is it related to beliefs? Is it a generalisation from particular beliefs? If it were, it should make sense to say that someone behaved as a human being on one occasion, but behaved like an automaton on all other occasions, whereas such a supposition is clearly meaningless. As an alternative view, we might think that our attitude to others as human beings is a summation of our particular beliefs. But that won't do either, since the implication would be that our attitude to others as human beings is more doubtful than the particular beliefs. But the attitude to others as human beings, so far from being doubtful, seems beyond the reach of doubt; it cannot be doubted. The attitude is not a hypothesis, not a belief, but shows itself in all our varied dealings with other people. But, then, what *is* this attitude? Is it a specific view which everyone shares? What *kind* of consensus are we talking about? Winch's answer is to say that it is one bound up with certain expectations with respect to each other that we can take for granted:

> We may for instance notice at once that someone in the street is joyful or distressed; and we have our expectations concerning their likely behaviour, at least to the extent that many things would astonish us. We should be aghast if someone were deliberately to approach a stranger and gouge out his eyes. But such recognitions and expectations, together with our own reactions to other people are on the same level, equally primitive. That is not to deny that often our reactions *are* based on reflections about others' states of mind or probable future behaviour. The point is, first, that it is not always so; and second, that our *un*reflective reactions are part of the primitive material out of which our concept of a human person is formed and which makes more sophisticated reflections possible (*ES*, p. 147).

By calling these unreflective reactions and expectations an attitude, there is a danger of thinking of them as something we could adopt or drop at will. Clearly, this is not the case. Winch asks us to consider the following example:

> Suppose you and I are present when a man is being given some terrible news – the death of someone he loves perhaps. I say 'Poor man! How he will suffer' and you ask, 'What makes you think he will suffer?' That would be a strange question and I should most naturally assume at first that you had not grasped the situation, did not realize what was going on, what he was being told, etc . . . At this point I am perilously close to formulating a syllogism: 'All men suffer at such news. This is a man hearing such news. Therefore . . .' (*ES*, pp. 151–2).

But Winch says that the real generality lies, not here, but elsewhere:

> The real generality in the present instance is that my reaction to the man I see receiving bad news is a typical, characteristic, constantly repeated feature of the human life in which I share . . . It is in the context of a shared life involving such a

consensus that our *Einstellungen* towards each other can be understood in the way they are. That does not *justify* them, but it does provide the conditions under which they can be called *intelligible* (*ES*, pp. 152–3).

The attitude towards others as human beings, then, cannot be taken up and dropped at will. It has its sense, shows itself, in the consensus of expectations in our dealings with each other that we can take for granted. What lies outside this consensus, Winch argues, is not an alternative attitude, but horror or madness. The horror to be located there is the point of Swift's *A Modest Proposal*. The madness to be located there is depicted by Swift by recounting Gulliver's experiences with the Yahoos and the Houyhnhnms. Gulliver is pursued, with lustful intent, by a female Yahoo. Winch says of Gulliver's reaction to this humanoid creature:

> His hysterically horrified flight registers the conflict between the *necessity* and the *impossibility* of acknowledging his own common humanity with one of these depraved creatures (*WN*, p. 165).

As for the Houyhnhnms, who are supposed to be completely rational, it is impossible to treat these horses seriously. Winch concludes:

> We should remember that the upshot of the combined influence of Yahoos and Houyhnhnms on Gulliver was years of madness after he left their country. I think Swift knew what he was doing when he ended his story like that (*WN*, p. 165).

In the general attitude to other human beings, the object of the attitude is not in doubt. We do not ask whether these beings are human beings.

As a further example of this lack of doubt, Winch mentions our unhesitating response to Jesus's question in the Parable of the Good Samaritan. We are in no doubt as to who acted as a neighbour, or as to the neighbour who was the object of his compassion. The Samaritan reacts to a fellow being. Who could doubt it? Winch wants to say of all the reactions to human beings we have considered:

> In all these cases, the situation is not that I first recognise my common humanity with others and that this recognition then

provides the intellectual justification of my response to certain modalities in my dealings with them. On the contrary, it is a recognition which is itself a function of these responses. . . . It is the point Wittgenstein is succinctly making in his remark: 'My attitude towards him is an attitude towards a soul. I am not of the *opinion* that he has a soul' (*WN*, p. 165).

So far I have done little more than rehearse what I take to be the main points of Winch's stimulating discussion. But I find the discussion puzzling in certain respects that I want to try to bring out. It seems to me that too many *different* examples are run together under the designation, 'our attitude to others as human beings'. Winch is right in emphasising that this attitude involves a general consensus, one we can take for granted. The difficulty is in seeing how this insight can be applied, in the way Winch thinks it can be, to certain moral reactions to other human beings, and, in particular, to the response of the Good Samaritan.

II

We have noted certain characteristics of our attitude to others as human beings which, according to Winch, are essential features of it. It is an attitude which shows itself in responses and expectations with respect to others which we can take for granted. We do not have these responses and expectations because we first believe that others are human beings. Rather, the very possibility of our concept of a human being is formed in these responses and expectations. For me, difficulties begin to emerge with Winch's claim that some of these responses and expectations are moral. He says:

My central point is that in questions concerning our under-standing of each other, our *moral* sensibility is indeed an aspect of our *sensibility*, of the way we see things, of what we make of the world we are living in (*WN*, p. 166).

By saying that our moral sensibility is an *aspect* of our sensibility, Winch is clearly recognising that the two are not equivalent or co-extensive. The difficulty comes when we discuss specific moral reactions and argue that these are constitutive of our attitude to others as human beings. If we can say of them what Wittgenstein says about 'an attitude towards a soul', these moral reactions should be beyond doubt, something we can take for granted. Winch's talk of *our* moral sensibility encourages us to think in that way about them.

Winch wants to say that certain moral reactions are primitive reactions, carrying with them equally primitive expectations. But the examples he provides are mixed and cannot be treated in the same way. On the one hand, there are examples concerning expectations with regard to human beings which we can take for granted. If I am told that someone has lost someone he loves, I know he will suffer. If I see someone hit himself with a hammer, I know he will feel pain. But if we put alongside these examples, as Winch does, the pity we may well feel in such circumstances, there is an obvious difference: it cannot be taken for granted. Once we remind ourselves of this obvious fact, we are faced with the question of whether such pity can be called 'an attitude towards a soul' in Wittgenstein's sense of that expression.

We will be encouraged to make a simple equation between pity towards others and 'an attitude towards a soul' if, like Winch, we tend to concentrate on our sympathetic reactions to others. He admits that our reactions to others are varied, but this is usually done in passing or in parentheses. For example, after saying that one natural expression on hearing someone receiving bad news is to say, 'Poor man! How he will suffer!', Winch says: It is in the context of relationships involving such expressions (amongst numberless others of course) that we understand what suffering is (*ES*, p. 153).

Note again, that as with Winch's talk of *our* moral sensibility, here, too, there is an emphasis on the way *we* understand what suffering is. But what if we remind ourselves of the numberless other expressions in face of suffering which Winch mentions in passing? In 1931, Wittgenstein wrote:

Nobody likes being confronted by a wounded spaniel. Remember that. It is much easier patiently – and tolerantly[2] – to avoid the person you have injured than to approach him as a friend. You need courage for that.[3]

One way of discouraging a one-sided diet of examples, in this context, is to put alongside each other sympathetic and unsympathetic responses to others as human beings which seem equally primitive. It is instructive to juxtapose Winch's examples with some of Swift's verses from his *Verses on the Death of Dr Swift*.

First, here is Winch describing one reaction to someone in pain:

> If for instance I see another person accidentally strike his thumb a heavy blow with a hammer, *I* will wince, cry out and clutch my thumb. I have not learned to do this, neither do I do it as the result of reflection on the pain my companion is in. It is itself *an expression* of my recognition of the pain he is in (*WN*, p. 163).

And now, these verses from Swift:

> Dear honest Ned is in the Gout
> Lies rackt with Pain, and you without:
> How patiently you hear him groan!
> How glad the case is not your own!

Can it not be said that this response, too, is not learned; that it is not the result of reflection on honest Ned's pain; and that it is itself *an expression* of the recognition of the pain Ned is in? Winch, of course, does not deny the possibility of knowing that someone is in pain without pitying him. He insists, however, that the place occupied in our understanding by such responses as 'Poor man! How he will suffer!' 'does mean that one cannot (unless a very special context is supplied) ask why the fact that someone is suffering should be a reason for pitying him' (*ES*, p. 153). But can it not be said that the place occupied by the relief, expressed in Swift's verses, in our understanding is such that we cannot (unless a very special context is supplied) ask why the fact that someone is suffering should be a reason for feeling relief that the suffering is not one's own?

The same can be said of Winch's other examples. Undoubtedly, we think people suffer at the death of friends. But, even in this context, primitive reactions vary enormously, if only because 'friendship' is not itself one thing. Since deep friendships are the exception rather than the rule, rare rather than common, it is hardly surprising that we recognise other natural responses that Swift brings to our attention:

> My female friends, whose tender Hearts
> Have better learn'd to Act their Parts
> Receive the News in *doleful Dumps*,
> The Dean is dead, (and what is Trumps?)

Swift goes on to ask:

> Why do we grieve that Friends should dye?
> No loss more easy to supply.
> One Year is past; a different Scene;
> No further mention of the Dean;
> Who now, alas, no more is mist,
> Than, if he never did exist.

Once we move outside the context of friendship, there are, of course, plenty of examples of primitive, unsympathetic responses to other human beings. Swift records responses to a poet's success, responses not unknown in academic and other circles:

> What Poet would not grieve to see,
> His Brethren write as well as he?
> But rather than they should excel,
> He'd wish his Rivals all in Hell.

We recall the reactions in Tolstoy's *The Death of Ivan Ilych* to the death of Ivan. Tolstoy says:

> besides considerations as to the possible transfers and promotions likely to result from Ivan Ilych's death, the mere fact of the death of a near acquaintance aroused, *as usual*, in all who heard of it the complacent feeling that it is he who is dead and not I.[4]

Swift's verses are meant to illustrate Rochefoucault's maxim: 'In the adversity of our best friends, we find something that doth not displease us.' Swift comments:

> As Rochefoucault his Maxims drew
> From Nature, I believe 'em true:
> They argue no corrupted Mind
> In him; the Fault is in Mankind.

Can we not apply Winch's words which we have already quoted, to the cases Swift draws to our attention?

> The real generality in the present instance is that [the reactions Swift outlines in relation to human fortune and misfortune, are] typical, characteristic, constantly repeated features of the human life in which I share.

Faced with these very different examples, we are tempted to start speculating on which, among them, are to be included in 'my attitude towards a soul'. Are we going to include only those reactions which can be taken for granted? We may think this is what we should do, since the 'attitude' is said to be beyond question, something about which no doubts are raised. In that event, however, my attitude towards a soul will include a very limited range of cases. We can take for granted that a man will suffer after hearing bad news, or that a man will feel pain if he hits himself with a hammer. Also pitying responses to suffering, on this view, will *not* be included in my attitude towards a soul, since, as we have seen, they cannot be taken for granted. My response to pity may be relief that I am free of it. The same can be said of the other cases we have considered. According to the view we are considering, they will be excluded from an attitude towards a soul.

On the other hand, it may be said, what we should be emphasising is not that my attitude towards a soul is something which can be taken for granted, but, rather, that this attitude is immediate and unreflective. The reactions involved are primitive reactions. But, then, noting how different these reactions are, we may be tempted to say that there are *many* attitudes towards souls involved. Indeed, someone may argue, it is positively misleading to speak of *our* attitude towards a soul or *our* attitude towards human beings, since there is no such thing. It implies a consensus where none exists. All we have are different attitudes towards human beings. It is interesting to note that, whereas Wittgenstein speaks of 'Eine Einstellung zur Seele', Winch refers to the responses he discusses as constituting a consensus in terms of which our *Einstellungen* towards each other are to be understood.

This would seem to give us a short way out of our difficulties, but the impression does not last for long. All we have to do is to think of the different responses we have discussed and note that they are all responses to human beings. In fact, to speak of 'noting' is odd, because no such activity is required. The matter is obvious. The question of whether the creatures we are responding to are human beings simply does not arise. We do not consider the possibility that we are responding to automata or some creatures of another kind. The obviousness of the fact that I am responding to a human being brings us back to the question of what is involved in Wittgenstein's remark that he is not of the *opinion* that the other is a human being. What is the nature of the obviousness that Wittgenstein is referring to?

Before suggesting an answer to this question, one ought to consider a preliminary objection. Someone may say that the different reactions I have considered are not all on the same level with respect to their relation to my attitude to the other as a soul. The responses Winch discusses, it may be claimed, are related to the attitude differently from the ones Swift mentions and enjoy a different logical status. The unsympathetic reactions are distortions of the sympathetic ones, and can only be appreciated in the light of them. Swift, after all, we are reminded, is not simply describing, he is satirising.

Given a priority to moral responses, these conclusions cannot be denied, but that priority cannot be taken for granted. Moral teaching may exhort us to give some of our reactions a priority, but the reactions themselves, sympathetic and unsympathetic, seem equally primitive. The latter are not parasitic on the others. For example, Winch emphasises pity as the conviction that someone is in pain. But is not recoiling also such a conviction? Moving away seems as primitive a reaction as moving towards, where pain is concerned. Primitive reactions to danger are also varied. Some will run to help someone in danger, while others will run away. An ambivalence in reacting seems equally primitive in this context. Think of someone running towards, checking, then moving forwards and backwards from someone in danger. All these reactions can be found in animals. If these reactions are equally primitive, it cannot be argued that only the sympathetic ones among them are involved in what is meant by an attitude towards a soul.

We seem, then, to be faced with a puzzle: what constitutes my attitude to the other as a human being? But isn't the puzzle one of our own making? By thinking that this attitude is a substantive one, one which can be distinguished from others, we get into the difficulties we have encountered when we try to determine its content. But my attitude towards another as a human being is not in *this* sense a substantive attitude at all. In that case, what is the attitude I have to the other which is not a general belief or hypothesis?

'That's a human being' is related to the diverse primitive responses we have noted in a way akin to that in which 'Physical objects exist' is related to our primitive reactions in physical surroundings. We do not sit on chairs, sit at tables, climb stairs, pick up objects, reach for objects, avoid obstacles, because we *first* believe in the existence of physical objects. Rather our conviction, our certainty, that physical objects exist has its sense in this context. They are the contextual surroundings which hold the conviction fast. Thus, if someone wanted to raise the possibility that physical objects do not exist, we would not know what to make of him, since he, though raising the possibility, would exhibit the same primitive reactions as ourselves.

In the same way, we do not react to others in the diverse ways we noted because we first believe in the existence of human beings. Rather, our conviction that the others are human beings is held fast by, and has its sense in the context of, the diverse reactions we have discussed. We would not know what to make of someone who suggested that the creatures we react to might not be human beings, since he, though raising the question, would himself exhibit characteristic reactions towards them.

Winch, of course, would not dispute this conclusion. The puzzles and difficulties his discussion created for me come from his concentration on *some* of our primitive reactions rather than others. The question then arises of how much light is thrown on *these* reactions by the conviction that the other is a human being. Winch is quite right to say that pity may be immediate and unreflective. But so can recoil from the suffering of another. Winch is quite right to say that our conception of a human being is determined *in certain respects* by the pity we feel, but the same can be said of the recoiling. Also, when some see others recoil or they see them pity, neither are in doubt that the responses are to human beings. The question, then, is how much light is thrown on the *distinctive* reaction by invoking our certainty that the others are human beings. Further, as yet we have not asked whether the reaction of the Samaritan to the man who fell among thieves *is* the kind of primitive reaction we have been discussing. Even if, for the moment, we assume that it is, further difficulties arise if we equate such a response with what Wittgenstein meant by an attitude towards a soul.

III

One important reason for distinguishing between a specific reaction to another, such as the reaction to the neighbour in the Parable of the Good Samaritan, and Wittgenstein's notion of 'an attitude towards a soul', emerges if we ask what the *absence* of either involves. To imagine a situation in which I could no longer respond to the creatures around me as human beings would be to imagine a radical break-up of the familiar expectations we have noted. Such imaginings take us to the limits of the human, to the kind of situation Swift depicts in relating Gulliver's experiences with the Yahoos and the Houyhnhnms.

No such conclusion follows from the absence of the Samaritan's response to the other as a neighbour. I shall argue later that, for the most part, we do not see others as neighbours as the Samaritan did. To see them in this way is the exception rather than the rule. Therefore, when we do not see the other as a neighbour, in the way Jesus taught us to, it does not mean that we have come to the limits of the human. The unsympathetic reactions to others we have discussed, while certainly outside anything that can be called an attitude to a neighbour, are part of what Wittgenstein meant by an attitude towards a soul. So far from threatening our attitude to other human beings, these unsympathetic reactions to others are all-too-frequent expressions of it.

What might tempt us to equate an attitude towards a soul with the specific moral response to others Winch discusses? The answer, I believe, lies in the fact that a denial of *certain* moral responses is often called a denial of humanity. Winch discusses the view that, while it could be said that the priest and the Levite did not see a neighbour in the injured man, it would be odd to say that they did not see a human being. Winch responds by reminding us that certain responses are accused of being failures or refusals to see others as human beings. Slavery is an obvious example. Winch says:

> Consider the attitudes of Europeans and white Americans to slaves in the seventeenth and eighteenth centuries. It was sometimes said of them – indeed, they sometimes said of themselves

– that they did not regard slaves as human. To say this is not to make a point about their competence at biological classification, though no doubt such matters were confusedly mixed up with what was really at issue, namely the nature of their moral sensibility (*WN*, p. 166).

The likely confusion, however, is not between biology and morality, but between a form of moral sensibility and our certainty regarding the existence of human beings. This latter confusion leads Stanley Cavell to want to revise the claim that slave-owners did not regard slaves as human beings. He argues that, unless the owners *did* regard slaves as human beings, they could not have enjoyed the *kind* of satisfaction which possession, subjection and domination gave them. What should be said, Cavell suggests, is not that the slave-owners failed to treat slaves as human beings, but that the slave-owners treated certain human beings as slaves.[5] This attempt to tidy up the language should be resisted. Neither is the necessity for doing so apparent once we distinguish between our certainty that others are human beings and the specific moral response to them Winch has in mind.

This distinction is not kept in mind sufficiently when Winch says that Simone Weil in 'The *Iliad*, Poem of Might', depicts circumstances in which my attitude towards another as a human being may be 'strengthened, weakened or modified' (*ES*, p. 149). Such a comment obscures the fact that what is here described as weakened or modified responses towards human beings, is just as much part of what Wittgenstein means by an attitude towards a soul as the responses described as strong. The response Winch is discussing is a moral response of a certain kind. *Within* that response, other responses will be seen as modifications of the respect due to human beings. Again, *within* such a response, some responses will be seen as limiting cases which amount to a denial of humanity. Slavery would fall into this latter category, as would the horrors of the Holocaust. In fiction, Swift's programme in *A Modest Proposal* would be put in the same category. But these limiting cases, said by some to be denials of humanity, are directed against human beings. Such cases need to be distinguished from Gulliver's experiences which call into question *the very possibility* of seeing a common humanity in the creatures by which he is confronted. Despite the bestial in man, Gulliver reacted very differently to the beasts of the field.

If we keep these distinctions in mind, we can see why, if the possibility of responding to others as human beings is ruled out, the possibility of responding to them as neighbours is also ruled out. On the other hand, if people do not react to others as the Samaritan did, their reactions would still hold fast an attitude to others as human beings.

IV

As we have seen, what Wittgenstein meant by an attitude towards a soul, does not admit of an alternative. When I come into contact with human beings in various contexts, the question whether these creatures are human beings, as distinct from say, automata, simply does not arise. My reaction to others as human beings is immediate and unreflective and it is a reaction I take for granted in others.

I know, from correspondence with Winch, that he does not want to say that the reaction of the Samaritan can be taken for granted in others. Winch, like many of us, is impressed by the unreflective, immediate character of the Samaritan's response: 'Nothing intervenes between the Samaritan's taking in the situation and his compassionate reaction' (*WN*, p. 156).

The Samaritan does not ask whether the injured person is a proper object for his compassion. He takes that for granted; he simply reacts. Winch could hardly think that the reaction can be taken for granted, since, after all, two out of the three who came across the injured person passed by on the other side. When Winch says that the Samaritan's response is immediate, he is characterising the kind of response it is, not claiming that we can rely on everybody to respond in the same way. On the other hand, it is easy to gain the impression from reading Winch's paper that he does think the reaction can be taken for granted. Why should this be so?

First, let us emphasise, once again, that there is an important distinction between stressing the immediately unreflective character of a response and claiming that the response can be taken for granted. To illustrate this, consider the following entry in *The Daily Telegraph* on 25 August 1987:

> *Trio saved woman from rape*: Three have-a-go heroes were rewarded by a judge yesterday for saving a young woman from being raped. The men, all strangers, joined forces after they had

heard her cries for help from an alleyway. One used his car to block the exit, while the other two tackled the man and made a citizen's arrest. One of the men said, 'We just had to save the woman. I would do the same thing tomorrow.' Commenting on their actions, the judge said that they had shown 'considerable bravery. Many people would have ignored what was going on and left.'

We cannot ignore the spontaneous and unreflective character of the men's actions without detracting from their impressiveness. But part of our admiration is also due to the fact that they acted as they did in a situation which many would have ignored and left. This ignoring and leaving may also be spontaneous and unreflective. Indeed, it often is. We cannot take the help for granted. This example cannot be treated in the same way as the confident expectations that a man who hears bad news will suffer, and that a man who hits himself with a hammer will hurt himself. The trouble is that Winch presents *all* these examples as illustrations of what is meant by 'an attitude towards a soul'. Unless we note important differences between them, it will be natural to assume that the claim is being made that the moral responses, too, can be taken for granted.

There is also a distinct feature of the moral response Winch is discussing which feeds the temptation to think that it can be taken for granted in more than one sense. In the example of the men who saved the woman from rape, one of them, as we saw, said, 'We just *had* to save the woman.' Winch says of the Samaritan's response:

> The Samaritan responds to what he sees as a necessity generated by the presence of the injured man. What I mean by introducing this word can be brought out by considering what someone in the Samaritan's position, and responding as he did, might say if urged by a companion to hurry on so as not to miss his important appointment. 'But I *can't* just leave him there to die.' The word 'can't' as used in such a context, expresses the kind of necessity – in this case an impossibility – I have in mind (*WN*, p. 157).

As Winch says, it would simply be a sick joke if someone said, 'Of course you can leave him there, you haven't got a broken leg, have you?' The necessity of which the Samaritan speaks is not an external one brought about contingently by circumstances. The necessity is internally related to his reaction to the situation, and is a feature of the purity of his compassion. The necessity is an expression of the moral reaction, not a claim that such a reaction will necessarily be forthcoming from anyone confronted by the same situation. The expression 'I can't just leave him there to die' might tempt one to think otherwise. On the other hand, the expression 'You can't leave him there to die', which might well be directed in criticism against the priest and the Levite, should keep us from yielding to such a temptation.

On the other hand, this same expression, 'You can't leave him there to die', while freeing us from one temptation, may make us susceptible to another. We might be led to think, not that the moral response can be taken for granted, but that, if there is a moral response, we can take for granted that it will take this form. The situation generates this *moral* necessity. Winch does not emphasise that the response to suffering he is discussing is *one* moral response among others. When Callicles said 'Suffering does not happen to a man', he was not being indifferent to suffering, but responding to it morally in a way very different from the response of the Samaritan.

Once we note that the Samaritan's response cannot be taken for granted, and that it is one moral response among many, the question arises of what light Wittgenstein's notion of an attitude towards a soul throws on the *specific* response Winch is discussing. I cannot see that anything very positive can be said in reply. In *some* ways the difficulties are similar to those Winch came to recognise in his paper 'Nature and Convention' as a result of criticisms by R. F. Holland. In that paper, Winch had argued that in any language, truth-telling must be a norm. Generally, people will be concerned to say what is the case. From this fact, however, Winch tried to argue that truth-telling must be regarded as a virtue. Holland protested,[6] pointing out that the general considerations Winch had appealed to led to no such conclusion. This can be seen, Holland argued, if we pay attention to what these general considerations cannot account for, for example, the difference between someone who tells the truth normally, but who would always have an eye for the main chance, and someone who would die for the sake of truth, and who sees transgressing it as a spiritual offence. How is one to account for the character of the latter disposition? Not in terms of a reference to any general practice of truth-telling. Agreeing with this, Winch concluded: 'I was looking for an account of such moral significance in altogether the wrong dimensions.'[7]

But has not the wrong dimension also been invoked by Winch in his treatment of responses such as those of the Samaritan? I am not suggesting that Winch is trying to establish a natural morality as he was in 'Nature and Convention'. What I *am* suggesting is that in *both* cases, an attempt is made to bring out what is impressive in a specific response by invoking a more general attitude. A specific regard for truth was related to the general practice of truth-telling. The Samaritan's response is related to a more general attitude called 'an attitude towards a soul'. But, as we have seen, 'an attitude towards a soul' is not one substantive response. If we emphasise the fact that our conviction that others are human beings is immediate and unreflective, this, in itself, does not throw light on what is impressive in the Samaritan's reaction. Of course, it is true that Winch has shown that the Samaritan does not react in the way he does because he first believes that the sufferer is a human being. Rather, his conception of a human being is partly determined by his response. But that *conceptual* point can also be made in terms of the 'turning aside' of the priest and the Levite. We cannot say that the Samaritan's compassion is significant because it is immediate and unreflective. The fact that the 'turning away' is immediate and unreflective is a mark against it, not a redeeming feature.

What is impressive about the Samaritan's response is that it is *immediate and unreflective pity and compassion*. To appreciate this we need not invoke Wittgenstein's more general notion of an attitude towards a soul.

V

Given the context in which Winch has discussed the Samaritan's response, it is not surprising to find it affecting his reading of the Parable of the Good Samaritan. For Winch, the Samaritan's response is one of common decency to a fellow human being. He says,

> In fact I should say that the lawyer – and also those of us who feel that his answer to Jesus' final question is the only possible

one – are making a response analogous to that of the Samaritan himself. It is tempting to say that we are all responding to the same thing: to whatever it is that falls under the concept 'fellow human being'; but this, though it is not wrong, misleadingly suggests that we have some access to this otherwise than through such responses (*WN*, p. 157).

Winch gives the impression that this response is a pervasive one. For example, he does not think that Jesus *tells* the lawyer anything. He *asks* him who his neighbour is. Winch compares it with the Socratic method of eliciting an answer in discussion: 'The suggestion in both cases is that each of us has within him or herself the resources for answering the question' (*WN*, p. 157). Winch's reference to 'those of us who feel' that the lawyer's answer to Jesus's question is the only possible answer, suggests that not everyone does respond in this way. It is also important to recognise, however, how many diverse states of affairs may be covered by 'identifying the neighbour' in response to Jesus's question.

What would a 'successful' identification show about the resources we have within us? No general answer can be given to this question. For example, it does not follow that anyone who can identify a fellow human being as a neighbour, is capable of actually responding to him as a neighbour. This is because there is a distinction between an actual moral response, and a response to the response. For example, if a person is asked whether the three men who went to the aid of the intended rape victim did what any decent man should do, he may answer affirmatively without hesitation. That is his response to their response. But it does not follow that *he* has the resources to respond likewise. He may witness such a scene, do nothing, and feel deeply ashamed as a result, even though he knows that given a similar situation, he would fail to act again. An immediate and unreflective response to Jesus's question does not mean that I am capable of an immediate and unreflective response to my neighbour in distress. So even with notions of common decency, it does not mean that the decency is common in the sense of being something we all have the resources to fulfil.

But *is* the reaction of the Samaritan one of familiar common decency towards a fellow human being? If it were, Winch is quite right in saying that it would not need some kind of foundation to make it intelligible. He disagrees with a view once expressed by

G. E. M. Anscombe,[8] according to which 'the intelligibility of the obligation to help the injured traveller to which the Samaritan responded depends on accepting that it is a divine law that one should act thus' (*WN*, p. 161). Winch argues, to the contrary, that the concept of a divine law can only develop on the basis of the moral responses to a fellow human being such as that of the Samaritan (see *WN*, p. 161). To illustrate his point, Winch stresses what he takes to be the connection between the first and second commandments:

> Thou shalt love the Lord thy God with all thy heart, and with all thy soul, and with all thy mind . . . And the second is like unto it. Thou shalt love thy neighbour as thyself (Matt. 22: 37,39).

Winch says,

> The second Commandment might indeed be regarded as an application, or even a particularly central case of the first. That is supported by remarks like St John's: 'If a man say, I love God and hateth his brother, he is a liar: for he that loveth not his brother whom he hath seen, how can he love God whom he hath not seen?'[9] The suggestion here, as it seems to me, is that we do not first have a conception of God on the basis of which we form our conception of the Commandment to love our neighbour. On the contrary the conceptual development goes the other way. The responses to moral modality that we share with the Samaritan (however much they are modified or stifled by circumstance) are amongst the seeds from which, in some people, grows the conception of divinity and its laws (*WN*, p. 161).

What Winch ignores is that the Parable of the Good Samaritan is not a moral teaching from which conceptions of the divine may grow. It is itself a *religious* parable. Because Winch does not consider the possibility that the response Jesus is talking about is *already a spiritual extension* from more familiar acts of common decency, he misses the religious point of the parable. This is why, too, Winch does not think the lawyer comes to see anything through the parable that he did not already know. He says: 'If the lawyer had needed to be *told* the answer to Jesus' last question he would have been in no position to understand it' (*WN*, p. 157).

Winch makes nothing of the fact that the lawyer is not an honest questioner. After all, it must be remembered that he is tempting Jesus, putting him to the test. So he stands *in need* of the parable. The parable shakes him out of his game-playing. But still, it might be thought, when he is shaken out of it, the parable tells him, or calls him back to, what he already knew. No doubt the lawyer cannot respond to the parable unless he shares some of the sympathetic and unsympathetic responses to other human beings we have discussed. But, surely, what the parable does is to extend these reactions radically. Teaching the parable does not presuppose the possession of what it shows. It is at least possible that, on this occasion, the parable creates the possibility of a possession for the first time for the lawyer. The parable does not *remind* him, it *disturbs* him. How does this come about?

There is a tension between Winch's saying that we share the Samaritan's response, no matter how much it is modified or stifled by circumstance, and his saying that the Samaritan's response 'is all the more striking, of course, given that the encounter is between a Samaritan and a Jew (as it were a Palestinian Arab and an Israeli): that is, just the sort of situation in which one might expect questions and hesitations' (*WN*, p. 156). Surely, the latter comment is the appropriate one. A member of one race comes across an injured member of another race between whom bitter enmity and hatred existed. It is in *this* context that the lawyer is invited to see a neighbour. He is told a startling story which disturbs his previous reactions by presenting a despised one as a neighbour. A better link with the second commandment than the one Winch provides can be found in Matt. 5: 43–8:

Ye have heard that it hath been said, Thou shalt love thy neighbour, and hate thine enemy.
But I say unto you, Love your enemies, bless them that curse you, do good to them that hate you and pray for them which despitefully use you, and persecute you:
That ye may be the children of your Father which is in heaven; for he maketh his sun to rise on the evil and on the good, and sendeth rain on the just and on the unjust.
For if ye love them which love you, what reward have ye? do not even the publicans the same?
And if ye salute your brethren only what do ye more than others? do not even the publicans so?

Be ye therefore perfect, even as your Father which is in heaven is perfect.

This is not a teaching which simply causes one to ask questions or hesitate. It is a disruptive teaching which disturbs our natural expectations. If I am able to respond by saying 'The Samaritan did what he had to do', it does not follow that I can respond in the same way. It may mean that I see his response as a challenge to or judgement on my own behaviour. Consider, for example, what Simone Weil had to say about the appeal made by the inhabitants of Melos to the Athenians who threatened to massacre them if they did not join them in their war against Sparta:

> The men of Melos said that in the case of a battle they would have the gods with them on account of the justice of their cause. The Athenians replied that they saw no reason to suppose so.
>
> 'As touching the gods we have the belief, and as touching men the certainty, that always by a necessity of nature, each one commands whenever he has the power. We did not establish this law, we are not the first to apply it; we found it already established, we abide by it as something likely to endure for ever; and that is why we apply it. We know quite well that you also, like all the others, once you reached the same degree of power, would act in the same way.'[10]

Here, it might be said, the Athenians' confident appeal is to primitive responses. Simone Weil certainly regards them as natural responses. What she regards as true religion breaks in on these natural responses in the form of what she calls supernatural virtue. She says that the Athenians who massacred the inhabitants of Melos did not have this conception of virtue. Yet, they were wrong in ruling out the possibility of such a conception. Simone Weil says:

> The first proof that they were in the wrong lies in the fact that, contrary to their assertion, it happens, although extremely rarely, that a man will forbear out of pure generosity to command where he has the power to do so. That which is possible for man is possible also for God.[11]

Winch is quite right in thinking that it is in the context of the natural that the supernatural is shown at work, but the context he invokes is very different from that invoked by Simone Weil. Winch speaks of the seeds of the divine being in those modalities 'we share with the Samaritan however much they are modified or stifled by circumstance' (*WN*, p. 161), whereas, for Simone Weil, the seeds of the divine are found in those extremely rare occasions, when, out of pure generosity of spirit, a person forbears to use the power at his disposal against a victim. 'A difference of emphasis', you might say. Quite so, but an important difference nevertheless.

Winch gives the impression that reactions, such as that of the Samaritan are, within a certain moral perspective, part of our normal expectations in our dealings with each other; expectations which leave us in no doubt about what we ought to do when confronted by a human being in distress. True, Winch says that these expectations and reactions are modified or stifled by certain circumstances, but this gives the clear impression that fulfilled expectations and reactions, in this respect, are the rule. For Simone Weil, supernatural virtue is the exception rather than the rule, unreflective and natural in a person though its exercise may be. That is why such naturalness is an occasion for wonder, challenge and judgement. That is why, too, Jesus thought we all stand in need of being told of it; why we need to hear of what a Samaritan did when he came across a Jew who had fallen among thieves on the road from Jerusalem to Jericho.[12]

18

Philosophy and the Heterogeneity of the Human

Philosophising about the concept of a human being is fiendishly difficult. *Part* of the difficulty lies in this very way of talking: in talk about *the* concept of a human being. Yet, we are not going to get very far in moral philosophy without reflecting on human beings and the lives they lead. But what kind of reflection is this? What difficulties stand in the way of it?

Cora Diamond tells us that when she has suggested to other philosophers in conversation 'that the notion "human being" is of the greatest significance in moral thought, the suggestion is met with puzzlement, or I am taken to have in mind by "human being" something like *decent* or *admirable* human being'.[1] Apparently, for the philosophers who reacted in this way, the notion 'human being' is, essentially, a biological notion: the concept *homo sapiens*. For them, moral evaluations and prescriptions are external appendages to this notion, via some such edict as, 'Protect its life'. The goods we advocate in connection with human beings and human life are said to be the product of our choices. But we do not all choose the same goods. According to the philosophers Diamond has in mind, we try to change choices by psychological means, but do not always succeed. When breakdown occurs, we simply have to admit that one man's meat is another man's poison.

The philosophical views Diamond refers to are essentially those advanced by C. L. Stevenson in his emotive theory of ethics. Most philosophers would agree that the theory presents an impoverished account of moral endeavour, but what does saying *that* amount to? According to Iris Murdoch, the impoverishment of the theory reflects a more general impoverishment in our culture: 'We have suffered a general loss of concepts, the loss of a moral and political vocabulary. We no longer use a spread-out substantial

251

picture of the manifold virtues of man and society. We no longer see man against a background of values, of realities, which transcend him. We picture man as a brave naked will surrounded by an easily comprehended physical world.'[2] The difficulty with such a general thesis is in determining who 'we' refers to. Cora Diamond argues that this conceptual loss in the culture to which Murdoch refers will show itself *in philosophy* in a distinctive way: 'Philosophers who accept such a picture of the soul will be blind to uses of words for which that picture leaves no room' (p. 264). Again, as in Murdoch's case, the problem is with the generality of this thesis.

Taking Stevenson's emotive theory of ethics as an example, Diamond recognises that the question of the *kind* of conceptual loss it involves is *itself* a matter of philosophical dispute. For example, Alasdair MacIntyre and Stanley Cavell disagree over the issue.[3] Diamond points out that they agree 'that a distinction between rational discussion and mere persuasion is internal to the notion of morality itself, where the necessary distinction is more than just an emotive labelling of the kind of discussion you like to approve of. They agree also that there have actually been forms of life in which a moral vocabulary has been alive and well, in which there has been a distinction between bringing a moral consideration to someone's attention and seeking to influence him by telling him things that you believe will affect his action' (p. 260). Diamond also points out that, for MacIntyre and Cavell, 'Stevenson's incapacity to make a contrast between moral thought and manipulative uses of language is tied to his more general philosophical misunderstandings about fact and value' (p. 260). On the other hand, as Diamond shows, MacIntyre and Cavell have a major disagreement about Stevenson's theory: 'given that Stevenson portrays a world in which the concept of morality is missing, is this, as MacIntyre would have it, a true portrayal of our world, or is it, as Cavell suggests, a reflection of Stevenson's blindness to what we still have?' (p. 260). Must we choose between these general theories? If we disagree with them, must we replace them with a general theory of our own?

There is an obvious difficulty with the generality of MacIntyre's thesis. If as MacIntyre claims, we have all lost our moral concepts, and have become centres of arbitrary will, from what source is MacIntyre informed of our state of moral deprivation?[4] Diamond shares these misgivings, but she also has misgivings about Cavell's views. Cavell depicts Stevenson as someone who 'does not suffer from incapacity to use moral vocabulary in ordinary life at any rate, Cavell does not suggest that he does'[5] but 'from an incapacity that shows itself in reflection on that use' (pp. 260–61). For Cavell, Stevenson is conceptually confused, but not morally confused.

Diamond offers a third account of Stevenson's confusion which, as we shall see, is presented as an alternative *general* thesis. She thinks 'it would be wrong to take the philosophical blindness to be a matter of philosophers' going on as if we had lost concepts which we have not lost at all, and which were perfectly happily *there* for everyone else, including the philosopher when he is not doing philosophy' (pp. 262–3). Instead, she argues that what Stevenson 'lacks the capacity for is itself a particular kind of use of the moral vocabulary' (p. 261). I do not deny that this *could* be so in Stevenson's case, but I do not know this. With *some* philosophers, what they say about certain moral perspectives shows that they are blind to them. In other cases, although one may think a philosopher conceptually confused, one could not draw this conclusion *from his work alone*. This is my view of Stevenson. Without knowing him, I simply do not know what moral vocabulary found a place in his life. Diamond exhibits no such caution. This is because she is charmed by Murdoch's idea of 'a form of conceptual loss . . . which affects the whole educated Western world and which affects philosophers in a particular way' (p. 263). On this view, a philosopher who argues like Stevenson 'suffers from a form of cultural deprivation rooted in philosophical practices. His case is not a case of *as-if* loss of concepts but a particular kind of *actual* loss or failure of mastery' (p. 261).

My misgivings about the generality of Diamond's thesis can be brought out in terms of the central example she uses to illustrate it: the concepts of a human being and a human life. Philosophical distortions of these concepts, she argues, do not emanate, as Murdoch thinks, simply from a deficient philosophy of mind. They come from a deficient philosophy of language: 'The criticism I am making could be put in this way: linguistic philosophers have brought to their study of language an impoverished view of what can be involved in conceptual life' (p. 266).

What is involved in grasping a concept? Diamond insists that it 'is not a matter of just knowing how to group things under that concept; it is being able to participate in life-with-the-concept' (p. 266). This applies to as ordinary a concept as 'chair'. Wittgenstein reminds us

'that it is part of the grammar of the word "chair" that *this* is what
we call "to sit in a chair", and that it is part of the grammar of the
word "meaning" that *this* is what it is like to *explain* a meaning'
(p. 264). What, then, is involved in life-with-the-concept 'human
being'? Diamond replies: 'To be able to use the concept "human
being" is to be able to think about human life and what happens in
it; it is not to be able to pick human beings out from other things or
recommend that certain things be done to them or by them'
(p. 266). Literature, she argues, helps us to think well about
human life. In myriad contexts, it can and does portray looks
which can pass between one human being and another, in such a
way that we are helped to appreciate 'the sharedness of human
life', 'denial of that solidarity', 'what the depth may be of recognition and its denial' (p. 265). Great writers

> give recognition and denial place in a narrative, and by doing so,
> and doing it in the particular way they do, they show us some-
> thing about human life which has nothing to do with our
> *choosing* to evaluate things one way or another. I cannot choose
> what weight it shall have that I fail you or betray you, or that I on
> some occasion look at you with a look that leaves you a mere
> circumstance and not a human being (p. 265).

Diamond says: 'Not to know what it is to look at another human
being with such recognition or with its denial, is not to have as
fully as one might and as one should the concept of a human
being' (p. 265). She concludes: 'What it is to grasp the biological
concept is nothing like what it is to grasp the concept of a human
being. But neither is the concept of a human being that of homo
sapiens plus an evaluative extra. The choice of concepts offered us
by contemporary analytical philosophy does not accommodate the
reality' (p. 265).

What, in the light of these remarks, is to be said of philosophical
uses of the notion 'human being'? These uses, too, for Diamond,
are instances of life-with-the-concept. According to her, when a
philosopher says, 'This is what it is *like* to use these concepts', this
'is itself a use, a philosophically reflective use, of the concepts'
(p. 261). For Diamond, philosophical reflection is thus a form of
moral reflection, one which may or may not 'accommodate reality'.
When the reflection does not accommodate the reality of what it is
to be a human being or to live a human life, the philosophical

failure and confusion, it seems, is at the same time a moral failure and confusion.

While I do not want to rule out the possibility of reaching such a conclusion in particular cases, the generality of Diamond's argument is dangerous and confusing. In wanting to avoid the emotivist conception of choice, thought of as externally related to factual states of affairs, she is in danger of embracing a homogeneous conception of what it is to be a human being and to live a human life, in which 'choice', in the sense of different readings and weighings of situations, plays little part. The adequacy of philosophical reflection is then measured against this non-existent homogeneous conception of human life. To say that to use the concept of a human being 'is to be able to think about human life and what happens in it', is to cover a multitude of differences.

Diamond's comparison between the concept 'chair' and the concept 'human being' encourages us to ignore these differences. Our participation in life-with-the-concept of something as definite as a chair, may lead us to think that our life-with-the-concept 'human being' concerns something just as circumscribed. It would have been better to compare the concept 'human being' with the concept 'physical object'. We do not have our various dealings with physical objects because we first believe in their reality. Rather, what we mean by their reality is shown in, held fast by, these dealings. Similarly, we do not act towards each other in the ways we do because we first believe in the reality of human beings. Rather, what we mean by human beings is given in, held fast by, these ways of acting.[6] Yet, what has to be recognised is that these ways of acting are *mixed*. We are related to each other *sympathetically and unsympathetically*. Furthermore, within these relations *there is further variety*. There is no way of showing that the sympathetic relations are the paradigmatic form of 'recognising a human being', the unsympathetic relations being, somehow, parasitic on, or deviations from, the sympathetic relations.[7] Thus, it seems to me, it is extremely misleading to talk as though grasping the concept 'human being' *is itself to adopt a specific substantive attitude*. Our sense of the human is held together by distances and differences, as well as by similarities and proximities. The same Wittgenstein who teaches us that to grasp a concept is to participate in life-with-the-concept, also teaches us differences. He teaches us that to grasp a concept philosophically is not the same as embracing it in one's personal life. We must remember, too, that we do not learn to speak by speaking to anyone about anything.

Let me illustrate further some of the differences Diamond's comments tend to obscure. Because she is tempted by a homogeneous conception of human life, she is led to say, as we have seen, that a person cannot choose what weight he gives to betrayal or failure. First, it has to be noted that people differ in their conceptions of what constitutes betrayal and failure. Further, the great literature Diamond invokes affords countless examples of the different ways people weigh betrayal and failure, some forgiving while others cannot, some thinking they render certain things pointless while others do not, and so on. In the course of these differences we have remarks such as 'How can a human being do that?' from *either* side of the various divides.

Consider another example. Diamond calls our attention to the looks in which human beings are recognised and others in which they are denied. She is unhappy to mark the difference by saying that certain looks express common decency while others lack it. To do so, she thinks, entails treating 'human beings' as essentially the biological concept, *homo sapiens*, with value judgements appended as an evaluative extra. This misgiving is misplaced. Neither our sympathetic nor our unsympathetic reactions to others belongs to the life of a biological concept. Both express what human relations can be like.

Another source of temptation towards a homogeneous conception of human life, is the moral use of the expression, 'That's a human being!'. It serves as an admonition to ourselves and others in certain circumstances. When despicable actions are contemplated, the expression indicates that a limit has been reached. Stanley Cavell calls it 'the lower limit'. Below it is found the horrific, as found in slavery, for example, or the atrocities of the Holocaust. Agreement on the lower limit is widespread among people who differ morally in many ways. Such agreement may lead us to think that the lower limit is *the base of a common morality* in which *the same* measure of agreement can be found. Once this assumption is made, it is a short step to speak, as Diamond does, of the sharedness of human life, and of failures to recognise it as forms of dissociation.

Diamond presents a view of philosophical confusion about the concept 'human being' as forms of dissociation. How does this come about? Suppose we say that philosophers fail to grasp the concept. Diamond has already defined such grasping as life-with-the-concept. Are we to say, then, that confused philosophers do not participate in a human life? To avoid the absurdity of *that* conclusion, Diamond says: 'The conceptual losses we have indeed suffered have not actually changed us into human beings limited to the interests and experiences and moral possibilities we can express in our depleted vocabulary' (p. 263). Philosophers who are in the grip of this impoverished vocabulary remain more than their words can tell. Only the articulate, outside this situation, will appreciate the predicament such philosophers are in. Thus, Diamond argues, 'someone's philosophical view itself may be subject to the criticism that it rests on a failure in the relation between his experience and his thought, of a kind which, on his philosophical view, there is no intelligible room for. Philosophical views which make certain kinds of dissociation invisible may themselves be described by others as cases of such dissociation' (p. 271). Diamond regrets that 'our practice of philosophy encourages the idea that such judgements have no part in philosophical thinking, that it does not call on a responsiveness involving the whole mind' (p. 275).

My aim in criticising Diamond is not, of course, to deny that philosophical confusion can *ever* be a form of dissociation. Rather, it is to show that the general way in which she presents her thesis obscures other possible relations between moral philosophy and the moral realities in people's lives. Because she wants to emphasise philosophical confusion as a form of dissociation, Diamond seeks to compare it with four examples of cultural deprivation manifested in a depleted vocabulary. The idea seems to be that the confused philosopher is in the grip of such a vocabulary, one which does not do justice to human beings and the lives they lead. We may call the four contexts of deprivation with which she wants to compare philosophical confusion, empty naming, misnaming, leaving unnamed, and renaming, respectively. While the examples to which Diamond draws our attention may apply to particular treatments of certain concepts by some philosophers, it is important in each case to point out possibilities the examples exclude. Diamond pays little attention to these other possibilities, a fact which encourages the generality of the picture she presents, namely that where the concept 'human being' is concerned, philosophical confusion concerning it is a form of dissociation from the human life we all share. This is just as much a generalisation from particular cases as would be my saying that when philosophers are confused about concepts of human life, they use the concepts without difficulty, when not philosophising. No general thesis is going to succeed in giving simply *one* overall account of the relation of moral philosophy to human life.

This conclusion is evident if we consider Diamond's first example of a comparison between philosophical confusion and cultural deprivation. The philosopher's language may amount to empty naming. By 'empty naming' she means a use of language which is cut off from the context which would give it sense; in short, idle language. The philosopher's language about human beings is empty, idle, when it is cut off from the realities of human life we share. Once we consider a particular example of empty naming, however, we see how tenuous such a general thesis becomes.

Diamond recalls Elizabeth Anscombe's example of empty naming, namely, the attempt to speak of unconditional, or absolute uses of 'ought', without reference to a divine-law ethics which, Anscombe claims, is the only context which gives such talk its sense. Already the particularity of the example creates difficulties for someone who speaks of the sharedness of human life in the way Diamond does. Anscombe points out, and Diamond concurs, that a divine-law ethics is no longer dominant in our culture. This is to say that for very many people there is no life-with-the-concept of divine law in their personal lives. But, as Diamond admits, one cannot speak in this way of the concept 'human being' or 'human life'. Here, it seems, we are all participants. If we ask, 'Participants in *what*?' we soon see how tricky a notion 'human life' is. It certainly cannot be identified with specific moral perspectives, since it will soon become evident that some people share these perspectives and others do not. Nevertheless, consideration of a specific example, such as divine-law ethics, illustrates the *different* relations which may obtain between conceptual analysis in philosophy and the lives which people lead. These differences cannot be captured in the one notion of philosophical confusion as a form of dissociation and cultural deprivation.

Even if we allow that talk of an unconditional 'ought' had religious origins, why should it not develop new, independent senses as it gradually severs from that context? This has, in fact, happened. We now have intelligible talk concerning absolute 'oughts' in religious and non-religious contexts. Not everyone talks in this way. The relations of philosophers to such talk vary. Some may be blind to it in either context. Others, while participating in such talk in their personal lives, may still give philosophically confused accounts of what they do. This does not mean that they are dissociated from the concepts concerned in their personal lives. For example, it may be argued that Anscombe's own philosophical account of divine-law ethics is confused, since it suggests an external relation between the content of God's commands and God's commanding of them. On the other hand, it may be said that such an analysis *does* reflect what divine-law ethics is for a person, involving a conception of God as, to use Simone Weil's expression 'a policeman in the sky'. People will differ in their reactions to these different conceptions of divine-law ethics. It must also be noted that a philosopher may give perspicuous representations of these conceptions in his search for clarity, *without* embracing any of them in his personal life. That being so, it cannot be said that philosophical reflection always concerns concepts the philosopher embraces personally when not philosophising. It follows that moral philosophy cannot always be said to be a reflective use of the moral concepts we employ when not philosophising, a view of moral philosophy which seems central to Diamond's argument.

Diamond's second example of cultural deprivation which is meant to throw light on the nature of philosophical confusion is what she calls 'misnaming'. In certain circumstances, 'we lack the capacity to use certain words but, if we had it, we could make intelligible to ourselves important parts of our life and experience' (p. 259). Philosophers, too, in their confusions, would be said to lack the words they need to make intelligible important aspects of their lives. As an example of misnaming, Diamond refers to the claim that 'the language used by Americans is not adequate for the articulation of [their] moral and political commitments . . . [they] sound more isolated than [they] are: [they] should like to be "arbitrary centers of volition" although [they] are not' (p. 258).

Diamond's use of the notion of 'misnaming' is problematic. Note that she is not referring to confused accounts of perspectives people do not embrace, but to confused accounts of the lives they *actually* lead. What does it mean to say that the experiences in these lives cannot be articulated? Surely, language is used in daily discourse. Are we to say that *this* discourse cannot capture the experiences of daily life? Such a claim would drive a wedge between language and experience in a way of which Diamond would surely not approve. Furthermore, reflection will also be part of daily discourse. After all, not all reflection is philosophical reflection.

What, then, are the confused attempts at articulation which Diamond calls 'misnaming'? The most natural answer, *in the above context*, in relation to philosophy, would be: philosophical mis-characterisations of those moral and political perspectives the philosophers in question embrace when they are not philosophising. But because Diamond conflates moral and philosophical re-flection she fails to leave sufficient logical space for these possibilities. For her, the philosophical lack is a lack of moral reflection, manifesting a dissociation from a moral form of life. Whether this is so, however, cannot be determined in abstraction. As I have already said, it depends on the perspectives the philos-ophers in question actually embrace. A philosopher may or may not be more than his misplaced philosophical accounts suggest.

I am not combatting Diamond's thesis with a general thesis of my own: that all philosophers, when not philosophising, have a sure grasp of the moral concepts about which they philosophise. On the contrary, I recognise that philosophical misunderstandings are not always misunderstandings of the logic of a language the philos-ophers use when not philosophising. The misunderstandings may be a sign that the language in question means nothing to the philosopher concerned.[8] I also recognise that prestigious philo-sophical accounts may help to erode moral perspectives they are blind to.[9] But these are *possibilities*. Diamond is tempted by a more general thesis: philosophers who are confused are blind to moral perspectives they need to make articulate important aspects of their lives. Our response should be: they may or may not be.

Diamond's emphases certainly rescue us from the intellectual conceit of thinking that no philosopher *could* be blind to certain moral perspectives. But to insist that confusion in moral philos-ophy must be a form of blindness or moral dissociation is simply the reverse side of the same intellectual conceit. As we have seen, no single account can be given of the relation of moral philosophy to human life. For example, further possibilities can also be borne in mind. A philosopher may display considerable subtlety in his account of human relationships and still be blind to what is wrong in his own. No appeal can be made to literature as though litera-ture *must* be of help. It may do more harm than good. Learning from a person is very different from learning from literature. Indeed, romanticism may take the form of wishing a person were like a poem. *Philosophical* recognition of the difference may not rescue one from the wish.

Diamond's third example to illustrate how a failure in or absence of an adequate vocabulary in moral philosophy is akin to a form of cultural deprivation and dissociation, concentrates on the consequences of such a failure or absence. The consequences are that central aspects of human life remain *unnamed*. Diamond illustrates the fate of being unnamed, by reference to Berger's claim that

> large sections of the English working and middle class . . . are inarticulate as the result of wholesale cultural deprivation. They are deprived of the means of translating what they know into thoughts which they can think. They have no examples to follow in which words clarify experience. Their spoken proverbial traditions have long been destroyed: and, although they are literate in the strictly technical sense, they have not had the opportunity of discovering the existence of a written cultural heritage. A great deal of their experience – especially emotional and introspective experience – has to remain unnamed for them.[10]

Berger's comments are, in some respects, problematic. This must be recognised if these comments are meant to illustrate the consequences of suffering from the depleted vocabularies of moral philosophers. Berger's remarks could refer to a literate people who lack a literature and other intellectual traditions. As a result, their lives may pass unchronicled, unnamed. This aspect of Berger's remarks is irrelevant for Diamond's purposes. A second aspect of his remarks seems to me to be incoherent. If intellectual articulation, 'naming', does not occur, the people concerned are said to be 'deprived of the means of translating what they know into thoughts which they can think'. But what is it to say that people know those things? That they do would show itself in the ways they live. To say that this knowledge needs translating is an over-intellectualised account of such knowledge and a possible over-estimation of the need for intellectual clarification.

Berger may be saying that the articulation which comes from intellectual reflection on human life is itself a good thing. To which it may be replied: that depends on the form such reflection takes. One is caught up in philosophical reflection whether one likes it or not, not because one thinks it is a good. If we look on much that has gone on in moral philosophy and the philosophy of religion, the wonder is that the forms of morality and religion about which philosophers speculate have survived despite the philosophers! After all, Diamond is not simply emphasising the unfortunate consequences which an *absence* of moral philosophy may have. She is more concerned to emphasise unfortunate consequences which may follow from the *presence* of a moral philosophy which trades in a depleted vocabulary; a vocabulary which does not do justice to human beings and the lives they lead. As a result of this vocabulary, aspects of these lives may go unnamed. To be deprived of *these* reflections is to be fortunate, not culturally deprived.

In Diamond's fourth example, she compares the benefits which can accrue from an imaginative moral philosophy with what might be called the task of *renaming*. What 'renaming' amounts to can be illustrated from the writings of the young Marx:

> The contrast is not between our present use of words and that of a tradition from which we are cut off (and which still at some level shapes our experience), but between the present use of words and one adequate to human nature. The criticism of our present conceptual life is not tied to what is embodied in our past but to a vision of human wholeness to which a mode of speech and thought unlike ours belongs (p. 259).

When a philosopher argues in this way, however, it is important to realise that he is *recommending* a renaming in terms of his vision of human life. It is misleading to speak of this new vision as one 'adequate to human nature', since this gives the impression that the vision can be *underwritten* by an appeal to human nature.

This impression is very much in evidence when Diamond comes to discuss the second major concern of her paper: How do we assess conceptual gain or loss in human beings or in human life? This question is closely connected with the matters we have been discussing. If Diamond accuses moral philosophers of conceptual loss in the way they argue about human beings and human life, it will be necessary to determine how such an accusation can be justified. How is conceptual gain or loss to be identified and assessed?

Diamond says that people may want to ask, 'What if we have lost concepts? Might we not have gained more than enough to counterbalance that loss, in the general shift of modes of thought and action, and forms of social life, of which the supposed conceptual loss was part?' (p. 266). Philosophers speak, sometimes, Diamond argues, as though they possessed a neutral method by which the conceptual gains and losses can be assessed. This is because they think, she suggests, that 'if a word has descriptive content at all, that content can be expressed by an evaluatively neutral term. Description itself is thought of as something that can be pulled out of the context of human life and interest within which descriptions have their normal place' (p. 267). This philosophical confidence takes no account of the possibility of conceptual blindness about human life. If someone is in the grip of such blindness, he will be in no position to judge whether there has been a conceptual gain or loss. The problem is that Diamond, in her treatment of these questions, assumes that human lives and human beings have a homogeneity they do not possess.

Consider, for example, Diamond's discussion of Alison Jagger's confident assertion that we would be better off without our present concept of sexual difference. The trouble is, Diamond argues, that Jagger has no idea of what this difference amounts to. For Jagger it amounts to no more than Maurice Chevalier singing 'Thank heaven for little girls'! Diamond comments: 'She does not see as a human good our having a range of concepts through which the characterising facts of human life enter our sense of who we are and what we experience' (p. 269). As a result, 'as she does not see that as a good at all (or even see that it is possible to see it so), she is simply not in a position to ask how such a good is related to possibilities of oppression, nor *a fortiori* to discuss the question whether such a good can be balanced against such evils and, if so, how' (p. 269). Diamond wants the example to illustrate a more general point: 'One difficulty in discussing whether the loss of certain concepts is balanced by some other gain is that there may be no recognition at all of what the good is of concepts, of possibilities of thought' (p. 269).

As we have seen, the central concept which concerns Diamond is that of 'being a human being' and 'living a human life'. To grasp these concepts is, according to her, to be able to think about human life and what happens in it. But I have insisted that 'human life and what happens in it' is not a homogeneous phenomenon. Rather, it refers to mixed activities with both cooperation and conflict between them. People, philosophers included, will vary in the extent of their appreciation of these various activities. In terms of her example, what Diamond has established is that Jagger may be blind to the importance of sexual differences in our lives and in our culture. But Diamond wants to establish a far more ambitious claim about Jagger: 'What is invisible to her is the structure of the story of her own life and the relation it has – given our concepts – to life's coming into the world through sexual difference' (p. 269). Because Diamond thinks that the appeal to *our* concepts is unproblematic, the structure of Jagger's life must be understood in terms of these *same* concepts. But since Diamond says that Jagger fails to see even the *possibility* of certain relations between men and women as a good, Diamond has to say that Jagger is blind to the possibility of a good which is part of the structure of her own life. But if we emphasise the heterogeneity of human perspectives, this conclusion is unjustified. For those who think that the notion of sexual difference Jagger defines is important, their criticism can be put differently. The trouble with Jagger, it will be said, is not that she is blind to the structure of a human life we all share, but that she gives all-too-accurate an account of the perspectives she embraces.

Similar tensions appear in Diamond's reactions to Judith Jarvis Thompson's claim that we need only feel responsible for that which we choose to be responsible for. No doubt Thompson's thesis cannot be maintained. But can it be countered in the way Diamond adopts? She chooses, as her example, what she calls the good of the concept of parenthood, which, she argues, is part of the structure of our lives whether we like it or not. Of course, for those for whom parents matter, a world in which people could simply choose to ignore them, would be as different from their world as the ancient world is from ours. But Diamond does not speak of *their* world, but of *our* world. Can she speak for everyone in this way?

When would we speak of the good of the concept of parenthood? Only, I suspect, in rather special circumstances. For example, certain groups might experiment with alternative ways of living to the family. Those who wanted to rid the world of parents as we know them, may speak of sperm banks, and so on. Someone may be torn between these values, unable to decide whether to leave his family to join one of these experimental groups. Diamond seems to think that such a conflict of values depends on suspect philosophical arguments:

'Each of us can decide whether to treat respecting one's parents and accepting responsibility for them as a good.' Such a philosophical view may be tied to a general philosophical account of the nature of human goods, in which conceptual goods are, as it were, *translated into* individual goods, and individual goods are themselves thought of as either chosen by ourselves or imposed on us. The good in question though is altered in the 'translation' (p. 272).

But a clash of communal concepts need not depend on any such argument. The values involved are not translated into individual values, nor need they be thought of as imposed or chosen. People are attracted by, get caught up in, different ways of living and thinking which have values which conflict with each other. We cannot say that some of these reflect human life while the others do not. This is true, not simply as between differing communal concepts, but of the variety which may well exist within any one of them. Relations between children and parents are themselves decidedly mixed affairs. One might say: human life is like that.

If there are different perspectives in human life, it is unsurprising that the criticisms they make of each other will often, but not always, be in terms of values internal to the respective perspective. Diamond sees this as involving a circularity she wants to avoid. She says: 'I do not want to claim that there is a problem with circularity here, that we appeal to our own concepts in judging the human significance of the change to the conceptual world of those very concepts' (p. 273). But why should the involvement of a certain circularity be thought to be problematic? If I want to express what I think would be lost or is lost in the evasion of certain attitudes to parents, why should I want to do something other than elucidate what these attitudes involve?

In avoiding this circularity Diamond, as we have seen, pursues a far more ambitious but problematic course. By invoking what Cavell calls 'the sharedness of human life', Diamond can speak confidently of those who grasp the concept of a human being and of human life. Those who disagree do not grasp some *other* con- · cept, since there is only the one human life we share. Their disagreement has to be understood as a state of deprivation or dissociation which someone who philosophises well may help to rectify. Only those who understand can discuss conceptual loss, since the possibility of such discussion depends, she claims, on 'one's sense of how one lives, what life is like' (p. 272). But is 'what life is like' exhausted by 'how *one* lives'? Surely not. But in that case, one may regard what another regards as a conceptual loss as a gain. Neither party in the disagreement need be in a state of dissociation in Diamond's sense. The disagreement cannot be resolved by an appeal to 'what life is like'.

Diamond tempts one to think of human life as a homogeneous phenomenon by emphasising examples where there would be widespread agreement that one had reached the limits of what is acceptable from a human being. Diamond, for instance, speaks of her reaction to someone who justifies experimentation on animals on the ground that, unlike human beings, they do not develop into rational beings capable of making worthwhile contributions to society: 'My distance from such a person is not a matter of a rejection of what he takes himself to be arguing for. I might find myself asking, "Who is he, and how can he think that that is what to adduce in discussing – but with whom exactly? – putting babies in cages? What life does he live within which such a discussion goes on?"' Diamond says: 'The point of that example was to illustrate the idea that part of life with concepts is responsiveness to ways of talking which make no sense within that life; in the example, what makes no sense in the life of moral discussion is talk of the putting of babies into cages as a question *like* the use of taxes for public education. When someone speaks as if he did not know or had somehow forgotten that these are questions of different sorts, a participant in the life in which they have a different character may respond: "What is this?" "What is going on?" "Huh?"' (p. 274).

The reactions of incredulity are prompted by the fact that the proposal being made, according to Diamond, makes no sense in the lives of human beings, 'makes no sense in the life of moral discussion'. This charge of senselessness has to be used carefully. Recall Wittgenstein's remark that Goering had a kind of ethics too when he replied to a charge of injustice by saying, 'Justice is what we do'. No doubt our response to Nazi atrocities is not one of understanding. We cannot understand how human beings could behave in that way. Yet, the cries of the afflicted down the centuries show us all too clearly that they do. 'What is this?' 'What is going on?' are reactions from within lives governed by certain perspectives, but not reactions from within the lives of the perpetrators of the atrocities. Hitler's dreams were not ours gone wrong!

There are other differences between us, but the vast majority of them are not differences between us and the monstrous. Moral differences of different kinds separate us. In some cases, we can appreciate other points of view although we disagree with them, while in others we fail to see how people could have such points of view. Which cases these are vary from person to person. We could not counter those we oppose by saying of what they say, 'It simply makes no sense in the life of moral discussion.'

This conclusion is important, given Diamond's elucidation of the role of the philosopher. The philosopher is to play a part in elucidating what is involved in living a human life. He provides words for the inarticulate. Diamond compares him with a doctor who put into words the lives of the villagers he lived with, 'putting his articulateness into their service' (p. 269). Anyone who offers such articulateness, philosophers included, has an onerous responsibility, since the words offered may be the wrong ones. Such was the fate of French workers whose trade unions and parties on the Left only offered them the language of economic bargaining to describe their predicament. Simone Weil says that it is as if 'the devil were bargaining for the soul of some poor wretch and someone, moved by pity, should step in and say to the devil: "It is a shame for you to bid so low; the commodity is worth at least twice as much."'[11]

If, as I have suggested, human life is characterised by the heterogeneity of its perspectives and practices, the philosopher will be mischaracterising this complexity if he takes himself to be articulating what is involved in *the* concept of a human being or *the* concept of a human life. According to Diamond, as we have seen, 'the capacity to use a descriptive term is a capacity to participate in the life from which that word comes' (p. 267). But if the philosopher teaches us differences, giving us perspicuous representations of different perspectives in discussions, say, of moral disagreement or moral dilemmas, his grasp of the descriptive terms involved cannot mean that he personally participates in the *diverse* life forms from which these terms come. These forms are often in conflict, so how could he participate in all of them? *We need to distinguish between philosophical elucidation and personal participation.*

At times, it seems that Diamond recognises the importance of this conclusion. She says: 'I now want to add that, although the terms we use will have a place in a network of evaluative thought, to participate in the life in which the terms are used does not mean that one must share those evaluations' (p. 267). All Diamond means, however, is that one need not agree with every particular evaluation which occurs in life-with-a-concept. This is not to address the issue of the clash *between* different moral concepts, and of how a concept may be recognised by someone who has no personal use for it. Thus Oscar Wilde responded to the charge of blasphemy by saying, 'Sir, "blasphemy" is a word I never use.'

Diamond seems to get closer to discussing the different moral perspectives in human life philosophy has to take account of when she says: 'noting . . . conceptual contrasts need not involve evaluation' (p. 275). But in this case, all she has in mind is the conceptual contrast between our times and times remote from our own. We can note these contrasts without a moral grading of these different times. She explicitly contrasts this situation with the one she is concerned with, in which a personal acknowledgement and commitment *is* called for. Diamond compares this demand with the one she believes great writers make on us: 'They invite conceptually critical judgements involving a kind of acknowledgement on the part of the reader' (p. 275). But in our responses to literature, as in our responses in moral philosophy, what we acknowledge is far wider and more varied than what we accept morally ourselves.

Diamond recognises the huge gap between the world of the ancients and ours, but does not seem to recognise the problems the possibility of conceptual change poses for her arguments. At the end of her paper, however, she does address the issue of conceptual change, admitting that her arguments to this point are insufficient to do so. This is because the issue involves 'a kind of judgement, comparing it to another mode of thought, a possibility which does not depend upon one's participating in the life to which that mode of thought belongs' (p. 276). The example she considers is a detail from Paulus Potter's painting *The Young Bull* which is on the jacket of R. G. Frey's book on animal rights, *Rights, Killing and Suffering*. In the book, 'the permissibility of eating meat is defended by utilitarian arguments, against the utilitarian arguments on the other side by people like Peter Singer' (p. 276). Diamond does not believe such arguments get to the root of the matter. Potter's painting comes from a perspective which does not depend on them. The painting comes from a Christian perspective: it shows 'a peasant with his beasts, separated from them by a fence and by a cross formed by two trees, on which he leans. He is with them but apart from them; he shares, but with a difference, their life. What is in the picture is Potter's sense of the mysteriousness of the life we share; it is an impressive mediation of what *dominion* means, on what it is for human life to be dependent in the ways it then was on animals' (p. 276).

Diamond says of the picture: 'that is not my conceptual world' (p. 276). On her arguments so far, how can Diamond grasp concepts when she does not participate in the life to which they belong? She replies that we use concepts from old forms of life no longer our own simply by reflecting on them. Thus, she argues, 'coming to understand a conceptual life other than one's own involves exercise of concepts belonging to that life' (p. 276). But what kind of exercise is this? Diamond replies: 'When I understand what you say I am using concepts internal to your thought. It is not the same as the use you make; and in one's relation to a conceptual world very different from one's own, one may be limited to a narrow range of uses of their concepts, how narrow depending on one's relation to that world' (p. 277). Old concepts, Diamond argues, can help us to understand our present concepts: 'In an obvious sense, it is true that I do not order my thought about animals in relation to human beings by using the notion of dominion tied to a general Christian understanding of human life. There is a sense though, in which I do use that notion. The thought that is alive in Potter's picture, and the picture itself, belong to my understanding of what it can be like to think about animals and ourselves; within my understanding they serve as a standard. The concepts internal to the picture then belong to my capacity to think about and to assess the life around me' (p. 277).

In her treatment of Potter's painting, Diamond treats what is shown as an old concept which can inform our present ones. She still does not address the issue of *mixed and conflicting concepts in our present life*. In her treatment of the example, Diamond oscillates between talking of 'our conceptual life' and 'my conceptual life'. If the latter refers to what I personally embrace, the former is a wider phenomenon. Part of our conceptual life involves a Christian perspective on our relation to animals which an individual may or may not share. Such a perspective may accuse an urbanised, city conscience of distorting the differences which separate us from animals. Here is one voice from this perspective:

> We see a reduction of spirit through sentimentality, a loss of discrimination in respect to brutality, in a passage [Flannery] O'Connor notes in William Lynch's *The Image Industries: A Constructive Analysis of Films and Television*. Parochial children are stopped by a legal injunction from launching a mouse in a rocket. Their Bishop says there would have been less public

outcry if they had wanted to launch the nun teacher. Lynch comments: 'It is the reign, this protest for the mouse, of absolute sentimentality. It is that kind of identification of the solemn levels of human feeling with anything and everything which produces tawdriness and stupidity.' (Just how pervasive the distortion, one may be sure, might be measured by the number of persons reading my own argument here who would conclude it a call for cruelty to animals. How many of them, the critic must ask himself, would consent to shipping the critic to Mars on the next rocket, while they remain behind and resolutely oppose the death penalty for mass murderers and champion abortion.) The failure of discrimination of which we speak is connected with that failure to recognise the obscenely violent, a grotesquery which equates mice and men and which Miss O'Connor sees as leading to a wide range of sentimentality. . . . Another: she writes Robert Fitzgerald: 'Did you see the picture of Roy Rogers' horse attending a church service in Pasadena? The horse was apparently not born again and is currently a stuffed exhibit in a Roy Rogers Museum, to which we may if we will compare J. Bentham's stuffed presence at the University of London.'[12]

I have not quoted these comments to endorse or advocate them, but to note their presence. I do not know whether Diamond would see in them the dissociation Montgomery sees in others. In her treatment of Potter's painting, assessment and personal acknowledgement remain her concern. In the course of assessing it she appeals to 'our conceptual life' and 'to what human life is like'. I cannot see how the perspectives she embraces are *underwritten* by such an appeal. The acknowledgement philosophy seeks in its search for clarity is surely different; namely, the acknowledgement of what we know when not philosophising: the mixed character of human life. That mixture is not going to be tidied up by appeals to the concept of a human being or the concept of a human life. *That* is the acknowledgement philosophical reflection should result in. As Wittgenstein said, what is ragged must be left ragged.

There is little less ragged than the heterogeneity of the human. Many use the expression, 'What a man!' Their elucidations will show that the expression is used in the service of very different concepts. An individual may lose some of these in such a way that he cannot assess the gain or loss in doing so. Another may not

be deflected from acting decently even under the pressure of misfortune. A man who has such an attitude to life sees that as long as afflictions do not thus deflect him, they do not harm him – not in relation to what he regards as really important in his life (pp. 206–7).

At the end of his paper, Winch raises a major difficulty for this view of what is meant by saying that a good man cannot be harmed. Although in saying that all will be well, the good man is not predicting that no misfortune or affliction will come his way; he *is* predicting that no misfortune or affliction will deflect him from his allegiance to the good. As Winch points out, what this ignores is the power of extreme affliction to do just that. As a result, how can the good man say that *nothing* can harm him? Winch concludes that as a result of pressure of this kind, 'the ethical requires completion by the religious' (p. 207). While not denying this in given instances, my aim is not to explore religious perspectives. Rather, I want to consider moral perspectives which may withstand the pressure Winch refers to in ways he does not explore.

Winch is right to identify a predictive element in the moral patience he elucidates. Socrates, after all, makes the prediction explicit: 'I am sure that you would see me facing my fate with serenity' (522). Winch is also right to point out that this agent perspective on action may be destroyed by affliction. In the event of death in such circumstances, the agent, unlike Socrates, will not die an informed death. He cannot, since the perspective which would have informed it has been destroyed. Yet, even in circumstances such as these, could there be a point in saying that a good man has not been harmed? I think there could be but, of necessity, it would be a judgement made by spectators.

To appreciate the possibility of such judgements, we need to see how certain forms of moral purity are not agent perspectives on action, and are therefore free from the kind of prediction Socrates makes about himself. I am thinking, for example, of someone who does something magnanimous, but does not think of his action himself in this way at all. Indeed, part of its magnanimity consists in the fact that he does not do so. He may think that what he has done is perfectly ordinary, or not think of his action *as* anything in any laudatory way. He simply acts magnanimously, that is all. I heard of a person who read somewhere that an inmate of Broadmoor could come out on parole if someone would take him into his home for some months. He offered to take him immediately. He did not think of himself as doing anything special. He thought any decent person would respond as he did. In fact, of course, very few people would even contemplate making such an offer.

What I want to emphasise is that the character ascribed to such moral purity by others, is *not* part of the agent's perspective on his own deeds. The judgement of him is a spectator judgement. There are cases where this is even more obvious. Ascriptions of humility come from spectators. 'I am the humblest of men' is a self-refuting remark. It remains true, however, that a pure person of this kind may succumb or be defeated by life's horrors and afflictions. I am thinking, for example, of the effects of prolonged torture: torture born of a hatred which such purity often calls forth. If this happens, what might it mean to say that goodness has been necessarily rewarded, or that it has not been touched? It cannot mean that a perspective, such as that of Socrates, has survived the trials, but not because it has been overthrown, since it was never a feature of the kind of purity I am talking about. Nevertheless, when such purity is destroyed, the terribleness of what has happened cannot be elucidated without mentioning the goodness which has been outraged. In face of the outrage, the goodness is dumb, silenced, but its story cannot be touched. It is what shows itself in the fate it undergoes. Those spectators who witness it and want to say that the person's goodness is necessarily rewarded have found *a way of saluting that story*. The salutation does not compensate for what has been destroyed, but it does not denigrate it either. The character of the agent and his story prompts this salutation in the spectator. Again, any attempt to confirm this salutation by the agent would be self-negating. 'I am a pure man' constitutes, in the cases I am considering, a self-refuting claim.

In 'Ethical Reward and Punishment', Winch turns to the issue of what it might mean to say that an evil man is necessarily punished. He argues in ways analogous to those he used in discussing what it might mean to say that a good man is necessarily rewarded. Winch suggests that the punishment of an evil act is only morally significant if it is related to *the agent's* moral perspective. He illustrates this claim by considering the attitudes of three criminals to their punishments. The first vows never to be caught again for his crimes. The second vows to give up his life of crime because he is getting caught too often. The third vows to lead a better life, accepting his punishment as something he deserves. Only in the third, as Winch says, is there a moral relation between the punishment and the agent. For him, the punishment is not a mere causal consequence of the crime. His imprisonment has a significance for him within his moral perspective. This helps us to understand how a person may feel that he must undergo punishment for his misdeeds, even though, prior to the punishment, he has repented of them and changed radically as a person. Insistence on the punishment is, for him, an expression of the seriousness of his repentance. Invoking 'remorse' as a reason why punishment should be excused is a reason for doubting the genuineness of the remorse. Winch is not suggesting, of course, that these attitudes are shared by everyone. He is well aware that they are not. He is pursuing the philosophical task of endeavouring to see what such attitudes and perspectives amount to.

Of course, a misdeed may not be followed by any punishment, formal or informal, inflicted by any authority. A person may, however, regard a natural disaster or misfortune which befalls him as punishment for his wrongdoing. Winch points out that such an attitude may be superstitious, involving a belief in a queer causal connection between wrongdoing and misfortune, but he also points out that this need not be so. The attitude may be an extension of the seriousness with which the agent regards what he has done.

Winch also points out that a person may feel remorse for what he has done without the occurrence of any of the punishments mentioned so far. The remorse itself, however, may be seen as a punishment for the wrongdoing. When this is so, remorse cannot be regarded as a sanction, contingently related to the action. If it were so regarded, it ought to be possible to say, 'Don't do that, you will only feel remorse', as though it were akin to saying, 'Don't eat that, it will only upset your stomach'. This would not be remorse at all. Further, as Winch says, even if we regard remorse as a sanction, 'unlike sanctions imposed by external authorities, such "sanctions" will only operate on someone who is himself able to see the wrongness of his action. For feeling remorse *is* a way of seeing the wrongness of one's action' (p. 225).

Winch concludes that in the three cases he has considered, the moral significance of punishment depends on the moral perspective of the agent. Without that perspective, the formal or informal punishments inflicted by authorities, simply become effective or ineffective deterrents, which have no moral significance for the agent. Without the agent's moral perspective, natural disasters may be viewed superstitiously as punishments: 'If you do that, something bad is sure to happen to you.' Without that perspective, it makes no sense to speak of remorse, since remorse *is* a moral perspective.

In the light of this conclusion, we can appreciate the difficulty involved in understanding what might be meant by the claim that an evil man is necessarily punished. Clearly, none of the punishments Winch has mentioned can be called 'necessary', since they need not occur. Such is the case with Archelaus, the evil tyrant discussed in Plato's *Gorgias*. He perpetrates evil on a grand scale and yet, it seems, is not punished. He is not punished by any authority. He does not regard his misfortunes as punishments for his crimes, nor does he feel any remorse for them. Yet, despite all this, someone may want to say that Archelaus is necessarily punished. What on earth can this mean? Winch says,

> The terms in which the problem presents itself preclude *ab initio* any attempt to find a solution by looking for relevant events in the life of the offender, for the supposition is that no relevant events are to be found there. Now the only other direction in which we can look is the life of the person who makes such a judgement as 'no crime goes unpunished'. We must try to understand, that is, exactly what such a judgement commits its author to (p. 226).

Winch argues that once we look in this direction,

> There is an extremely simple short answer to this question: namely, that one who believes that all wrong-doing is punished is committed in all cases to pitying wrongdoers, not only when they are subsequently visited by worldly misfortunes (including pangs of remorse) but also, and even more especially, when they seem to have escaped any consequences of their crimes (p. 226).

Winch is right to point out that we may find it morally and psychologically difficult to accept such an attitude to wrongdoing, one in which 'the beastlier the wrong-doing, the greater the demand for compassion towards the wrongdoer' (p. 227). Following Winch, however, I shall concentrate on the intellectual difficulties presented by such an attitude.

For many people, their difficulties come from wanting *more* than the wrongness of actions, to justify the pity felt for them. The difficulty, Winch says, is 'to see how the fact that a man has committed a wrong can be a justification for pitying him at all. It is a difficulty in attaching sense to a certain way of thinking' (p. 227). Winch wonders, however, whether the difficulty should arise if we keep in mind his discussion of various forms of punishment. In this discussion, to appreciate the moral significance of the rewards and punishments which actually occur,

> our attention is focused, not on the specific character of those happenings considered in themselves, but on the moral character of the actions which are being thought of as rewarded or punished. In other words, *even in those cases*, the actual character of the consequences drops out of consideration as irrelevant and we are left with the nature of the agent's actions. We still have those actions, together with a certain view of their nature and significance, where no further consequences in fact ensue. That is, we have all that we need to justify congratulations of, or pity for, the agent (p. 227).

Perhaps this conclusion is justified, but does it help us to see what is meant by saying that someone like Archelaus is necessarily punished? Can this judgement be equated with the pity felt for wrongdoers *in all cases*? I do not think so. Something is left unaccounted for. A person may pity someone who fails to feel remorse for some petty behaviour, but he does not think that the possibility of remorse is ruled out. The immorality is not such as to make that likely. With Archelaus, it is different.

When Winch discussed actual punishments, he argued that their moral significance was to be found in the moral perspective of the agent. But the moral significance of saying that Archelaus is necessarily punished is to be found in the moral perspective of certain spectators. It is the spectator who is the author of the judgement, 'no crime goes unpunished'. When Winch discussed the judgement, 'The good man is necessarily rewarded' he did so in terms of the agent's moral perspective. I suggested that recognition of a certain kind of moral purity showed why the judgement had to be a spectator judgement. Similar considerations will enable us to see why, given a certain kind of evil, the judgement, 'Evil is necessarily punished' must also be a spectator judgement.

As Winch recognises, actual punishments may be seen in a non-moral way by the agent, but they may come to have moral significance for him. A punishment carried out by some authority, or a natural disaster, may come to have moral significance for the agent. Ambivalent mental disturbances after a misdeed may develop into remorse. These possibilities are absent in Archelaus. He revels in his wrongdoing. What, then, is his punishment? The answer is: what he has become. From a spectator perspective it may be said that Archelaus is necessarily punished because he is in a kind of hell. It is for this reason that this spectator judgement cannot be equated with pity for *all cases* of wrongdoing. Just as the judgement, 'The good man is necessarily rewarded' meant something distinctive in the case of exceptional moral purity, so the judgement, 'The evil man is necessarily punished' may mean something equally distinctive in the case of extreme evil.

What I have in mind can be elucidated by exploring further the difficulties which may be felt about saying that Archelaus is necessarily punished. If we say that Archelaus is in a kind of hell, someone may wonder how someone can be in hell without knowing it. Does not hell necessarily involve torment? What is hell without it?[4]

At the outset of his paper, 'Can a Good Man Be Harmed?', Winch quotes Claudius's confession from Shakespeare's *Hamlet*:

> My words fly up, my thoughts remain below,
> Words without thoughts never to heaven go.

This is something Claudius *says*, but Archelaus says no such thing. He revels in evil, believing himself to be in paradise. But, as Simone Weil has pointed out, this is precisely what one kind of hell consists in: thinking you are in paradise when you are not. When that 'paradise' takes the form of extreme evil, it may be thought that this is the worst hell of all. One who is in it is necessarily punished.

At the outset of his paper, in elucidating what might be meant by saying that a good man is necessarily rewarded and cannot be harmed, Winch also quotes Wittgenstein's reference to an experience in which a person is inclined to say, 'I am safe, nothing can injure me whatever happens.'[5] This remark shares the confidence of the Socratic prediction we discussed earlier. The morally pure man of whom I spoke, says no such thing. He simply acts, and others marvel at what he does. They may say of such a man, even if afflictions destroy him, 'He is necessarily rewarded.'

Shakespeare's Claudius says that he had most need of blessing, but that 'Amen' stuck in his throat. But 'Amen' does not stick in Archelaus's throat. In Benjamin Britten's opera , *Billy Budd*, Claggart, when confronted by Billy's innocence, is made to say that a light has shone in darkness, and that the darkness comprehended it and trembled. Archelaus, on the other hand, fits the Biblical paradigm: when light shone in darkness, the darkness comprehended it not. Archelaus continues to think his hell is paradise. Spectators reacting to him may say that he is necessarily punished.

In the judgements of moral purity and moral depravity we have discussed, we have seen how they involve notions of necessary reward and necessary punishment respectively. The judgements are responses to the characters of the persons judged. As such, they are spectator judgements. They cannot be judgements made from the perspectives of the agents. The morally pure man and the evil man I have referred to, do not see themselves as others see them. Any measure of assent to the spectator judgements on the part of the agents, would show immediately that such judgements are mistaken.

Notes

1 On Morality's Having a Point

1. G. E. M. Anscombe, 'Modern Moral Philosophy', *Philosophy*, Jan. 1958, reprinted in *Ethics, Religion and Politics, Collected Philosophical Papers*, Vol. III (Oxford: Blackwell, 1981).
2. See 'Moral Beliefs', *Proc. Arist. Soc.*, 1958; 'Moral Arguments', *Mind*, 1958; 'Goodness and Choice', *Proc. Arist. Soc.*, Supp. Vol. XXXV, 1961, reprinted in *Virtues and Vices* (Oxford: Blackwell, 1978).
3. See Mary Warnock's Introduction to *Utilitarianism* (London: Fontana, 1962), p. 31.
4. Max Black, 'The Gap Between "Is" and "Should"', *Philosophical Review*, April 1964.
5. G. H. von Wright, *The Varieties of Goodness* (London: Routledge & Kegan Paul, 1963).
6. See R. S. Peters and A. S. Phillips Griffiths, 'The Autonomy of Prudence', *Mind*, 1962.
7. See Richard Wollheim's Introduction to Bradley's *Ethical Studies* (Oxford: Oxford University Press, paperback 1962), p. xvi.
8. See Mrs Foot's excellent paper, 'When Is a Principle a Moral Principle?', *Proc. Arist. Soc.*, Supp. Vol. XXVIII (1954), which, interestingly, she did not want included in *Virtues and Vices*.
9. I owe this example to Dr H. S. Price.
10. 'Moral Beliefs', in *Virtues and Vices*.
11. I owe it to Mr Rush Rhees.
12. Georges Sorel, *Reflections On Violence*, trans. T. E. Hulme (London: Collier, 1961), pp. 229–30.

2 Moral Practices and Anscombe's Grocer

1. G. E. M. Anscombe, 'On Brute Facts' (*Analysis*, Vol. 18, 1957–8), reprinted in *Ethics, Religion and Politics, Collected Philosophical Papers*, Vol. III (Oxford: Blackwell, 1981).
2. Ibid., p. 70.
3. This mistake appeared in my paper, 'Miss Anscombe's Grocer', *Analysis*, July 1968, and was pointed out by Colwyn Williamson in 'Miss Anscombe's Grocer and Mr Phillips's Grocer', *Analysis*, July 1968. For the reply to this latter paper see 'The Limitations of Miss Anscombe's Grocer', *Analysis*, January 1969.

3 The Possibilities of Moral Advice

1. Max Black, 'The Gap Between "Is" and "Should"', *Philosophical Review* LXXIII, 1964, pp. 165–81.

2. Ibid., p. 166.
3. Ibid., p. 181.
4. Ibid., p. 175.
5. Ibid., p. 178.
6. Ibid., p. 179.
7. Ibid., p. 179.
8. Ibid., p. 180.

4 Allegiance and Change in Morality: A Study in Contrasts

1. Peter Winch, 'The Universalizability of Moral Judgments', *Ethics and Action* (London: Routledge & Kegan Paul, 1972), pp. 154–5.
2. Ibid., p. 155.
3. See Chapter 15.
4. I am grateful to Mr D. L. Sims for emphasising this point in a discussion of this paper at the University College of Swansea English Society.
5. 'The Universalizability of Moral Judgments', p. 155.
6. Blake Nevius, 'On *The Age of Innocence*', in *Edith Wharton: A Collection of Critical Essays*, ed. Irving Howe, p. 166.
7. Ibid., pp. 168–9.
8. Edmund Wilson, 'Justice to Edith Wharton', ibid., p. 26.
9. Ibid., p. 29.
10. Lionel Trilling, 'The Morality of Inertia', ibid., p. 145.
11. Louis Auchincloss, 'Edith Wharton and Her New Yorks', ibid., p. 38.
12. Edith Wharton, *The Age of Innocence*, p. 139.
13. Ibid., pp. 139–40.
14. Ibid., p. 141.
15. Ibid., p. 192.
16. 'Edith Wharton and Her New Yorks', *Edith Wharton*, p. 38.
17. *The Age of Innocence*, p. 283.
18. Louis O. Coxe, 'What Edith Wharton Saw in Innocence', *Edith Wharton*, p. 159.
19. *The Age of Innocence*, p. 283.
20. Edith Wharton, *The Custom of the Country*, p. 70.
21. 'What Edith Wharton Saw in Innocence', *Edith Wharton*, pp. 157–8.
22. Irving Howe, 'A Reading of *The House of Mirth*', ibid., p. 122.
23. 'What Edith Wharton Saw in Innocence', ibid., p. 160.
24. Edith Wharton, *A Backward Glance*, p. 207.
25. These points were made by H. O. Mounce in the discussion referred to in note 4.
26. C. W. K. Mundle, *A Critique of Linguistic Philosophy* (Oxford: Clarendon Press, 1970), p. 14.
27. E. Kamenka, *Marxism and Ethics* (London: Macmillan, 1969), p. 35.

6 The Presumption of Theory

1. Peter Winch, *The Idea of a Social Science* (London: Routledge & Kegan Paul, 1958).

2. Reprinted in Winch, *Ethics and Action* (London: Routledge & Kegan Paul, 1972). All references to Winch's papers are from this volume.
3. 'Understanding a Primitive Society', p. 9.
4. 'Moral Integrity', p. 191.
5. 'The Universalizability of Moral Judgements', p. 154.
6. The necessity of such connections if the word 'moral' is to mean anything is excellently brought out by Philippa Foot in 'When is a principle a moral principle?', *Proc. Arist. Soc.*, Supp, Vol. 1954.
7. 'Understanding a Primitive Society', p. 43–4.
8. 'Human Nature', p. 77.
9. Ibid.
10. Ibid., p. 82.
11. Alasdair MacIntyre, *A Short History of Ethics* (New York: Macmillan, 1966), p. 148.
12. 'Human Nature', p. 80.
13. For related criticisms of MacIntyre's later work, *After Virtue* (London: Duckworth, 1981), see Chapter 5 above.
14. 'Human Nature', p. 84.
15. 'Moral Integrity', pp. 172–3.
16. For similar criticisms, see Chapter 9.
17. 'Moral Integrity', p. 175.
18. Ibid., pp. 175–6.
19. Ibid., p. 177.
20. Ibid.
21. Ibid., p. 178.
22. 'Human Nature', p. 88.
23. Ibid.
24. Onora O'Neill, 'The Power of Example', *Philosophy*, Vol. 61, Jan. 1986. All references will be to this paper. Her footnote referring to the tradition she detects reads as follows: 'A basic source for this writing is Wittgenstein's "Lecture on Ethics", which was published together with reports of conversations Wittgenstein later had with F. Waismann and Rush Rhees, *Philosophical Review*, Vol. LXXIV, 1965, pp. 3–12; 12–36. Wittgenstein's discussion of examples in non-ethical contexts are also influential. In addition to the papers in Winch, op. cit., Wittgensteinian approaches to ethics include: Rush Rhees, *Without Answers* (London: Routledge & Kegan Paul, 1969); D. Z. Phillips and H. O. Mounce, *Moral Practices* (London: Routledge & Kegan Paul, 1970); R. W. Beardsmore, *Moral Reasoning* (London: Routledge & Kegan Paul, 1969); Rodger Beehler, *Moral Life* (Oxford: Blackwell, 1978); various articles in *Philosophical Investigations*, including C. Diamond, 'Anything But Argument?' (1982), 23–41; some papers in R. F. Holland, *Against Empiricism* (Oxford: Blackwell, 1980); and some in D. Z. Phillips, *Through a Darkening Glass* (Oxford: Blackwell, 1982).
25. 'Moral Integrity', p. 182.
26. Ibid., p. 184.
27. Ibid.
28. Ibid., p. 185.
29. 'Understanding a Primitive Society', p. 42.

30. 'Nature and Convention', p. 71.
31. Alice Munro, *Something I've Been Meaning to Tell You* (Harmondsworth: Penguin, 1985).
32. For my fuller discussion of this example see 'Meaning What We Say' in *From Fantasy to Faith: Philosophy of Religion and Twentieth Century Literature* (London: Macmillan, 1990).
33. See J. P. Sartre, 'Existentialism is a Humanism' in *Existentialism from Dostoyevsky to Sartre*, ed. W. Kaufmann (Cleveland, Ohio: World Publishing, 1956).
34. See G. E. M. Anscombe, 'Modern Moral Philosophy', *Philosophy*, 1958, reprinted in *Ethics, Religion and Politics, Collected Philosophical Papers*, Vol. III (Oxford: Blackwell, 1981).
35. R. W. Beardsmore, 'Consequences and Moral Worth', *Analysis*, June 1969, p. 183, n.
36. 'Moral Integrity', p. 185.
37. Ibid.
38. Ibid., pp. 186–7.
39. Kant, *The Critique of Pure Reason*, trans. N. Kemp Smith (London: Macmillan, 1961), A 132–133/B 171–172. Quoted by O'Neill on p. 8.
40. Ibid., A 134/B 173.
41. 'The Universalizability of Moral Judgements', p. 163.
42. Ibid., pp. 163–4.
43. Ibid., p. 170, n. 16.
44. 'Moral Integrity', p. 191.
45. Kant, *Logic*, trans. Robert Hartmann and Wolfgang Schwartz (Indianapolis: Bobbs-Merrill, 1974), p. 48.
46. Kant, *The Critique of Judgement*, trans. James Meredith (Oxford: Oxford University Press, 1978), p. 293.
47. Kant, ibid., 294.
48. This was one of the main themes of my collection, *Through a Darkening Glass* (Oxford: Blackwell, 1982); see Chapter 4 of this collection.)
49. 'The Universalizability of Moral Judgements', p. 164.
50. Ibid., p. 165.
51. Ibid., p. 166.
52. Ibid.

7 What Can We Expect From Ethics?

1. Bernard Williams, *Ethics and the Limits of Philosophy* (London: Fontana Press/Collins, 1985), p. 21. All quotations from Williams are from this work.
2. See, for example, Philippa Foot, 'Moral Beliefs' in *Virtues and Vices* (Oxford: Blackwell, 1978).
3. See, for example, Alan Donagan, *The Theory of Morality* (Chicago: University of Chicago Press, 1977), p. 7.
4. I argue for this conclusion in Chapter 9.
5. See Chapter 1.
6. J. L. Stocks, 'The Limits of Purpose', in J. L. Stocks, *Morality and Purpose*, edited with an Introduction by D. Z. Phillips (London:

Routledge & Kegan Paul, 1970), p. 27. The Introduction to this work forms Chapter 13 below.

7. J. L. Stocks, 'Can Philosophy Determine What is Ethically or Socially Valuable?' op. cit., p. 124. I shall refer to this paper as *CPD*.
8. Annette Baier, 'Theory and Reflective Practices' in *Postures of the Mind* (London: Methuen, 1985), pp. 208–9.
9. Peter Winch, 'Moral Integrity' in *Ethics and Action* (London: Routledge & Kegan Paul, 1972), p. 181.
10. J. L. Stocks, 'The Need for a Social Philosophy', op. cit., p. 109. I shall refer to this paper as *NSP*.
11. Annette Baier, 'Doing Without Moral Theory?' op. cit., p. 231. All quotations from Baier are from this paper unless otherwise indicated.
12. Annette Baier, 'Caring About Caring', op. cit., p. 94.
13. See Nicholas Wolterstorff, 'Is Reason Enough?', *The Reformed Journal*, Vol. 34, no. 4, April 1981, p. 23.
14. I owe this way of putting the matter to Rowan Williams. See his, 'The Suspicion of Suspicion: Wittgenstein and Bonhoeffer' in *The Grammar of the Heart*, ed. Richard Bell (New York: Harper and Row, 1988).
15. Ludwig Wittgenstein, *Culture and Value*, ed. G. H. von Wright, trans. Peter Winch (Oxford: Blackwell, 1977), p. 77. For my criticisms of Rorty see *Faith After Foundationalism* (London: Routledge, 1988), Part Two, Chapters 10–12, pp. 131–66.
16. Ludwig Wittgenstein, *Culture and Value*, p. 42.
17. Peter Winch, 'Moral Integrity', op. cit., p. 178.
18. I owe this example to Rush Rhees.
19. *Letters of Flannery O'Connor: The Habit of Being*, edited with introduction by Sally Fitzgerald (New York, 1980), p. 220.
20. Alasdair MacIntyre, *After Virtue* (London: Duckworth, 1981), p. 24.
21. Rush Rhees, 'Politics and Justification' in *Without Answers* (London: Routledge & Kegan Paul, 1969), pp. 84–5.
22. Rush Rhees, '"Natural Law" and Reason in Ethics', *ibid.*, p. 96.
23. I am indebted to R. F. Holland and John Edelman for emphasising the importance of such contributions in ethics. Annette Baier stresses the temptation for the contributors to think that their observations are the results of disinterested enquiry or pure reason. See Baier, op. cit., p. 230.
24. See Peter Winch, 'The Universalizability of Moral Judgements', *op. cit.*

9 Does It Pay To Be Good?

1. Reprinted in *Virtues and Vices* (Oxford: Blackwell, 1978).
2. See Peter Winch: 'Nature and Convention', *Proc. Arist. Soc.*, Vol. LX (1959–60). Reprinted in *Ethics and Action* (London: Routledge & Kegan Paul, 1978). I no longer hold this view for reasons given by R. F. Holland in 'Is Goodness a Mystery?', reprinted in *Against Empiricism* (Oxford: Blackwell, 1980), and acknowledged by Winch in his introduction to *Ethics and Action*. See pp. 244–5 of this collection.
3. Mrs Foot herself has argued that what is to count as a moral principle cannot be a contingent matter. See 'When Is A Principle A Moral

Principle?' *Proc. Arist. Soc.* Supp. Vol. XXVIII, 1954. My objections are to the way she has tried to develop her arguments there in later papers.
4. The translation by W. Lowrie (Oxford: Oxford University Press, 1946).
5. See J. L. Evans, 'Grade Not', *Philosophy*, Jan. 1962.
6. 'The Limits of Purpose', in J. L. Stocks, *Morality and Purpose*, ed. D. Z. Phillips (London: Routledge, 1970), p. 27.
7. 'Is There A Moral End?', ibid., p. 77.

10   In Search of the Moral 'Must': Mrs Foot's Fugitive Thought

1. See 'Morality as a System of Hypothetical Imperatives', *Philosophical Review* 81 (1972): 'Reasons for Action and Desires', Supp. Vol., *Proc. Arist. Soc.*, 46 (1972): 'Is Morality a System of Hypothetical Imperatives? – A Reply to Mr Holmes', *Analysis*, 35 (1974–5), reprinted in *Virtues and Vices* (Oxford: Blackwell, 1978) Quotations are from the original, p. 305.
2. 'Morality as a System of Hypothetical Imperatives'.
3. 'Is There a Moral End?', in J. L. Stocks (ed.), *Morality and Purpose* (London: Routledge, 1970), p. 73.
4. Søren Kierkegaard, *Purity of Heart*, trans. Douglas Steere (London: Fontana, 1961).
5. Ludwig Wittgenstein, 'Lecture on Ethics', *Philosophical Review*, 74 (1965).
6. J. L. Stocks, 'The Limits of Purpose', in *Morality and Purpose*, op. cit.
7. Kant, 'Fundamental Principles of the Metaphysics of Morals', in *Critique of Practical Reason*, trans. Abbott (London, 1948), p. 17.
8. F. C. S. Schiller, 'Belief and Action', in *Problems of Belief* (London, 1924), pp. 138–9.
9. See R. W. Beardsmore, *Moral Reasoning* (London: Routledge, 1969); D. Z. Phillips and H. O. Mounce, *Moral Practices* (London: Routledge, 1970); R. F. Holland, 'Is Goodness a Mystery?', *The Human World*, No. 9, Nov. 1972; Peter Winch, *Ethics and Action* (London: Routledge, 1978).
10. 'Is Morality a System of Hypothetical Imperatives? – A Reply to Mr Holmes', p. 53.
11. See 'Moral Beliefs', *Proc. Arist. Soc.*, 1958–9; 'Moral Arguments', *Mind*, 1958', reprinted in *Virtues and Vices*.
12. See 'Moral Beliefs'.
13. For criticism of the attempt to establish a link between morality and self-interest see Chapters 1 and 9.
14. 'Moral Beliefs', p. 37 in *Theories of Ethics*, ed. Philippa Foot (Oxford, 1967).
15. For an excellent attack on the view that commendation is externally related to its object see Philippa Foot, 'When Is a Principle a Moral Principle?', *Proc. Arist. Soc.*, 1954.
16. Introduction to *Theories of Ethics*, ed. Philippa Foot, p. 9.
17. 'Morality as a System of Hypothetical Imperatives', p. 310. For further effective criticism see 'Reasons for Action and Desires', p. 207.

18. 'Is Morality a System of Hypothetical Imperatives – A Reply to Mr Holmes', p. 55.
19. See pp. 126–7.
20. 'Morality as a System of Hypothetical Imperatives', p. 308.
21. 'Is Morality a System of Hypothetical Imperatives? – A Reply to Mr Holmes', p. 56.
22. I am grateful to my colleague Mr H. O. Mounce, in a discussion of an earlier draft of this paper, for pointing out the need to make this clearer than I would otherwise have made it.
23. 'Morality as a System of Hypothetical Imperatives', pp. 308–9.
24. The fact that the observance of many rules of etiquette depends on the presence of more than one person does not affect the substance of my point.
25. See Chapter 15.
26. See Rush Rhees, 'Some Developments in Wittgenstein's View of Ethics', *Philosophical Review*, 74 (1965).
27. See Chapter 4.
28. 'Reasons for Action and Desires', p. 209.
29. Introduction to *Theories of Ethics*, p. 9.
30. 'Morality as a System of Hypothetical Imperatives', p. 313.
31. J. L. Stocks, 'Moral Values', in *Morality and Purpose*, p. 58.
32. J. L. Stocks, 'Is There a Moral End?', in *Morality and Purpose*, p. 79.
33. Kierkegaard, *Purity of Heart*, p. 177.

11 Do Moral Considerations Override Others?

1. Philippa Foot, *Virtues and Vices* (Oxford: Blackwell, 1978).
2. See Chapter 10.
3. The relevance of the examples which follow was pointed out to me by David Reeve when I read an earlier version of the paper at Reed College, Portland, Oregon.
4. D. Z. Phillips and H. S. Price, 'Remorse Without Repudiation', *Analysis*, 28 (1967).
5. See Chapter 15.
6. A. I. Melden, *Rights and Right Conduct* (Oxford: Blackwell, 1959).
7. For further discussion of this failure see Peter Winch, 'Moral Integrity', in *Ethics and Action* (London: Routledge, 1978). See p. 78 of this collection.

12 An Argument From Extreme Cases?

1. William Davie, 'The Extreme Case in Ethics', *Philosophical Investigations* 3, no. 1 (Winter 1980).
2. On this whole issue see J. L. Stocks, *Morality and Purpose*, ed. with an Introduction by D. Z. Phillips (London: Routledge & Kegan Paul, 1969). The Introduction forms Chapter 13 below.
3. See John Anderson's papers on ethics in *Studies in Empirical Philosophy* (Sydney: Angus and Robertson, 1962) and Rush Rhees, 'Responsibility to Society' in *Without Answers* (London: Routledge & Kegan Paul, 1969).

4. See Chapter 11.
5. For the latter possibility see Peter Winch, 'Moral Integrity' in *Ethics and Action* (London: Routledge & Kegan Paul, 1972). Again, see p. 78 of this collection.
6. See Chapter 15.

13   Morality and Purpose

1. J. L. Stocks, *Morality and Purpose*, ed. with an Introduction by D. Z. Phillips (London: Routledge & Kegan Paul, 1972). All references are to this work.
2. I am thinking especially of Philippa Foot's and G. E. M. Anscombe's writings on ethics. See P. R. Foot's 'Moral Beliefs', *Proc. Arist. Soc.* LIX (1958-9) and G. E. M. Anscombe's 'Modern Moral Philosophy', *Philosophy* XXXIII (1958).
3. Such talk is prominent in R. M. Hare's writings on moral philosophy.
4. For a discussion of such reductionism see Chapter 9.
5. See Rush Rhees, 'Some Developments in Wittgenstein's View of Ethics', *Philosophical Review*, January 1965, pp. 22–3.

14   How Lucky Can You Get?

1. B. A. O. Williams and T. Nagel, 'Moral Luck', *Proc. Arist. Soc.*, Supp. Vol. L, 1976. All quotations from Williams and Nagel are from this source. Williams and Nagel have reprinted their papers in their respective collections, *Moral Luck* (Cambridge: Cambridge University Press, 1981) and *Mortal Questions* (Cambridge: Cambridge University Press, 1979). With one exception, in Williams's case, noted at the end of the paper, the reprinted versions do not affect the points in the original symposium which I have relied on.
2. An equally interesting and related topic, in view of the different forms of rationalism in ethics, is the involvement of luck in the study of ethics itself; in the ways one met one's teachers and how one's attention was directed to what they took to be of central importance in the subject. It was the good fortune of students at Swansea from 1952 to 1964 to have R. F. Holland, J. R. Jones, Peter Winch and – above all – Rush Rhees, who came to Swansea in 1940, teaching philosophy there at the same time.
3. Nagel's point does not depend on our sharing these moral judgements. Similar considerations would apply given moral perspectives radically different from these. The pervasiveness of certain moral points of view may lead us to miss this point. It was characteristic of Wittgenstein that he was alive to the possibility of radically different perspectives. As in 1945:

> When the war was nearly over and the Russian armies were closing in on Berlin, I spent a few hours with Wittgenstein in London, on my way back to Germany after a period of leave in England.

Wittgenstein: 'What a terrible position a man like Hitler is in now.' He said this with compassion. I thought it remarkable that at a time when we were all gloating over the fall of Hitler, Wittgenstein, although detesting everything that Hitler had stood for, could at the same time see the suffering involved in such a terrible situation. (M. O'C. Drury, 'Conversations With Wittgenstein' in *Ludwig Wittgenstein: Personal Recollections* edited by Rush Rhees (Oxford: Blackwell, 1981), p. 163)

4. Ludwig Wittgenstein, *Philosophical Investigations* I, I:620.
5. Winch expounds these difficulties and the way Wittgenstein worked through them in 'Wittgenstein's Treatment of the Will', first published in *Ratio* in 1968. The neglect of this paper and his paper 'Trying', adapted from a 1971 symposium with Peter Heath, *Proc. Arist. Soc.*, Supp. Vol. XLV on 'Trying and Attempting' is rather surprising. Both papers were reprinted in Winch's *Ethics and Action* (London: Routledge & Kegan Paul, 1971). They deal with the central issues which concern Williams and Nagel. Even the same examples are discussed. It might be said that Winch's philosophising begins where Nagel's expression of philosophical puzzlement ends.
6. Ludwig Wittgenstein, *Notebooks 1914–1916*, p. 73.
7. Winch, 'Trying', pp. 137–8.
8. Ludwig Wittgenstein, *Philosophical Investigations* I, I:615.
9. Peter Heath, op. cit., p. 196.
10. Winch, 'Trying', p. 140.
11. Ibid., p. 141.
12. But it is not a case of what we want, but of what we have. As to whether it could be otherwise, 'we' in this context refers to many, but not to all, people. There are those, for example, who, in defence of injuries inflicted on the old and defenceless, have said that they did not really do it, but that 'society' made them do it.
13. 'Moral Integrity', *Ethics and Action*, p. 184. Because Winch does not say it was irrational for Oedipus to blame himself, this does not commit him to saying that it was rational for him to do so.
14. Ibid., p. 185.
15. This is not to say that nothing can be done to nurture moral dispositions. For example, when I am tempted to be ungenerous I may pull myself up, saying, 'Come now, think of what you're doing. Be generous!' From such moral reminders natural generosity may develop.
16. Winch, 'Wittgenstein's Treatment of the Will', pp. 128–9.
17. Wittgenstein, *Philosophical Investigations* I, I:622–3. Quoted by Winch, ibid.
18. Winch, 'Moral Integrity', p. 183. Winch is not insisting his readers to condone this moral judgement, but to recognise its possibility.
19. For a more detailed discussion of this and related matters see 'What the Complex Did to Oedipus' in my collection *Through a Darkening Glass* (University of Notre Dame Press and Oxford: Blackwell, 1982).
20. Simone Weil, *Gravity and Grace*, trans. Emma Cranford, Introduction by Gustave Thibon (London: Routledge & Kegan Paul, 1947) p. 22.

21. There are, of course, other difficulties connected with the freedom of the will which are not considered in this paper.
22. Rush Rhees, 'What are Moral Statements Like?' in *Without Answers* (London: Routledge & Kegan Paul and New York: Schocken Books, 1969), p. 103.
23. Rush Rhees, 'Knowing the Difference between Right and Wrong', ibid., p. 97.
24. Ibid., p. 101.
25. Ibid.
26. Ibid.
27. 'What are Moral Statements Like?', ibid., p. 104.
28. Ibid.
29. 'The Study of Philosophy', ibid., pp. 169–70.
30. Ibid., pp. 171–2.
31. Ibid., p. 172.
32. See Chapter 15 below and 'Moral Dilemmas' in D. Z. Phillips and H. O. Mounce, *Moral Practices* (Routledge & Kegan Paul, 1970).
33. See below, p. 219.
34. See Thomas Mann, *Doctor Faustus*.
35. 'What are Moral Statements Like?', op. cit., p. 104.
36. Rush Rhees, 'Some Developments in Wittgenstein's View of Ethics', *Philosophical Review*, Jan. 1965.
37. Ibid.
38. Ibid.
39. Owen Flanagan, 'Admirable Immorality and Admirable Imperfection', *The Journal of Philosophy*, Vol. LXXXIII, no. 1, Jan. 1986, p. 53, n. 9.
40. For further discussions of this possibility see 'Mental Gymnastics', 'Following a Rule' and 'Only Words' in my collection, *From Fantasy to Faith: Philosophy of Religion and Twentieth Century Literature* (London: Macmillan, 1991).
41. I benefited from a discussion of an earlier version of the paper at a graduate discussion at the University College of Swansea, and especially on that occasion, as on so many others since 1952, from comments by Rush Rhees.

15 Some Limits to Moral Endeavour

1. J. L. Stocks, *Morality and Purpose*, edited with an introduction by D. Z. Phillips (Routledge & Kegan Paul, 1970), pp. 39–40.
2. Peter Winch, *Moral Integrity* (Oxford: Blackwell, 1968), p. 4. Reprinted in *Ethics and Action* (London: Routledge, 1972). See p. 172.
3. While they do not claim to be accurate in every detail, the three accounts I examine were suggested to me by the writings of R. M. Hare, Philippa Foot and A. I. Melden, respectively.
4. See D. Z. Phillips and H. O. Mounce, *Moral Practices* (London: Routledge & Kegan Paul, 1970), Chap. 8, 'Moral Dilemmas'. See also D. Z. Phillips and H. S. Price, 'Remorse Without Repudiation', *Analysis*, Vol. 28, no. 1, 1967.

5. *The Gambler/Bobok/A Nasty Story*, (Harmondsworth: Penguin Classics, 1976), pp. 189–90.
6. Ibid., pp. 237–8.
7. *Tess of the D'Urbervilles* (London: Macmillan: 1912), pp. 53–4.
8. I owe this example to Peter Winch. See *The Idea of a Social Science*, (London: Routledge & Kegan Paul, 1958), p. 123. The quotation is from Penelope Hall's *The Social Services of Modern England* (London: Routledge & Kegan Paul, 1955).
9. Of course, I am not denying that there are a host of intermediate cases about which different things would have to be said.
10. Hardy, op. cit., p. 91.

16 Self-Knowledge and Pessimism

1. Ilham Dilman, 'Self-knowledge and the Reality of Good and Evil' in *Value and Understanding: Essays for Peter Winch*, edited by Raimond Gaita (London: Routledge, 1990). All quotations are from this paper unless indicated otherwise.
2. Ilham Dilman, 'Self-Knowledge and the Possibility of Change' in *Rules, Rituals and Responsibility: Essays Dedicated to Herbert Fingarette*, ed. Mary Bochover (London: Open Court, forthcoming).
3. Ilham Dilman, *Freud: Insight and Change* (Oxford: Blackwell, 1988), p. 188.
4. Rush Rhees, 'What are Moral Statements Like?', *Without Answers* (London: Routledge & Kegan Paul, 1969), p. 104.

17 My Neighbour and My Neighbours

1. Peter Winch, *Trying to Make Sense* (Oxford: Blackwell, 1987). I shall refer to the two papers from the collection mentioned above as *ES* and *WN* respectively.
2. In the German there is a play on the words *geduldig* and *duldend*, which intensifies the irony and which I have been unable to catch in English. (Tr.)
3. Ludwig Wittgenstein, *Culture and Value*, trans. Peter Winch (Oxford: Blackwell, 1984), p. 11.
4. Leo Tolstoy, *The Death of Ivan Ilych and Other Stories*, trans. Aylmer Maude (New York: Signet, 1960), p. 96. My italics.
5. Stanley Cavell, *The Claim of Reason* (Oxford: The Clarendon Press, 1980), pp. 372f.
6. R. F. Holland, 'Is Goodness a Mystery?' in *Against Empiricism* (Oxford: Blackwell, 1980).
7. Peter Winch, *Ethics and Action* (Routledge & Kegan Paul, 1972), p. 4.
8. G. E. M. Anscombe, 'Modern Moral Philosophy', in *Ethics, Politics and Religion, Collected Philosophical Papers*, Vol. III (Oxford: Blackwell, 1981).
9. 1 John 4: 20.
10. Simone Weil, *Waiting on God*, trans. Emma Crauford (London: Fontana, 1959), pp. 98–9.
11. Ibid., p. 101.
12. I have benefited from comments and criticisms made by Raimond

Gaita, Walford Gealy, Geoffrey Hunt, Norman Malcolm, Rush Rhees, Peter Winch and Colwyn Williamson. They are not responsible, of course, for the conclusions I have reached.

18 Philosophy and the Heterogeneity of the Human

1. Cora Diamond, 'Losing Your Concepts', *Ethics*, Jan. 1988. All quotations from Diamond are from this paper.
2. Iris Murdoch, 'Against Dryness: A Polemical Sketch' in *Revisions*, ed. Stanley Hauerwas and Alasdair MacIntyre (Notre Dame, Ind.: University of Notre Dame Press, 1983), p. 46.
3. Alasdair MacIntyre, *After Virtue* (London: Duckworth, 1981); Stanley Cavell, *The Claim of Reason* (Oxford: The Clarendon Press, 1979).
4. For my detailed criticism of MacIntyre, see Chapter 5. For a related discussion of conceptual and ethical forgetfulness see my *Belief, Change and Forms of Life* (London: Macmillan, 1986), Ch. 3: 'Reminders of What We Know?'
5. But Diamond calls our attention to Cavell, *The Claim of Reason*, pp. 172–3.
6. This was one of Wittgenstein's main emphases in his treatment of 'basic propositions' in *On Certainty*. For my discussion of these see *Faith After Foundationalism* (London: Routledge, 1988).
7. I have argued for these conclusions in Chapter 17 in criticising Peter Winch's claim, in *Trying To Make Sense*, that Wittgenstein's talk of 'an attitude towards a soul' throws light on the response of the Good Samaritan. In most of his work, however, Winch has argued against claims for the homogeneity of human nature and human life. See Chapter 6 above.
8. See my paper, 'Primitive Reactions and the Reactions of Primitives', *Religious Studies*, Vol. 22, and *Belief, Change and Forms of Life* (London: Macmillan, 1986), Ch. 3: 'Reminders of What We Know?'.
9. See my *Belief, Change and Forms of Life*, Ch. 4: 'The Challenge of What We Know', and 'Only Words' and 'Mental Gymnastics' in *From Fantasy to Faith* (London: Macmillan, 1991).
10. John Berger, author, and Jean Hohr, photographer, *A Fortunate Man* (New York: Pantheon Books, 1982), pp. 98–9. Quoted by Diamond on pp. 258–9.
11. Simone Weil, 'Human Personality' in *Selected Essays 1934–43*, ed. Richard Rees (London: Oxford University Press, 1962), p. 18. Quoted by Diamond on p. 270.
12. Marion Montgomery, *Why Flannery O'Connor Stayed Home*, Vol. I of *The Prophetic Poet and the Spirit of the Age* (La Salle, Illinois: Sherwood Sugden and Company, 1981), pp. 137–8.

19 Necessary Rewards, Necessary Punishments and Character

1. In Peter Winch, *Ethics and Action* (London: Routledge, 1972).
2. Søren Kierkegaard, *Purity of Heart*, trans. Douglas Steere (New York: Harper and Row, 1956). See § 6.

3. I have discussed some of them in Chapter 15. For an example of exceptional self-sacrifice which has destructive results, see Edith Wharton's short story, *Bunner Sisters* in *Madame de Treymes* (London: Virago, 1984). I have discussed this story in 'Displaced Persons' in *From Fantasy to Faith: Philosophy of Religion and Twentieth Century Literature* (London: Macmillan, 1991).

4. I am indebted to my former colleague, David Sims, for putting these questions to me in this form.

5. Ludwig Wittgenstein, 'Lecture on Ethics', *Philosophical Review*, Jan. 1965, p. 8.

Bibliography

Anderson, John, *Studies in Empirical Philosophy* (Sydney: Angus and Robertson, 1962).

Anscombe, G. E. M., *Ethics, Politics and Religion, Collected Philosophical Papers*, Vol. III (Oxford: Blackwell, 1981).

Auchincloss, Louis, 'Edith Wharton and Her New Yorks' in *Edith Wharton: A Collection of Critical Essays*, ed. Irving Howe (Englewood Cliffs, NJ: Prentice-Hall, 1962).

Baier, Annette, *Postures of the Mind* (London: Methuen, 1985).

Beardsmore, R. W., *Moral Reasoning* (London: Routledge, 1969).

——, 'Consequences and Moral Worth', *Analysis*, June 1969.

Beehler, Roger, *Moral Life* (Oxford: Blackwell, 1978).

Black, Max, 'The Gap Between "Is" and "Should"', *Philosophical Review*, April 1964.

Cavell, Stanley, *The Claim of Reason* (Oxford: The Clarendon Press, 1980).

Coxe, Louis O., 'What Edith Wharton Saw in Innocence', in *Edith Wharton: A Collection of Critical Essays*, ed. Irving Howe (Englewood Cliffs' NJ: Prentice-Hall, 1962).

Davie, William, 'The Extreme Case in Ethics', *Philosophical Investigations*, no. 1, 1980.

Diamond, Cora, 'Anything But Argument', *Philosophical Investigations*, 1982.

——, 'Losing Your Concepts', *Ethics*, January 1988.

Dilman, Ilham, *Freud: Insight and Change* (Oxford: Blackwell, 1988).

——, 'Self-Knowledge and the Reality of Good and Evil' in *Value and Understanding*, ed. R. Gaita (London: Routledge).

——, 'Self-Knowledge and the Possibility of Change', in *Rules, Rituals and Responsibility: Essays Dedicated to Herbert Fingarette*, ed. Mary Bochover (London: Open Court, forthcoming).

Donagan, Alan, *The Theory of Morality* (Chicago: University of Chicago Press, 1977).

Dostoyevsky, Fyodor, *The Gambler/Bobok/A Nasty Story*, (Harmondsworth: Penguin Classics, 1976).

Drury, M. O'C., 'Conversations with Wittgenstein', in *Ludwig Wittgenstein: Personal Recollections*, ed. Rush Rhees (Oxford: Blackwell, 1981).

Evans, J. L., 'Grade Not', *Philosophy*, January 1962.

Faulkner, William, *Sanctuary* (Harmondsworth: Penguin, 1955).

Flanagan, Owen, 'Admirable Immorality and Admirable Imperfection', *Journal of Philosophy*, Vol. LXXXIII, 1986.

Foot, Philippa, *Virtues and Vices* (Oxford: Blackwell, 1978).

——, 'When is a Principle a Moral Principle?', *Proceedings Aristotelian Society*, Supp. Vol. 1954.

—— (ed.), *Theories of Ethics* (Oxford: Oxford University Press, 1967).

Hall, Penelope, *The Social Services of Modern England* (London: Routledge, 1955).

Hardy, Thomas, *Tess of the D'Urbervilles* (London: Macmillan, 1912).

Heath, Peter, 'Trying and Attempting', *Proceedings Aristotelian Society*, Supp. Vol. XLV.

Holland, R. F., *Against Empiricism* (Oxford: Blackwell, 1980).

Howe, Irving, 'A Reading of *The House of Mirth*' in *Edith Wharton: A Collection of Critical Essays*, ed. Irving Howe (Englewood Cliffs, NJ: Prentice-Hall, 1962).

James, William, *The Varieties of Religious Experience* (London: Longmans, Green & Co., 1941).

Kamenka, Eugene, *Marxism and Ethics* (London: Macmillan, 1969).

Kant, Immanuel, *The Critique of Pure Reason*, trans. Norman Kemp Smith, (London: Macmillan, 1961).

——, *The Critique of Practical Reason*, trans. Abbott (London, 1948).

——, *The Critique of Judgement*, trans. James Meredith (Oxford: Oxford University Press, 1978).

——, *Logic*, trans. Robert Hartmann and Wolfgang Schwartz (Indianapolis: Bobbs Merrill, 1974).

Kierkegaard, Søren, *Either/Or*, trans. W. Lowrie (Oxford: Oxford University Press, 1946).

——, *Works of Love*, trans. Edna and Howard Hong (London: Collins, 1962).

——, *Purity of Heart*, trans. Douglas Steere (New York: Harper & Row, 1956).

MacIntyre, Alasdair, *A Short History of Ethics* (New York: Macmillan, 1966).

——, *After Virtue* (London: Duckworth, 1981).

Melden, A. I., *Rights and Right Conduct* (Oxford: Blackwell, 1959).

Montgomery, Marion, *Why Flannery O'Connor Stayed At Home* (La Salle, Illinois: Sherwood Sugden, 1981).

Mounce, H. O., *Moral Practices*, with D. Z. Phillips (London: Routledge, 1970).

Mundle, C. W. K., *A Critique of Linguistic Philosophy* (Oxford: Clarendon Press, 1970).

Munroe, Alice, *Something I've Been Meaning To Tell You* (Harmondsworth: Penguin, 1985).

Murdoch, Iris, *The Sovereignty of Good* (London: Routledge and Kegan Paul, 1970).

Nagel, Thomas, *Mortal Questions* (Cambridge: Cambridge University Press, 1979).

——, 'Moral Luck', *Proceedings Aristotelian Society*, Vol. L, 1976.

Nevius, Blake, 'On *The Age of Innocence*' in *Edith Wharton: A Collection of Critical Essays*, ed. Irving Howe.

O'Connor, Flannery, *Letters of Flannery O'Connor: The Habit of Being*, edited with introduction by Sally Fitzgerald (New York: Farrar, Strauss, Giroux, 1969).

O'Neill, Onora, 'The Power of Example', *Philosophy*, Vol. 61, 1986.

Peters, R. S. and Griffiths, A. P. Phillips, 'The Autonomy of Prudence', *Mind*, 1962.

Phillips, D. Z., *Moral Practices*, with H. O. Mounce (London: Routledge, 1970).

——, *Through A Darkening Glass* (University of Notre Dame Press, 1982).

——, *Faith After Foundationalism* (London: Routledge, 1988).

——, *From Fantasy to Faith: Philosophy of Religion and Twentieth Century Literature* (London: Macmillan, 1991).

——, 'Miss Anscombe's Grocer', *Analysis*, July 1968.

——, 'The Limitations of Miss Anscombe's Grocer', *Analysis*, January 1969.

——, 'Remorse Without Repudiation' (with H. S. Price), *Analysis*, Vol. 28, 1967.

Price, H. S., 'Remorse Without Repudiation' (with D. Z. Phillips), *Analysis* Vol. 28, 1967.

Rhees, Rush, *Without Answers* (London: Routledge & Kegan Paul, 1969).

——, 'Some Developments in Wittgenstein's Views of Ethics', *Philosophical Review*, 1965.

Sartre, J.-P., 'Existentialism is a Humanism' in *Existentialism from Dostoyevsky to Sartre*, ed. W. Kaufmann (Cleveland, Ohio: World Publishers, 1956).

Schiller, F. C. S., 'Belief and Action' in *Problems of Belief* (London, 1934).

Sorel, Georges, *Reflections on Violence*, trans. T. E. Hulme (London: Collier Books, 1961).

Stocks, J. L., *Morality and Purpose*, ed. with introduction by D. Z. Phillips (London: Routledge, 1970).

Trilling, Lionel, 'The Morality of Inertia', in *Edith Wharton: A Collection of Critical Essays*, ed. Irving Howe.

Tolstoy, Leo, *The Death of Ivan Ilych and Other Stories*, trans. Aylmer Maude (New York: Signet, 1960).

Warnock, Mary, Introduction to *Utilitarianism* (Fontana, 1962).

Weil, Simone, *Waiting on God*, trans. Emma Crauford (Fontana, 1959).

Wharton, Edith, *The Age of Innocence* (London: Lehmann, 1953).

——, *The House of Mirth* (London: Lehmann, 1953).

——, *The Custom of the Country* (London: Lehmann, 1954).

——, *Bunner Sisters*, in *Madame de Treymes* (London: Virago, 1984).

——, *A Backward Glance* (London: Constable, 1972).

Williams, Bernard, 'Moral Luck', *Proceedings Aristotelian Society*, Vol. L 1976.

—— *Moral Luck* (Cambridge: Cambridge University Press, 1981).

——, *Ethics and the Limits of Philosophy* (London: Fontana/Collins, 1985).

Williams, Rowan, 'The Suspicion of Suspicion: Wittgenstein and Bonhoeffer' in *The Grammar of the Heart*, ed. Richard Bell (New York: Harper and Row, 1988).

Williamson, Colwyn, 'Miss Ancombe's Grocer and Mr Phillips's Grocer', *Analysis*, June 1968.

Wilson, Edmund, 'Justice for Edith Wharton', in *Edith Wharton: A Collection of Critical Essays*, ed. Irving Howe.

Winch, Peter, *Ethics and Action* (London: Routledge, 1978).

——, *Trying To Make Sense*, (Oxford: Blackwell, 1987).

Wittgenstein, Ludwig, *Philosophical Investigations*, ed. G. E. M. Anscombe and Rush Rhees, trans. G. E. M. Ascombe (Oxford: Basil Blackwell, 1953).

——, *Notebooks 1914–1916*, ed. G. H. von Wright and G. E. M. Anscombe, trans. G. E. M. Anscombe (Oxford: Basil Blackwell, 1961).

——, *Culture and Value*, ed. G. H. von Wright, trans. Peter Winch (Oxford: Blackwell, 1977).

——, *On Certainty*, ed. G. E. M. Anscombe and G. H. von Wright, trans. D. Paul and G. E. M. Anscombe (Oxford: Basil Blackwell, 1969).

——, 'Lecture on Ethics', *Philosophical Review*, Vol. LXXIV, 1965.

Wollheim, Richard, Introduction to F. H. Bradley's *Ethical Studies* (Oxford: Oxford University Press, 1962).

Wolterstorff, Nicholas, 'Is Reason Enough?', *The Reformed Journal*, Vol. 34 no. 4, April 1981.

Wright, G. H. von, *The Varieties of Goodness* (London: Routledge, 1963).

Index of Names

Index of Subjects

suffer such a loss and say 'Good riddance!' to the concept he no longer personally embraces. The philosopher, if he wants to give perspicuous representations of human life, in reflecting on what human life is like, will have to take account of this diversity. His task will be to teach us differences.

19

Necessary Rewards, Necessary Punishments and Character

It has been said that a good man is necessarily rewarded, and that an evil man is necessarily punished. What does such a claim amount to? There is no one answer to this question. In this chapter, I shall simply explore what is involved in some possible answers to the question.

Peter Winch has argued, in 'Ethical Reward and Punishment',[1] that discussions of reward and punishment in moral philosophy have placed too great an emphasis on spectator perspectives on action, and not sufficient emphasis on the agent's perspective on his actions. The notions of necessary rewards and necessary punishments I want to explore, however, necessarily involve spectator moral perspectives. Further, these spectator judgements cannot be assented to by the agents to whom they refer. Any attempted assent by the agents would show the judgements to have been mistaken.

From a spectator perspective, rewards and punishments have often been seen as consequences which are causally related to actions. On such a view, rewards are characterised as inducements to action, and punishments are characterised as deterrents. An obvious objection is that if an agent is concerned with reward or punishment in this sense, he is not concerned with the morality or immorality of his actions. Winch argues that if we take account of an agent's moral perspective, rewards and punishments are seen in a very different light.

In the case of rewards, Winch illustrates this difference with an example of a soldier who is rewarded for gallantry. If the soldier cares only for the reward, he would accept the medal even if his actions had not been gallant. In a rather different case, a soldier, while being concerned to perform the gallant act, subsequently

272

glories in the reward the action brings. It is one of the curious features of Kant's ethics that it pays no attention to this familiar phenomenon. Kant, rightly, emphasises the difference between acting in conformity with duty and acting out of respect for duty. But he says little, if anything, about the bearing which one's thoughts after a deed have on the character of the deed. For many, a self-congratulatory attitude towards one's accomplishments modifies, or even nullifies, their moral character. Another case would be that in which a soldier has what Kierkegaard called, an egocentric service of the good.[2] He is extremely hard to distinguish from the genuinely gallant soldier, since he may be prepared to sacrifice far more than an averagely decent soldier. His trouble is that he insists that gallantry should be manifested through *him*. *He* must be the vehicle of the virtue. Such insistence shows that he cannot have the very virtue he wants to possess.

Such cases should not lead us to conclude that there is no proper sense in which a good action can be rewarded without detracting from its goodness. The way in which a soldier accepts a medal for gallantry may show why. Winch says that such rewards

> are *one* way (but not the only possible way) of filling out, of expressing the judgement that a good action has been performed. It is a form of expression which emphasises that the good action is not an isolated event in the life of the agent, but is something which, as it were, spreads out and affects the character of the rest of his life. But someone who thinks about good actions in this way will do so whether or not such actions as a matter of fact attract what are commonly called rewards. The good action will be thought of as having a certain sort of bearing on the rest of the life of the agent anyway, in itself, whether or not this bearing is actually symbolized in the form of tangible benefits. It is what is symbolized that is important to the notion of reward rather than the actual occurrence of the beneficial consequences themselves (pp. 216–17).

Within the perspective I want to explore, however, the good man is said to be *necessarily* rewarded. Clearly, this cannot refer to actions where there are tangible rewards, since the presence of such rewards is contingent and therefore cannot be said to be necessary. Wherein, then, does the necessity of the reward reside? In his paper, 'Can a Good Man Be Harmed?', also in *Ethics and*

Action, Winch tries to answer this question in terms of the moral perspective of the agent. In some sense or other, the reward is to be found in the action itself. Everything depends, however, on what this sense amounts to. The reward will not be seen as a consequence of the action. We say of a host of activities that they can be rewarding. This is a reference to the character of the activities, not to their consequences. We say that we have found something to be a rewarding experience. Why should we not say that a good action is a rewarding one? There are difficulties if this is presented as a general thesis. Good actions, through no lack of foresight on the part of the agent, may have lamentable consequences from which the agent cannot distance himself. It cannot be assumed that goodness begets goodness. I am not going to pursue these difficulties here, formidable though they undoubtedly are.[3] Instead, I want to continue exploring what might be meant by saying that a good man cannot be harmed.

To say that a good man cannot be harmed is not to deny that all sorts of misfortunes and disasters may befall the good man. Because he thought otherwise, Callicles, in Plato's *Gorgias,* fails to understand Socrates. He says: 'You seem to me, Socrates, as confident that none of these things will happen to you as if you were living in another world and were not liable to be dragged into court, possibly by some scoundrel of the vilest character' (521). It is clear from Socrates' immediate response that this is not the kind of confidence that the good man has: 'I should be a fool, Callicles, if I didn't realize that in this state anything may happen to anybody' (521). But despite being aware of all the disasters which may befall him in Athens, including his own execution, Socrates says, 'All will be well.' This *is* a kind of confidence; a confidence which asserts that if he is faithful to goodness, nothing can touch him no matter what his lot may be.

In 'Can a Good Man Be Harmed?' Winch argues that this confidence is a kind of patience; a patience which enables us to appreciate the connection between

> the absolute demand of the moral 'ought' and the absolute impossibility of harming a good man. A man who accepts the first of these *is* a man who accepts the second. For to accept the first is to think that, compared with the importance of acting honourably and justly (for instance), nothing else matters. And this *is* to bear the afflictions that life brings patiently – i.e. not to

Child Care

Options

A Workplace Initiative
for the 21st Century

Date Due

NOV 2 9 1995			
DEC 1 5 1995			
APR 2 1 1996			
JAN 3 1 '97			

BRODART, INC.   Cat. No. 23 233   Printed in U.S.A.